Michael Seibold

European Tennis: A Comparative Analysis of Talent Identification and Development (TID)

Michael Seibold

EUROPEAN TENNIS:

A COMPARATIVE ANALYSIS OF TALENT IDENTIFICATION AND DEVELOPMENT (TID)

ibidem-Verlag
Stuttgart

Bibliografische Information der Deutschen Nationalbibliothek
Die Deutsche Nationalbibliothek verzeichnet diese Publikation in der Deutschen Nationalbibliografie; detaillierte bibliografische Daten sind im Internet über http://dnb.d-nb.de abrufbar.

Bibliographic information published by the Deutsche Nationalbibliothek
Die Deutsche Nationalbibliothek lists this publication in the Deutsche Nationalbibliografie; detailed bibliographic data are available in the Internet at http://dnb.d-nb.de.

Coverbild: Emily Seibold. Foto: Michael Seibold.

∞

Gedruckt auf alterungsbeständigem, säurefreien Papier
Printed on acid-free paper

ISBN-13: 978-3-8382-0330-0

© *ibidem*-Verlag
Stuttgart 2011

Alle Rechte vorbehalten

Das Werk einschließlich aller seiner Teile ist urheberrechtlich geschützt. Jede Verwertung außerhalb der engen Grenzen des Urheberrechtsgesetzes ist ohne Zustimmung des Verlages unzulässig und strafbar. Dies gilt insbesondere für Vervielfältigungen, Übersetzungen, Mikroverfilmungen und elektronische Speicherformen sowie die Einspeicherung und Verarbeitung in elektronischen Systemen.

All rights reserved. No part of this publication may be reproduced, stored in or introduced into a retrieval system, or transmitted, in any form, or by any means (electronic, mechanical, photocopying, recording or otherwise) without the prior written permission of the publisher. Any person who does any unauthorized act in relation to this publication may be liable to criminal prosecution and civil claims for damages.

Printed in Germany

Abstract

This thesis critically examines and assesses how Talent Identification and Development (TID) programmes for tennis are organised and implemented in four European countries. The thesis is based upon a multi-disciplinary and comparative research design, using both quantitative and qualitative research strategies, and the research methods of literature surveys, documentary research and semi-structured interviews, supplemented by a self-completion questionnaire. The study directly compares the views of key actors (players, coaches, administrators and parents) involved in TID practice in tennis in two of the countries: the Czech Republic and Germany. Two additional European countries, the United Kingdom (but focussing on England) and France, also form part of the research for comparative purposes. Following an original analysis of published and unpublished national and international literature, websites, documents and data in each of these countries, interviews were conducted in English and German with 39 key informants from the Czech Republic and Germany. The results indicated gaps between the theory and practice of TID and that tennis in the countries examined is likely to remain and become an even more socially exclusive sport within the next few years. Talent Development will be funded either by the public sport system, by private initiative, or both, but talent identification and development in tennis will remain limited to children from families with above average financial backgrounds.

Acknowledgements

There are three groups of people I want to pay acknowledgement to here that have guided and assisted me during the production of this thesis. Firstly, at the University of Edinburgh, I would like to thank my supervisors Professor Dave Collins, who encouraged me to enroll with the University in the first place, Dr. Pat McLaughlin, who contributed many valuable insights along the way, and Professor John Horne (now of the University of Central Lancashire) without whom I could not have completed this project. Secondly, I want to pay tribute to the many people in the four European countries I studied, who gave me their time and comments freely in response to my questions and requests for information about the sport of tennis and talent identification and development. Thirdly and finally, but by no means least, I owe the biggest debt of gratitude to my wife Birgit and my daughter Emily. They have supported and encouraged me in their different ways over the full length of this long 'championship'. Hopefully in the future, junior tennis players like Emily, will benefit from some of my research findings.

Table of Contents

Abstract v

Acknowledgements vii

List of Tables... x

List of Figures and Images xii

Abbreviations.. xiii

Chapter 1 Comparing approaches to talent identification and development in tennis 1

Chapter 2 The World of Tennis/ Tennis in the World........................... 15

Chapter 3 Tennis in Four European Countries 33

Chapter 4 Talent Identification and Development in sport and tennis. 67

Chapter 5 Methodology... 97

Chapter 6 Tennis and TID in Four National Systems: Major Similarities and Differences 111

Chapter 7 Comparing Views of TID in European Tennis....................... 153

Chapter 8 Discussion and Critical Analysis 181

Chapter 9 Interpretation and conclusions 195

Bibliography 207

Appendices 227

List of Tables

Table 2.1:	Regional Tennis Federations	24
Table 2.2:	Level of junior tennis at international tournaments	25
Table 2.3:	Details of the professional tennis tour	26
Table 2.4:	Elite Women's Tennis	27
Table 2.5:	Differences in sports participation	30
Table 3.1:	Membership development in selected years	44
Table 3.2:	Membership figures in tennis 2008 by age and gender	44
Table 3.3:	Overview of the sport practice of people between the ages of 15 and 75 in the year 2000	48
Table 3.4:	The most popular sport activities of the French population in the year 2000	49
Table 3.5:	Participation rates in tennis	58
Table 3.6:	Participation rates in tennis social distinction	59
Table 4.1:	Sport talent detection using a five-step approach	71
Table 4.2:	Talent analysis from three perspectives by Gimbel (1976)	71
Table 4.3:	Talent Development Model modified from Bloom (1985)	73
Table 4.4:	Distinct stages of participation in sport proposed by Côté (1999)	74
Table 4.5:	Most important determinants of talent development	75
Table 4.6:	Long-term development of a tennis player recommended by the International Tennis Federation	80
Table 4.7:	Mean highest professional ranking of Top 20 junior boys, and mean age at which it was achieved	86
Table 4.8:	Likelihood (in percentage terms) of top 20-ranked juniors reaching a top 100, 50, 20 and/ or 10 professional ranking 2005	86
Table 4.9:	Mean age statistics of TOP 100 ATP players	87
Table 4.10:	Characteristics of Talented Athletes, Coaches and Parents	90

Table 5.1:	Interviews with key actors in Germany and the Czech Republic (names are anonymised)	101
Table 5.2:	Number of respondents in the research	104
Table 5.3:	Characteristics of the respondents of the research	104
Table 6.1:	GDP and budget for the national tennis federation in four European countries	112
Table 6.2:	Cross section of the Tennis infrastructure of four European countries	113
Table 6.3:	Total Participation	116
Table 6.4:	Members registered with NTFs	118
Table 6.5:	The relationship of numbers of tennis courts to world ranked players	119
Table 6.6:	Relation clubs to world ranked players	120
Table 6.7:	Conversion rate from coach to world-ranked players	120
Table 6.8:	Coaches' training systems in the countries selected	122
Table 6.9:	National Talent Identification and Development programmes	123
Table 6.10:	Start of Talent Identification	125
Table 6.11:	Total hours of training within the federation	127
Table 6.12:	Progressive Development in four national tennis federations	128
Table 6.13:	Elite player participation	137
Table 7.1:	Organisation of Talent Detection in the different countries, and people involved	155
Table 7.2:	Target groups for talent search in tennis	158
Table 7.3:	Financial support	159
Table 7.4:	National Centres	160
Table 8.1:	An Under 12 Player's annual expenses for tennis	184

List of Figures and Images

Image 2.1:   The death of the Hyacinth from Giambattista Tiepolo(1752-1753).. 17

Image 2.2:   Major Wingfield aged 40 (1873) 19

Image 2.3:   First rule book (cover page from 1873) 19

Figure 3.1:   Relations between the Ministry of Education and Sport and civic associations (sports organisations) in the Czech Republic 35

Figure 4.1:   Correlation between performance development and age in tennis 82

Figure 6.1:   Progressive development stages in the Czech Tennis Federation (modified from an interview with the Czech Administrator 'Miroslav' 2008) 134

Figure 6.2:   Progressive development stages in the French Tennis Federation «La Pyramide Du Haut Niveau» (modified from Fédération Française de Tennis 2008c) 136

Figure 6.3:   Progressive development stages and cadre selection in German tennis (modified from Deutscher Tennis Bund 2008) 141

Figure 6.4:   Progressive development stages in the Lawn Tennis Association (modified from Lawn Tennis Association 2008b) 146

Abbreviations

Abbreviation	Meaning
AGM	Annual General Meeting
ATF	Asian Tennis Federation
ATP	Association of Tennis Professionals
BBC	British Broadcasting Corporation
BMI	Body Mass Index
BNP	Banque National de Paris
BOA	British Olympic Association
BTV	Bayerischer Tennisverband/ Bavarian Tennis Federation
CAPI	Computer-Assisted Personal Interview
CAT	Confederation of African Tennis
CCPR	Central Council of Physical Recreation
CCRPT	Central Council of Recreation Physical Training
CIA	Central Intelligence Agency
CNOSF	Comité National Olympique et Sportif Française
COS	Czech Sokol Community
COSAT	Confederacion Sud-Americana de Tenis (Tennis South America)
COTECC	Confederacion de Tenis de Centroamerica y Caribe
CR	Czech Republic
CSA	Czech Sports Association
CSSR	Czechoslovakia
CTS	Czech Tennis Association
CZK	Czech Kronen
DEL	Deutsche Eishockey Liga/ German Ice Hockey League
DHB	Deutsche Handball Bund/ German Handball Association
DOSB	Deutscher Olympischer Sport Bund/ German Olympic Sports Association
DSB	Deutscher Sport Bund/ German Sports Association

Abbreviation	Meaning
DTB	Deutscher Tennis Bund/ German Tennis Federation
DTN	Direction Technique Nationale
EU	European Union
FFT	Federation de Tennis Française
FLTA	First Line Tennis Academy
FNDS	Fonds Nationale pour le Development du Sport
FRA	France
FRG	Federal Republic of Germany
GBP	British Pound
GDP	Gross Domestic Product
GDR	German Democratic Republic
GER	Germany
GHS	General Household Survey
HPC	High Performance Centre
ILTF	International Lawn Tennis Federation
INSEP	Institut National du Sport et de l'Education Physique
ITF	International Tennis Federation
ITN	International Tennis Number
KJS	Kinder- und Jugendsportschulen/ children's and Junior sport schools)
LTA	Lawn Tennis Association (United Kingdom)
MJS	Ministre de Jeunesse et des Sports
NATO	North Atlantic Treaty Organization
NF	National Federation
NGO	Non Governmental Organisation
NOC	National Olympic Committee
NOK	Nationales Olympisches Komitee (Germany)
NTF	National Tennis Federation
OECD	Organisation for Economic Co-operation and Development

Abbreviation	Meaning
ONS	Office for National Statistics
OTF	Oceania Tennis Federation
PTI	Performance Tennis Initiative
RF	Regional Federation
RTF	Regional Tennis Federation
RUS	Russland/ Russia
SCO	Scotland
SOGCA	Swaziland Olympic Games & Commonwealth Association
TA	Tennis Australia
TCN	Tennis Club Nagold
TE	Tennis Europe
TI	Talent Identification
TID	Talent Identification and Development
UNSS	Union Nationale du Sport Scolaire
UGSEL	Union générale sportive de l'enseignement libre
UK	United Kingdom
USA	United States of America
USTA	United States Tennis Association
WR	World Ranked Player
WTA	Women's Tennis Association
WTB	Württembergischer Tennis Bund/ Regional Tennis Federation

Chapter 1 Comparing approaches to talent identification and development in tennis

Introduction

Today tennis is a global sport and is enjoyed by millions of recreational and competitive players of all age groups following the same rules world wide. The four Grand Slam tournaments (sometimes referred to as the 'majors'): the Australian Open, the French Open, Wimbledon, and the US Open, attract many millions of spectators in several continents. Names like Roger Federer, Rafael Nadal and Andrew Murray are known by most people interested in sport. Through the popularity and the spread of tennis, and the existence of many other popular sports, it must be one of the main goals of any national tennis federation to make the sport popular and to identify and select young people for the sport of tennis at a very early stage. To achieve this, a systematically organised talent identification and development programme (TID) is essential for any tennis nation wishing to develop future professional players. Without the implementation of a structured TID programme, a would-be tennis nation will probably fail to have successful tennis players.

Considering TID and the amount of research and publications on sport, we have to mention that tennis has not received the same amount of attention in research as some team sports in recent years. As an individual sport, tennis has not attracted the masses like soccer and it appears in the media only during the Grand Slam tournaments; thus it is not possible to identify cross-cultural comparative research about TID programmes in tennis in different countries which could help coaches, parents and players understand talent identification and development in tennis. Talent identification and development should be a key point in most national federations and implemented in any tennis policies of developed countries world-wide.

In sum, interest in the topic and practical experience as an international tennis coach lead me to believe that there might be a big gap between the theory and the practice of national TID programmes in tennis in European countries. This thesis is therefore concerned with comparing approaches to talent identification and development in tennis in four European countries.

1.1 Aims and Objectives of the Research Programme

In this section of the chapter I will provide an introduction to the research themes and to the research design and state how I will answer the research questions. Further, I will outline the central aims and objectives of research and give the reader an overview of the aims and message of each chapter. Firstly, I will introduce the research themes and the research design; secondly, the thesis overview will give the reader knowledge about the procedure of this research and thirdly, the reader will find an introduction to modern sport and the development of modern tennis, and the importance of TID programmes. The message of this chapter is to make the reader understand under what conditions of structural and societal development sport in general and tennis in particular has been developed and how important talent identification and development programmes can be for any tennis nation.

My decision to focus on tennis in this thesis and especially on talent identification and development is motivated by a number of practical and theoretical considerations. On the practical side, comparable data is available. The sport of tennis has umbrella organisations from international to regional and district level which keep records of participation and communicates with their members through various websites. In most European countries, the figures are published by the national tennis federations, sometimes broken down by age, sex, and region. Additionally, I have worked as a tennis coach nationally and internationally over the last 15 years, thus having good access to experts and other people involved in the sport. Besides these practical arguments, there are some theoretical arguments in favour of the focus on this sport. My personal experience as a coach has shown that even 7-year-old girls are aware of a possible tennis career. Some of these children dream of winning tournaments and can motivate their coaches to make them future stars, and if the coach has the necessary skills (which could be the most difficult part) to identify a 7-year-old child as talented, it can practise even on a small court somewhere in a rural area. If they (the child and the coach) understand the long-term talent development process from childhood up to the highest level, the child could later represent his/ her country internationally.

In this thesis I argue that coaches play a highly important part in the development of talented children. Players, parents and administrators expect quality in coaching. An 'effective' coach should show many characteristics like patience, experience, communication, motivation, flexibility and organisation (Cassidy et al. 2004, 47). In the context of my research, the coach should understand the learning process of an athlete in the same way as she/ he knows how to develop the athlete's skills from beginner level to performance level. Coaches should know through literature and training how to identify talent in tennis and how to develop this talent. But the insecure factor will be that talented players may be lost because of the facts that they are unable to attend any Talent Identification 'events', or because during development the coach may not learn how to develop this talent. There are many reasons for this, perhaps the environment is not effective, or the financial resources of the parents are not very sound. These factors have been identified as crucial (De Bosscher et al. 2003, Côté 1999, Abbott 2005). The research of Van Bottenburg (2001, 2005) and Guttmann (2004, 1994, 1978) into the popularity and development of different sports in European countries, the International Tennis Federation with their attempt to implement world-wide programmes, the socio-historical view of tennis of Gillmeister (1997) and Clerici (1987), and my personal experience regarding current TID practice have significantly influenced this thesis. In my research I cannot deal with the whole field of the talent identification and development process for tennis, but I understand talent development as a multidisciplinary process in which the sociology and psychology of sport can help to understand talent identification and development in different sports as well as the development of talented children (for example see the recent work of Christensen 2009). The thesis compares national TID programmes and not the success of individual athletes. The immediate environment of the athlete, the published TID programmes and the social and cultural context in which people live are treated as of central importance in this research.

Research Themes

Tennis has not received the same amount of research as team sports in recent years. As an individual sport, it has not attracted the masses; occasionally the sport has attracted the upper or the middle class. Some researchers, such as Gillmeister (1997) and Clerici (1987), have done historical research into the long-term development of tennis over the last 500 years. Sociologists of sport, like Robert Lake (2008), have focused on the issue of social exclusion in British tennis with the conclusion that differences in age and class are less central in playing tennis in a club. Van Bottenburg (1992, 2001, 2005), has done sociological research in which tennis has figured in participation in sport and the development of sport as a global game. One researcher (Gabler 1993) has identified psychological features of tennis players and their importance during the development process into top players. There is no real cross-cultural comparative research on TID programmes in tennis in different countries. This thesis is about comparing approaches to talent identification and development in tennis in four European countries and sets out to find out how Talent Identification and Development (TID) programmes in tennis in four European countries (the Czech Republic, Germany, France and the United Kingdom) are organised and implemented. To compare and evaluate such TID programmes in different countries, several factors need to be considered. These involve the mechanisms and the implications of national TID models, general data about productivity (rankings of players, the number of coaches and players), population, culture, specific tennis history, participation and retention, resources, competition, training/practice, national tennis federations' goals, players, financial implications, the role of the coach and of the parents, as well as follow-up programmes. Specifically, concentrating on the main research question, the thesis overall investigates:

- How are TID programmes in tennis organised and implemented in different European countries?

To find answers to this main research question, we have to investigate three subsidiary questions:

- What is TID, when did it emerge as a concern and how is it discussed in the context of sport?
- How does TID operate in tennis in the four European countries selected?
- What influence do different social contexts have on the meaning of tennis and especially approaches to TID in tennis?

The first research question is referred to in the current chapter, taking into account the emergence of the concern with and discourse on TID, as well as throughout the thesis. The second research question will be addressed partly in chapter 3, and partly in chapters 6 and 7. To answer the question we provide a background to the organisation of sport and especially tennis in the four countries (chapter 3) using secondary sources, and then more detailed accounts of the organisation and implementation of TID (chapter 6), and critical reflections from key agents involved in two of the countries (chapter 7). The third research question will be considered in chapters 2, 3, 6, 7 and 8. The critical discussion of this question takes place at three levels of social analysis: societal/national (chapters 2, 3); institutional/organisational (chapter 6); and individual/agents (chapter 7).

Research Design

The thesis is based upon a comparative research design, using both quantitative and qualitative research strategies, and the research methods of surveys, interviews, documentary research and observation. The multi-disciplinary approach of this thesis is informed by historical, sociological and coaching studies literature on sport in society, and tennis in society specifically. Looking at European tennis, the study directly compares talent identification and development practices in tennis in two European countries: the Czech Republic

(CR) and Germany (GER). Two additional European countries, the United Kingdom (UK, but focussing on England) and France (FRA), also form part of the research for comparative purposes. The selection of these countries was made for the following reasons. Firstly, there was broadly comparable and systematic data available in each of them. Secondly, there was the linguistic ability of the candidate, and access to materials and key informants for primary research. Thirdly, these countries offer an effective cross-section of world opinion about TID in tennis. Fourthly, 80% of the top ranked 100 male and female players are from Europe. In addition, each of these countries offered various contrasting features, as I briefly recount next.

For the Czech Republic as a former 'communist' society and a new member of the EU from eastern Europe, sport in general, and tennis in particular, are seen as more than merely part of a leisure tradition. For the lucky few, tennis is seen as providing the opportunity to travel and develop a potentially lucrative career, and the Czech Republic has a strong history of excellence in tennis even through the communist era (1948-1989), when only Olympic sports were supported (tennis was not an Olympic sport from 1924-1988). Germany is a tennis powerhouse at recreational/club level and has for the past 20 years had the highest number of registered members (1.7 million in 2007) of any tennis federation worldwide. It has recently produced some very successful junior players (Deutscher Tennis Bund 2009a), although there is, currently at least, a comparative dearth of top-class senior players (Association of Tennis Professionals 2008a; Women's Tennis Association 2009a). Between 2004 and 2008, when the research for this thesis was undertaken, France was one of the most successful countries in Junior Tennis and Senior Tennis, and its Talent Development programme seems to be the most successful worldwide; it furthermore runs the most famous clay court tournament in Paris (French Open). The All-England Lawn Tennis and Croquet Club, based in Wimbledon, meanwhile runs the most important tennis tournament in the world, and the various tennis associations in the United Kingdom currently claim high participation rates for non-registered players, as well as a number of world-class juniors, although the UK have three woman and only one man in the world class rankings (Women's Tennis Association (2009d); Association of Tennis Professionals 2009d).

Why were Spain, the USA, or some up and coming tennis countries like China and Argentina not included in the survey? Regarding the production of senior world class players, the Spanish and American tennis athletes have certainly been among the most successful worldwide for years (De Bosscher et al. 2003). The reasons for the non-selection of these countries and other national tennis federations and systems for this thesis were organisational, linguistic, and a matter of time. Constraints on time and resources prevented the obtaining of qualitative and productive information required for the research from other nations. The focus of the research presented in this thesis, then, was finally on four European tennis federations. We shall return to the limitations of this project and the potential for further research in this area in the concluding chapter.

1.2 Modern Sport and Modern Tennis and TID

In the following section we will give a brief overview of the development of modern sport and modern tennis to understand the historical context and the way that sport and tennis have become globalised. In 2008, there were more than seventy international sport organisations which function in most countries world-wide. A national and international network connects athletes all over the world to their chosen sport. Today, the different types of championships up to the world championship and the Olympic Games are the main symbols of the global character of sport (Digel & Fahrner 2003a, 15).

Modern sport

For the purposes of this thesis, sport can be defined as '...autotelic physical contest...' (Guttmann 2004, 2). In the past century, modern sport has been developed into one of the most important communication platforms in our world (Guttmann 2004, 4). Sport is part of global culture. The first period in modern sport in which standardised rules were developed was between 1870 and 1880 (van Bottenburg 2001, 4); but without people who transformed sport from local variation to international standardisation, sport could not have achieved its global position. In daily life in the nineteenth century, the hours of the day, coins, units of measurement, and customs all varied according to local regulations. People from lower social classes spoke only dialect and were not aware of events outside their own regions. There had been little opportunity to travel or to learn different types of cultural behaviour, in contrast to the highest circles of society who could afford travel. Foreign journeys (in the 19th century mainly in Europe) became more common. Better travel conditions, newspapers and the telephone informed people more about different types of cultural behaviour (van Bottenburg 2001, 3). These differences between the social classes were reflected in their recreational activities. In England and Scotland, the change in society happened before that in most other countries (before the mid-nineteenth century). There was an increasing trend for the upper classes to found exclusive associations country-wide, which gave them the opportunity to regulate and standardise local and variable activities (e.g. hunting, cricket, fencing, boxing, and golf) (van Bottenburg 2001). The development from local variation to international standardisation was rapid. After 1870 nearly all Western countries emulated England in setting up sports clubs and national organisations (Guttmann 2004). Sport and its organisations grew very rapidly within one generation. Official statutes, regulations and membership fees made sports more comparable. It was easier to agree on rules and their enforcement and to introduce regularity in competition between competitors. One of the activities which underwent this transformation into a modern sport became the game of tennis.

Modern tennis

Tennis is a sport played between two players (singles) or between two teams of two players each (doubles). Each player uses a strung racquet to strike a ball covered with felt (most of the time nowadays Optic Yellow) over a net into the opponent's court. It is a game with a long traditional background (Gillmeister 1997, Clerici 1987). In the later Middle Ages, a complicated game of royal (court) tennis came into favour, first among royalty (for servants and labourers it was forbidden to play the game), and then among the urban bourgeoisie. From France, court tennis went to England, and south and east as well as west. 'Ballhäuser' (similar to indoor courts) also became part of the urban landscape throughout German-speaking Europe (Guttmann 2004).

The modern game of tennis originated in the United Kingdom in the late 19th century as 'lawn tennis', which has strong connections to the ancient game of real tennis. After its creation, tennis spread throughout the upper-class English-speaking population before spreading around the world. Tennis is an Olympic sport and is played at all levels of society by people of all ages. The sport can be played by anyone who can hold a racket, including people in wheelchairs. The rules of tennis have changed very little since the 1890s. Two exceptions are the fact that from 1908 to 1960 the server had to keep one foot on the ground at all times, and then the adoption of the tie-break in the 1970s. A recent addition to professional tennis has been the adoption of electronic review technology coupled with a point challenge system, which allows a player to challenge the line (or chair) umpire's call of a point.

Today tennis, with its specific features (organised play and competitive games) is played by around 45 million people (Guttmann 2004, van Bottenburg 2001). In 2008, at the most important tennis tournament (Wimbledon) players from more than 50 nations were present at the tournament main draw. Most of these world class players have their own coaches, from various countries. The final (All England Championship 2008) between Roger Federer and Rafael Nadal was one of the best games in the last 20 years. Television cameras and communication satellites made it possible for nearly 1 billion people all over the world to follow the finals as a live event. Most of the spectators and viewers understand the techniques and tactics of the game. Anyone who is familiar with this sport can practise it anywhere. The rules, number of players, size of the court, clothing, and symbols of the sport are virtually the same in every country. Whether we are talking about a Wimbledon final or a friendly tennis match between two middle-aged European men or women, these participants follow the international rules. Tennis exists worldwide in a standardised form. From Prague to Paris and Berlin to London, tennis players know all about volleys, smashes and double faults, and count from love, through fifteen, thirty, and forty to game. This global system connects people throughout the world. The rise of the global tennis sport system is an important development, as people in 205 countries (in 2008) are affiliated to the International Tennis Federation (note that, like football, there are more tennis federations than nations in the United Nations) and they have adopted the same rules. This would not have been possible without the formation of organisations to set the rules. Another argument for the development into a modern sport is the important role of competition. This internationally organised and standardised competition has been one of the most important characteristics of tennis over the past hundred years (van Bottenburg 2001). On the other hand, the rules and regulations make the development of the sport very slow; trends and further developments are slowed down by bureaucratic issues. However, tennis is still a global sport (see Chapter 2) and hundreds of thousands of young people all over the world enjoy participation in this sport. However, without a doubt tennis is not by far the most popular sport in the global perspective. Other sports are developing in the same way, and each continent, country or even social group has its own popular trends in sports development. There is a boom in sport everywhere (Guttmann, 2004), with the consequence that there is more competition between the different sports federations to make their sport attractive to the public. For this a modern and competitive TID programme has to be an essential part of each national or even regional tennis federation's development strategy.

Talent Identification and Development (TID)

National and regional tennis federations publish Talent Development plans, and many parents believe that their children can achieve the top level in the chosen sport. It sounds easier than it is in practice, however, and parents today have difficulty in evaluating whether their child is exceptional at tennis or not. 'If a child hits one good ball, they remember it. If he/ she hits 500 bad balls, they do not remember' (Agassi 2008, 46). So a proper evaluation of the children's skills and stages of development should be key points for every interested coach or parent, and be implemented in a development plan. This process can take more than 10 years (Abbott 2005, Ericsson et al. 1993, Schwarzer 2007) and goes through different stages (Abbott 2005, Bloom 1985, Gabler 1983, Gimbel 1976). From the coaches' point of view, it is very difficult to develop a child from the beginning to adult level. Even well-known international coaches like Nick Bollettieri (of the IMG-Bollettieri Tennis Academy) have not coached any player from the start all the way to professional status, but most parents, coaches and players dream of seeing a child/talent play in international tournaments.

Any tennis player who has taken part in 'big' tournaments will have started somewhere in his/her country at an early age, in most cases without a master plan to achieve world professional standard. Perhaps they found in their environment the facilities and conditions that brought them to this level. It is possible that their federation supported their parents or coaches with an effective Talent Development (TD) programme. However, practice has shown that most parents or coaches are not keen on talent identification and talent development; it is more by chance (being in the right place at the right time) that a talented player makes his/her way to the top level. Without a doubt, top player development in European tennis countries is the most successful in the world (MacCurdy 2008); if we take De Bosscher's (2003) method for measuring success into account we have to mention France, Germany, and the Czech Republic as three of the most successful countries in tennis in the world in 2008. In her study she compared success in tennis among countries and found that tennis success can be measured objectively through the ranking system.

It is undisputed that the success of any country or player is dependent solely on the quality of the identification and development of the talent. There are many concerns about current talent identification procedures and programmes (Abbott 2005). The problems for the talented do not decrease after they are identified; because the development process of talent is a long-term task (see Chapter 4). Any model is only as good as the programme in which this model is implemented by a tennis federation. However the programme is implemented, coaches and parents in the first stages have the most influence on the development of the player, and the coach should know what to do 'on court' with them (Bloom 1985). In her research, Abbott lists several talent development stages like positive family support (initiation stage), family commitment (development stage), family moral support and additional financial support (mastery stage) as key factors during talent development (Abbott 2005). Talent identification and talent development are not thinkable without taking into account the social environment of children.

1.3 Thesis overview

The rest of the thesis has the following structure. Chapter 2 offers a brief overview of the history, system and structures and the socio-structural and socio-cultural background of tennis. The aim of the chapter is to introduce the world of tennis in more detail and show how social conditions can have a central influence on the probability of success of national tennis federations' talent identification and development. In Chapter 3, the identification of the four countries and the consideration of certain national, socio-cultural and political-economic characteristics are therefore important for understanding under what circumstances talent identification and development takes place. It is also necessary to examine some social structural aspects in view of their sport-promoting or sport-impeding effect. These include population and development size, age groups, the ethnic and social composition of the players as well as the background specific to the sport of tennis, like financial means, the number of coaches, tournament participation and squad training, which have been noted as success defining factors for the productivity (and ranking in tennis terms) of the countries described.

In Chapter 4, I provide a broad overview of research on Talent Development and expertise and discuss general and tennis-specific views on this topic. Various accounts of the multidimensionality and dynamic nature of Talent Development in tennis are provided. The message of this chapter is that talent is not an all-or-nothing phenomenon. It is a dynamic manifestation that appears to be determined by both innate and environmental factors, and without family support, competent coaches and good physical resources an athlete will not achieve world class performance.

In Chapter 5, I consider the research design, the strategy and research methods I have used. I discuss the methods used to carry out this research. Through interviews and questionnaires conducted with parents, administrators, coaches and players, mainly in two countries (CR and GER), I collected information about what they do, why they do it and what they think would be best regarding TID programmes. This data enables me to investigate in more detail how talent identification and development in tennis is organised and implemented in the two European countries. Once again, findings are contextualised against research in talent identification and development.

In Chapter 6, I present the findings from my secondary data research into tennis in the selected European countries, and give a picture of four national tennis systems: major similarities and contradictions and their productivity are highlighted. In Chapter 7, I present findings discovered through primary research, including interviews with key actors in tennis in two of the selected countries. This deepens my knowledge about structures and systems in sport and tennis specifically and how they are related to the central research questions. This reveals a contradiction between the theory and the practice of talent identification and development in tennis, and complements the outline of the function and implementation of programmes in organised structures in tennis presented in chapters 1-3. In Chapter 8, the findings from the interviews with coaches, parents, players and administrators are critically assessed in relation to the research questions. Finally, in Chapter 9, conclusions are drawn and recommendations are made. The overall aim of this thesis is to provide the basis for a resource concerning talent identification and development in tennis, as well as an in-depth comparative analysis of different European TID programmes in tennis.

1.4 Conclusion

To summarise this chapter, I have outlined the aims and objectives and the practical and theoretical considerations underpinning this thesis, how modern sport has been developed into a global communication platform and the circumstances under which tennis has been developed into a modern sport and the difficulties and importance of a TID programme. In the next chapter I will highlight the world of tennis and its historical and cultural development, with its institutionalisation and popularisation in the world of sport, and thus provide an understanding of the cultural and societal conditions under which tennis has been developed and implemented in the past and today.

Chapter 2 The World of Tennis/ Tennis in the World

Introduction

This chapter offers a brief overview of the historical, social and cultural development of tennis, and the institutionalisation and popularisation of tennis systems and structures. At the beginning of the chapter I will discuss the world of tennis today and how the sport is organised. In the second part, I will show how the sport of tennis has developed from the Middle Ages into the modern sport at the end of the 19th century. Further, I will discuss the institutionalisation and popularisation of tennis systems and structures, and finally I will outline the structural and socio-cultural factors underpinning the development of expertise. A key message of this chapter is that there are different social and historical contexts that have an influence on the meaning of tennis, and especially approaches to TID in tennis. The next section begins by considering the historical development and structure of tennis worldwide and how the main organisations fit into this.

2.1 The Development of Tennis

2.1.1 The historical, social and cultural development of tennis

The winner of the first base line rally in tennis will never be known, nor will the server of the first ace. The responsible parties may, in fact, have produced their shots in ancient Egypt, Greece or Rome, as ball games existed in all of those cultures (Clerici 1987, 1). Although it has several centuries of development preceding it, the modern sport of (lawn) tennis was essentially an English 'export' formed at the end of the 19th century, as were so many other modern forms of sport (van Bottenburg 1992, 2001). Through its development from a form of the sport essentially played by kings and the aristocracy, it retained its association with royalty and the upper and middle classes. Despite considerable social change, industrialisation and the increase in social status, this association continues to mark its social and cultural significance today in most European countries and elsewhere in the world where it is played.

Tennis can be traced as far back as the ancient Greek game of 'sphairistike' (translated from Greek: 'play ball' or 'ball game') (Clerici 1987, 63, International Tennis Federation 1998a, 16), and is mentioned in literature in the Middle Ages in 'The Second Shepherd's Play'. Sir Gawain, a knight of King Arthur's round table, plays tennis with a group of giants in 'The Turke and Gawain' (Hahn 1995). The medieval form of tennis is termed 'real tennis'. 'Real' in this sense (presumably from Spanish) means 'royal' – i.e. a game for kings (Clerici 1987, 2). Royal, and from the late 19th century, 'real' tennis evolved over three centuries from an earlier ball game played around the 12th century in France. This had some similarities to 'palla, fives, pelota or handball', involving hitting a ball with the bare hand and later with a glove. One theory is that this game was played by monks in monastery cloisters, based on the construction and appearance of early courts (Gillmeister 1997, 9). In the course of time, the glove had become a 'racquet', the game had moved to an enclosed playing area, and the rules had stabilised. Royal tennis spread throughout royalty in Europe and reached its greatest popularity in the 16th century (Gillmeister 1997, 35).

In France, François I (1515-47) was an enthusiastic player and promoter of royal tennis, building courts and encouraging play among courtiers and commoners. His successor, Henri II (1547-59) was also an excellent player and continued the royal French tradition (Clerici 1987, 24). During his reign, the first known book about tennis, 'Trattato del Giuoco della Palla', was written in 1555 by an Italian priest (Antonio Scaino da Salo) (Clerici 1987, 36). Two French kings are believed to have died from tennis-related episodes – Louis X of a severe chill after playing, and Charles VIII after being struck by a door frame (Clerici 1987, 24). King Charles IX granted a constitution to the Corporation of Tennis Professionals in 1571, creating the first professional tennis 'tour', establishing three levels of professionals – apprentice, associate, and master. The first codification of the rules of 'royal tennis' was written by a professional named Forbet and it was published in 1599 (Clerici 1987, 25).

Royal interest in England began with Henry V, who reigned between 1413 and 1422 (Clerici 1987, 26), but it was Henry VIII (1509-47) who made the biggest impact as a young monarch, playing the game at Hampton Court on a court he had built in 1529 (Clerici 1987, 29), and on several other courts in his palaces. It is believed that his second wife, Anne Boleyn, was watching a game of real tennis when she was arrested and that Henry was playing tennis when news was brought to him of her execution. During the reign of James I (1603-25), there were 14 courts in London (Gillmeister 1997). 'Royal tennis' is also recorded in literature by Shakespeare, who mentions 'tennis-balls' in his play 'Henry V', when a basket of them is given to King Henry V by the Dauphin Louis of France (King Henry V, Act 1, Scene 2, 34-35) (Reclam 1978, 34-35), as well as 'hazard, courts and chases', thus using a number of tennis-specific metaphors in his play. One of the most striking early references to the game of tennis appears in a painting by Giambattista Tiepolo entitled 'The Death of Hyacinth' (1752-1753) in which a stringed racquet and three tennis balls are depicted.

Image 2.1: The death of the Hyacinth from Giambattista Tiepolo(1752-1753)

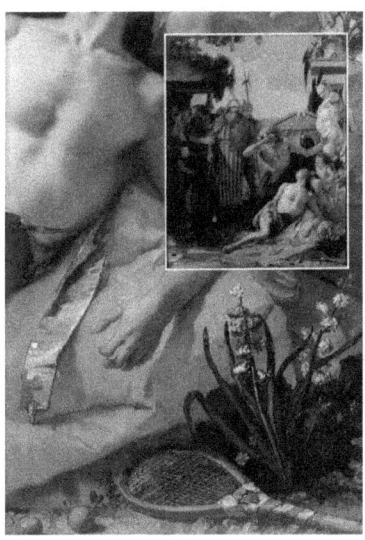

Source: Clerici 1987, 57

The theme of the painting is the mythological story of Apollo and Hyacinth, written by Ovid and translated into Italian in 1561 by Giovanni Andrea dell'Anguillara, who replaced the ancient game of discus throwing in the original text by that of 'pallacorda' or tennis, which had achieved a high status as a form of physical exercise at the courts in the middle of the sixteenth century. Tiepolo's painting, displayed at the Museo Thyssen Bornemisza in Madrid, was commissioned in 1752 by a German count, Wilhelm Friedrich Schaumburg-Lippe, who was known to be a tennis player (Clerici 1987, 56).

The game thrived in the 17th century among the nobility in France, Spain, Italy, and the Austro-Hungarian Empire, but suffered under English Puritanism. By the Age of Napoleon, royal tennis was largely abandoned. Royal tennis is also thought to have played a minor role in the history of the French Revolution, through the Tennis Court Oath, a pledge signed by French deputies in a royal tennis court, which formed a decisive early step in starting the revolution (Clerici 1987, 53). In England, during the 18th century and early 19th century, as 'royal tennis' died out, three other 'racquet' sports emerged – racquets, squash racquets and lawn tennis (the modern game) (Clerici 1987, 57).

The establishment of tennis as a modern sport can be dated back to two separate inventions. Between 1859 and 1865, in Birmingham, England, Major Harry Gem, a solicitor, and his friend Augurio Perera, a Spanish merchant, combined elements of the game of rackets and the Spanish ball game 'pelota' and played the resulting game on a croquet lawn in Edgbaston (Gillmeister 1997; Tyzack 2005). In 1872, the two men moved to Leamington Spa and in 1874, with two doctors from the Warneford Hospital, founded the world's first tennis club. In December 1873, Major Walter Clopton Wingfield (see Figure 2.2) devised a similar game for the amusement of his guests at a garden party on his estate of Nantclwyd, in Llanelidan, Wales (Clerici 1987). He based the game on the older 'real' tennis.

Image 2.2: Major Wingfield aged 40 (1873)

Source: Clerici 1987, 61

Wingfield named it 'lawn tennis', (Gillmeister 1997, 180) and patented the game in 1874 with an eight-page rule book, titled 'Sphairistike or Lawn Tennis,' (Gillmeister 1997, 175).

Image 2.3: First rule book (cover page from 1873)

Source: Clerici 1987, 60

From the old game Wingfield retained the basic rules (strokes on the volley and the rebound) and equipment (the net, lopsided rackets) and the obligation of serving from one side only, but he did away with the too complicated chase rule, walls and galleries and their hazards and, for the stuffed balls of old, substituted air-filled rubber balls. These could be manufactured as a result of Goodyear's discovery of vulcanization and bounced sufficiently even on the short-trimmed croquet lawns, the favourite venue for the new society. Wingfield's innovation reached France before 1875 and Germany in 1876, when English visitors experimented with it on the lawns of the Royal Victoria Hotel in Bad Homburg.

Wingfield borrowed both the name and much of the French vocabulary of real tennis, as the following list of five features of the modern game indicates:

1. Tennis comes from the French 'tenez', the imperative form of the verb 'tenir', to hold: This was a cry used by the player serving in royal tennis, meaning 'I am about to serve!' (rather like the cry 'Fore!' in golf).
2. The English word 'racket' is developed from the French word 'raquette', which derives from the Arabic word 'rahat', meaning the palm of the hand (Stemmler 1988).
3. Deuce comes from 'à deux du jeu', meaning 'to both is the game' (that is, the two players have equal scores) and a player needs two points to win (French: 'deux' means two) (Stemmler 1988).
4. Love originates not from 'l'oeuf', the French word for egg, representing the shape of a zero, but developed from the expression that 'for love' means there have been no winning points made by a player (Stemmler 1988).
5. The convention of numbering scores '15', '30' and '40' comes from 'quinze, trente' and 'quarante', which to French ears make a euphonious sequence, or from the quarters of a clock (15, 30, 45) with 45 simplified to 40 (Masters 1997). Another historian mentions that the scoring goes back to French influence in the 14th century, where one coin ('1 gros denier') had the value of 15 deniers (Stemmler 1988; Clerici 1987).

The modern game of tennis was institutionalised at the end of the 19th century and the beginning of the 20th century – in Germany, the German Lawn Tennis

Association (later in the 1950s named 'Deutscher Tennis Bund' (DTB) was founded in 1902, in the UK the Lawn Tennis Association (LTA) was founded in 1888 and is located at Roehampton in London, the Fédération Française de Tennis ('French Tennis Federation' in English), also known as the FFT, is an organisation set up in 1920 that takes charge of the organisation, co-ordination and promotion of tennis in France. In the Czech Republic, the first Lawn Tennis club was opened in Prague in 1892 (Ministry of Foreign Affairs 2008). The International Lawn Tennis Federation (ILTF) was set up after the turn of the century in 1913, with the US abstaining from joining it because they denied the Wimbledon tournament (in 1877, the first time played) the title of World Championships. The USA eventually became a member in 1923, when all parties were eventually reconciled by the introduction of the four major events in the game which since the 1930s have become known as the 'Grand Slam' tournaments. Germany, one of the founding members of the ILTF, but at the time banned from the organisation as a result of the Great War (1914-18), came away empty-handed in this process (Gillmeister 2008). Lawn Tennis was an Olympic sport from the beginning (1896 in Athens), but was banned from 1924 until 1988 during the conflict between amateurism and professionalism. However, this was part of the formation of modern sport or 'sportization' that Guttmann (1978) and Van Bottenburg (2001) describe. In tennis today, there are three main bodies responsible for overseeing the sport of tennis globally: The International Tennis Federation (ITF), the Association of Tennis Professionals (ATP) for men and the Women's Tennis Association (WTA).

2.1.2 The Institutionalisation and Popularisation of Tennis systems and structures

Sport, like most activities involving groups of people, requires an organisational structure to function successfully. To meet this need, sport organisations exist at international, national and regional levels. These organisations include those which concentrate on a single sport (e.g. tennis), as well as umbrella bodies for team sports (e.g. soccer). Most of these organisations share a number of similarities.

Each sport is controlled on the international level by a world governing body or international federation whose membership is comprised of national federations. International federations exist to serve their sport and their key activities usually include promoting their sport, setting technical rules, training referees and judges, maintaining lists of records and organising major championships and other competitions. Generally, international federations hold a regular assembly such as a congress or annual general meeting (AGM) where constitutional and technical matters are decided. The assemblies also elect a number of committees which oversee the various programmes of the federation.

National federations (sometimes called associations) make up the membership of the international federations. National federations serve their sport and are responsible for the competition and programmes within the political boundaries of their country. They are also responsible for organising teams to take part in international competitions. The basic organisational unit for sport in most countries is the sports club. Clubs exist to provide services to sportsmen and sportswomen, and they are the bodies through which most training and competitive activities are organised. They are affiliated to the relevant national federation. Schools, colleges, universities and other educational institutions often fulfil the role of the sports club, particularly for younger athletes.

Tennis

In most European countries, tennis in the 2000s is one of the top ten sports. This is a result of a boom in the 1960s and 1970s, when tennis increased its popularity in absolute members more than any other sport. Van Bottenburg (1992) identified three independent factors to explain this popularity. Female participation has risen, especially of women of the middle and upper class, the age restrictions have largely been eliminated (in the 1950s and 1960s the minimum age fell), and the professional and middle class increased structurally in Western Europe (van Bottenburg 1992). This could explain why tennis ranked higher than any other sport aside from soccer in many European countries (van Bottenburg 2001). However, another reason for the popularity of tennis is the balance of male and female participation. According to van Bottenburg the social exclusivity of tennis was more a matter of culture than money. Tennis monopolised the preference of a specific group of sports enthusiasts: adults with a high social status. Working-class boys started playing soccer, boys from higher social classes also often played soccer too. During their time at university, they started playing field hockey or rugby, and after university they focused mainly on tennis or golf. Women from the elite ended up on the tennis court after playing hockey at public schools (Van Bottenburg 2001).

International Tennis Federation

The International Tennis Federation (ITF) is the governing body of world tennis, made up of 205 (2008) national tennis associations. It was established as the International Lawn Tennis Federation (ILTF) by 12 national associations meeting at a conference in Paris, France on 1 March 1913. In 1924 it became the officially recognised organisation with authority to control lawn tennis throughout the world, with official 'ILTF Rules of Tennis'. In 1977 it dropped the word 'lawn' from its title, recognising that most contemporary tennis was not actually played on grass.

The funds of the ITF, which was originally based in Paris, were moved to London during World War II. From that time onwards the ILTF/ITF has been run from London. Until 1987, the ITF was based at Wimbledon; it then moved to Barons Court, near the Queen's Tennis Club, and then moved again in 1998 to the Bank of England Sports Ground, Roehampton (International Tennis Federation 2006a).

Member nations come from every continent, and each association is involved in organising tennis and promoting the interests of the game. The ITF also has six regional associations distributed geographically (see Table 2.1 below), which work within their regions and continents to assist the development and co-ordination of tennis:

Table 2.1: Regional Tennis Federations

Continent	Organisation
Asia	Asian Tennis Federation (ATF)
South America	Confederacion SudAmericana de Tenis (COSAT)
Africa	Confederation of African Tennis (CAT)
Central America and the Caribbean	Confederacion de Tenis de Centroamerica y El Caribe (COTECC)
Oceania	Oceania Tennis Federation (OTF)
Europe	Tennis Europe (TE)

Source: International Tennis Federation 1998a, 27.

The ITF's involvement in competitions extends from top professional events such as the Olympic Tennis Event and the four so-called 'Grand Slams' – the Australian Open (Australia), Roland Garros (France), Wimbledon (England) and the US Open (USA) – to the entry-level ITF Men's Satellite and Futures Circuit and the ITF Women's Circuit. There are also ITF tournaments and team events for juniors, seniors and wheelchair tennis players.

The ITF organises the men's team competition, the Davis Cup, and the Federation Cup for women, both sponsored by BNP Paribas, which give players the chance to represent their country. The annual Australian competition, the Hyundai Hopman Cup, which the ITF owns, also offers competitors the opportunity to play mixed team tennis at the start of the season. The ITF-sanctioned Nations Senior Cup was first held in 1999, and became the first nations senior tournament to bring together the most successful elite tennis players, retired from ATP and Davis Cup playing. The ITF also co-hosts and co-owns the Tennis Masters Cup, the event which concludes the ATP season (International Tennis Federation 2006b). Additionally, the ITF organises the international world junior ranking for players aged 18 and under.

Table 2.2: Level of junior tennis at international tournaments

Levels of Tennis	Placement of ITF, ATP, WTA
The Junior Grand Slams - ITF sanctioned	Australian Open Roland Garros Wimbledon US Open
Grade A Events	Grade A Grade 1 Grade 2 Grade 3 Grade 4 Grade 5
Team competitions – ITF	14 & Under 16 & Under 18 & Under

Source: International Tennis Federation 2002, 32.

The Junior Grand Slams are the most important junior tournaments. Only players ranked in the top 100 ranking of the ITF can participate. The Grade A events are the second highest tournaments and they are split up into 6 categories. The lower the category the fewer points can be won toward the rankings. This ranking system is updated every week by the ITF and published on their website (www.itftennis.com/junior).

The Association of Tennis Professionals (ATP) organises the men's professional tour (excluding the four Grand Slams). The ATP season culminates in the end of season Tennis Masters Cup, co-hosted and owned by the ITF, Grand Slams and ATP and played in Shanghai. The ATP also has a year-end doubles championship. The ATP is also responsible for the Challenger Circuit, the level of tournaments just below the Tour, and is also the men's union and was formed in 1972 to protect the interests of male professional tennis players. From 1990 on, the association has organised the principal worldwide tennis tour, the ATP Tour (International Tennis Federation 2006c).

The ATP Tour comprises tennis tournaments with ATP Masters Series, ATP International Series Gold, ATP International Series and ATP Challenger Series. The ATP tour also oversees the World Team Cup played in Düsseldorf (Germany) in May and the seniors' Tour of Champions. Players and Doubles Teams with the most ranking points play in the season-ending Tennis Masters Cup, which is run jointly with ITF. The week-long introductory level Futures tournaments are ITF events and count towards ATP Entry Ranking. The four-week ITF Satellite tournaments were discontinued in 2007. Grand Slam tournaments are overseen by the ITF and count towards the players' ATP rankings. The details of the professional tennis tour (2007) are outlined in Table 2.3

Table 2.3: Details of the professional tennis tour

Event category	Number	Total prize money (USD)	Winner's ranking points	Governing body
Grand Slams	4	6,784,000 to 19,000,000	1,000	ITF
Tennis Masters Cup	1	4,450,000	550-750	ATP & ITF
ATP Masters Series	9	2,450,000 to 3,450,000	500	ATP
ATP International Series Gold	9	755,000 to 1,426,250	250 to 300	ATP
ATP International Series	43	416,000 to 1,000,000	175 to 250	ATP
ATP Challenger Series	115	25,000 to 150,000	50 to 100	ATP
Futures	420	10,000 and 15,000	12 to 24	ITF

Source: International Tennis Federation 2007, 22.

The ATP publishes weekly rankings of professional players, ATP Entry Ranking, a 52-week rolling ranking and ATP Race, a year to date rankings list. The Entry Ranking is used for determining qualification for entry and seeding in all tournaments for both singles and doubles. The Entry Ranking is the cumulative points earned in the past 52 weeks, except for the Tennis Masters Cup, whose points are dropped following the last ATP event of the year. The player with the most points by season's end is the World Number 1 of the year. The ATP Race is an annual race from season start to season end. Every player starts collecting points from the beginning of the season. At the end of the season, the ATP Race determines which players and teams (first eight for singles and first four for doubles) can compete in the Tennis Masters Cup.

The Women's Tennis Association (WTA), formed in 1973, is the principal organising body of women's professional tennis and is the counterpart organisation of the men's professional tour (ATP). It organizes the WTA Tour, the worldwide professional tennis tour for women, which has for sponsorship reasons been known since 2005 as The Sony Ericsson WTA Tour (Women's Tennis Association 2009). The Women's Tennis Association can trace its origins back to Houston, Texas when the inaugural Virginia Slims event was won on 23 September 1970. Billie Jean King was a major figure in the early days of the WTA. Over 1,000 female players, representing 76 nations, are ranked on the WTA Tour ranking. The WTA Players Association, the tournaments and the ITF make up the WTA Tour Board. The ITF, ATP and WTA Tour work together to agree on calendar dates and are also responsible for the anti-doping programme.

Table 2.4: Elite Women's Tennis

Levels of tennis	Placement of ITF, ATP, WTA
The Grand Slams – ITF Sanctioned	Australian Open-Roland Garros-Wimbledon US Open
Olympic Tennis Event	Managed by the ITF on behalf of the IOC
Team competitions – ITF	Fed Cup by BNP Paribas Hyundai Hopman Cup (mixed) (owned by the ITF)
WTA	Tier I to Tier V
ITF Events	ITF Women's Circuit

Source: International Tennis Federation 2002, 37.

Regarding my main research question "How are TID programmes in tennis organised and implemented in different European countries?" it is important to know how tennis is institutionalised and popularised worldwide. A strong internationally standardised organisation of member nations from world tennis down to club level makes tennis comparable for people in South America to the same extent as for those in Asia and Europe (van Bottenburg 2001, 22). Taking socio-structural and socio-cultural factors into account, it is of relevance what kind of people play tennis and develop their possible talent.

2.2 Structural and socio-cultural factors

Cultural factors are a significant and often overlooked component of the environmental equation and development of expertise. The importance that a country or society attaches to a particular sport can have a dramatic influence on any success achieved. For instance, in Canada, where there is a long and well documented history of ice hockey, the game has become an integral component of national identity (Russell 2000). Ice hockey has featured on the national television network each Saturday evening for more than 50 years. In Austria I find the same factors for alpine skiing (Coakley 2001). Similarly, the sporting culture in Nordic countries places a high value on cross-country skiing. The natural environment in these nations, combined with the public interest and adulation, provides fertile ground for developing skiing expertise. For example, the dominance of American basketball by black athletes, and the recent pre-eminence of Kenyans in middle and long-distance running events, has sparked the belief in a genetic advantage, which often ignores the various cultural and psychological factors involved in the sport (Hamilton 2000). In addition, the sports that Black America has come to dominate, consisting primarily of basketball, football, and track and field sports, reflect a cultural emphasis made evident by the support these sports receive through the state school system. Black athletes have access to coaching, facilities, and competition in publicly funded school sports to a much greater extent than for traditionally more exclusionary endeavours. Sports taught primarily in a country club setting, like golf and tennis, provide a significant barrier to entry for blacks, as private clubs have historically denied membership to certain minority groups for economic and social reasons (Hamilton 2000).

Societal conditions frame success in sports in any nation (Jokl et al. 1956). For the identification of such external conditions in sport, the investigation of certain characteristics of a country is important (Digel 2001, 72). Political structures, the economic situation, the educational system and socio-cultural aspects are the most important factors which can influence development in sport, both positively and negatively. Furthermore, social stratification (the hierarchical arrangement of social classes, castes and strata within a society and the social position in which children are integrated in their early years (Bourdieu 1982), plus increases in leisure time available to the population, are also key factors which influence the choice and the popularity of sports (van Bottenburg 2001). Some sociologists (e.g. Bourdieu 1982) believe that the social backgrounds from which people emerge are important influences on the choice and the popularity of sport. When people choose a sport they are not just deciding between different forms of competition and physical exertion; they are also deciding between different groups of people. As Van Bottenburg (2001, 41) noted, people choose a sports or other recreational club because they feel 'at home', so such considerations as power relations and differences of status between countries and social classes, but also between men and women, the young and older people, and people from different regions become valuable in understanding the place of sport within any society.

Tennis is played all over the world. The International Tennis Federation includes 205 member nations. In Europe, tennis is part of the sports culture. As we have noted van Bottenburg (1992, 2001) has identified the growth of popularity in tennis since the 1960s as owing to three social factors. Firstly, the increase in female participation – related to the changing position of women in society; secondly, a reduction in the age restrictions placed on tennis (the numbers of both younger and older players have grown); and thirdly, the growth owing to occupational structure changes in professional and managerial workers, who tend to value and play such individualised sports (van Bottenburg 1992). In 1999, tennis was the sport with the second highest number of members in 15 European countries, with 4,572,139 registered members. According to van Bottenburg (2001) tennis in Europe in general is socially structured and is more an upper-middle class sport. In all EU members as well in the countries selected (United Kingdom, France, Germany and the Czech Republic) the degree of participation in tennis differs between social categories like gender, age, level of education, profession and income. Van Bottenburg (2005) also mentions that 'despite the popularisation and democratisation of sport, it appears that these differences remain very persistent'. He notes a higher participation in tennis for men than for women, but he also notes that the balance of participation in tennis is one reason for the increase in its popularity (van Bottenburg 1992). Furthermore, he mentions that participation in sport is proportionally related to age: age increase means that participation decreases; and finally a higher percentage of participation in groups with a higher educational, professional and/ or income level (Van Bottenburg 2005). See Table 2.5.

Table 2.5: Differences in sports participation

	Men	41%
Gender	Women	35%
Age groups	15-24	60%
	25-36	41%
	40-54	34%
	55+	28%
Education level	Finished studies at:	
	Age 15 or younger	20%
	Between 16-19	32%
	Age 20 or older	50%

Source: European Commission, Eurobarometer 213, 2005, 5.

Van Bottenburg (1992, 2001 and 2005) identified sport and tennis as part of a global culture and he noted a relation between the development of social class and the development of a sport like tennis. The changes in social classes and the increase of the middle and upper class are the main reasons for the spread of sport and tennis specifically. In general tennis was in the 1990s a sport for the upper class (van Bottenburg 1992). Contrary to soccer, tennis did not filter down from the upper to the middle class, and in contrast to other upper-class sports like golf or cricket, tennis is today (2008) the second English sport in Western Europe (van Bottenburg 2001). As I stated, there are three reasons for this popularity (female participation, the elimination of the age restriction, and professional and middle class growth). The social position of participants and the cultural context of the researched countries, mainly under which circumstances it is possible to play tennis in the different countries, form an important argument for the execution of any talent identification and development of tennis players. I look at this later on in the thesis. While the social factors that influence the acquisition of high levels of sport proficiency have only being briefly presented here, I suggest that it is very important to acknowledge that the environmental constraints on expertise can be broad (e.g., socio-cultural factors) and/or narrow (e.g., family or coaching factors).

2.3 Conclusion

To summarise this chapter, I have noted how in historical context tennis has been a sport for kings and the aristocracy; even during its development into a modern sport in the late 19th century, it was effectively closed to people from the lower social classes. It is obvious that tennis today, in the same manner as in history, is a sport for predominantly middle and upper class people. These different social contexts could have an influence of the meaning of tennis and especially their approaches to TID in tennis up to today; however, tennis today is related to age and gender, which have an influence on the TID programmes of any nation. Playing tennis is possible for everybody from the technical point of view, but to get access to clubs and courts (most of which are private or too expensive) is impossible for many people. This has consequences for the identification and development of talented children. I will discuss how these programmes are implemented in European countries and how talent identification and development in tennis works in the next chapter, which focuses on the four European countries (Czech Republic, Germany, France and the United Kingdom) and their political and cultural characteristics. I will briefly focus on the social structure of these countries, and the significance of sport, especially the sport of tennis, and how it is organised, in them.

Chapter 3 Tennis in Four European Countries

Introduction

The popularity of tennis has undoubtedly grown since the 1960s. It has become part of the sports culture of most European countries. After an increase in membership up to the early 1980s, a slow decline of membership has been obvious over the last 20 years: this could be explained by the shift of interest of older people towards other prestigious sports like golf, since, as I have indicated, sport preference is related to social background (van Bottenburg 2005, 204). However, tennis is still one of the top ten sports in the four countries in our research project (van Bottenburg 2005, 205).

For the purposes of this project, the Czech Republic, Germany, France and the United Kingdom (in particular England) are the main countries selected. The aim of this chapter is briefly to provide a background to the organisation of sport and especially tennis in the four countries, using secondary sources. I will give answers to the research topic of how TID operates in tennis in the four European countries selected. I start with a societal overview of each country to understand under what circumstances sport, in particular tennis, and their talent identification programmes, takes place. Secondly, I shall analyse sport and briefly show participation rates and the most popular sports. Thirdly, the position of tennis will be described in each of these countries. At the end of the chapter, I will give an account of the macro (societal), and meso (tennis/ sports organisations) levels, and identify the influence of different social, historical and cultural contexts. The message from this chapter is that the TID programmes of tennis can only take place under certain societal and sport structural conditions– and, more important, that tennis is still not a sport for all. It is more or less dependent on the social status of the population.

3.1 The Czech Republic

The Czech provinces have existed for more than 10 centuries. Due to their position in the centre of the European continent, they have played an important part in all eras of history (Czech Republic 2008a). After 1948 for more than 40 years Czechoslovakia was part of the communist bloc, following a different economic path than its western European neighbours (Altmann & Baratta 2006a). After 40 years of communist rule, the Velvet Revolution began on November 17, 1989. The communist regime intervened against demonstrations organised by students on the occasion of the anniversary of the closure of Czech schools by the Nazis. People came out on the streets to protest against the brutality of the intervention, and organized demonstrations and strikes. During the Velvet Revolution the communists relinquished their political power. The regime had exhausted itself and did not have the strength to engage in a power struggle with the whole of society. Political parties were reinstated, and the first free elections were held in 1990 (Czech Republic 2008b).

In 1993 Czechoslovakia was split into the Czech and the Slovak Republics. In 2004, the Czech Republic became a member of the European Union and took over the presidency in 2008. Up to 2008 and before the financial crisis, the Czech Republic was one of the fastest-growing economies in the EU. However sport during the communist period continued to provide one avenue for mutual contact with the non-communist world. In 2008 the Czech Republic has 10,489,183 inhabitants (Czech Statistical Office 2008a).

3.1.1 Sport in the Czech Republic

In 1999, 14% of the Czech population between 16 and 74 years of age participated in sport within an organised or competitive framework. According to the Leibniz Institute of Social Science (2008), a total of 34% of Czech people between the ages of 16 and 24 were sports club members. A number of organisations in the Czech Republic work in the area of sport, both governmental institutions and non-governmental organisations. The Ministry of Education, Youth and Sport is at the head of the governmental institutions (see figure 3.1). Among the non-governmental organisations (NGOs) in the CR, there are a number of large sport associations as well as small independent sports organisations.

figure 3.1: Relations between the Ministry of Education and Sport and civic associations (sports organisations) in the Czech Republic

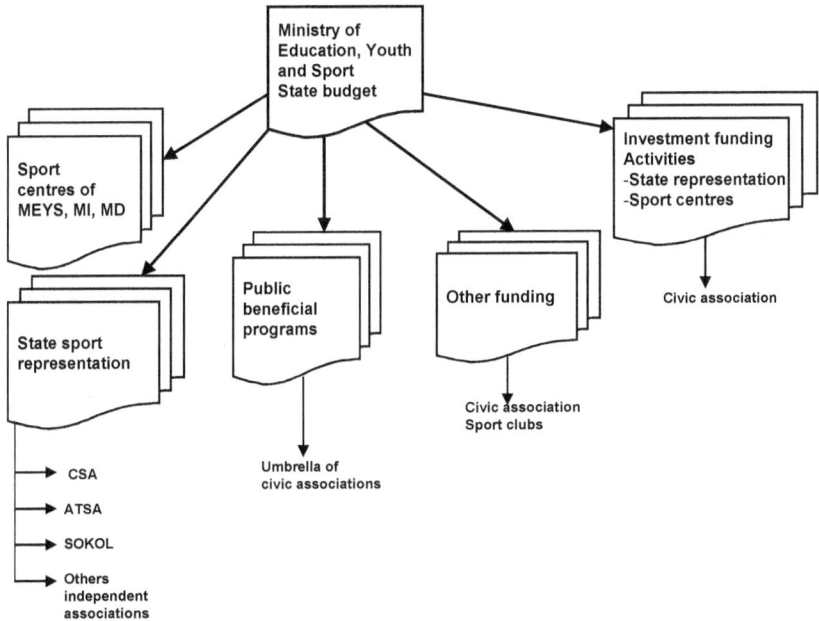

Source: Youth Sport Net 2008

Legend:
MEYS – Ministry of Education, Youth and Sport
MI – Ministry of Internal Affairs
MD – Ministry of Defense
CSA – Czech Sport Associations
ATSA – Association of Technical Sports and Activities
Sports centres – responsible for the preparation of top-level sportsmen
Sokol – Mass participation organisation founded in the 19th century

From the 13th century (invasion of the Teutonic knights) until the 20th century, when the Soviet Union struggled to survive the German invasion, Germans and

Slavs contended for political and cultural domination in Eastern Europe. In the last decade of the 19th century, the Czechs appropriated the German gymnastic movement to use it in their fight for national liberation. The most famous Czech sports grouping was the mass participation organisation Sokol (English translation: 'Falcon' (Guttmann 2004, 280) founded in the 19th century. The main goal of Sokol was to promote national health and sports and it played a key role in the national resistance to the Austrian Empire, the Nazi occupation and the Communist regime. Soon after it was founded in 1862, colourful gymnastic games were held regularly in Prague until the German occupation in 1938. The Communist regime banned the organisation after its 1948 rally, but Sokol continued to exist abroad. In July 1994, Sokol staged a triumphant return with games in Prague (Czech Republic 2008e).

Nowadays, Sokol supports sporting activities with regard to 57 sports, which are organised in the Czech Sokol Community. The Sokol Organization has also significantly influenced the broadening of a humanitarian event, the Terry Fox Run[1] (a charity event) in the Czech Republic, which together with Canada, is No. 1 in the world as far as the number of participants in the run is concerned. These days, the Czech Sokol Community (COS) has almost 1,100 units and 190,000 members. The last Sokol rally took place in July 2006. Sokol is one of the oldest organisations of this type in the world (Czech Republic 2008e).

The Czech Sports Association (CSA) is a voluntary association of sports, physical training, and tourist formations operating nationwide and of physical training unions and sports clubs including their associations. Established on 11 March 1990, the Czech Sports Association's mission is to support the sports, physical education, tourism and sports representation of the Czech Republic, including their preparation, to represent and protect the rights and interests of those involved in sport, to provide them with the required services, as well as to create

---

[1] Named in honour of Canadian amputee runner Terry Fox who at 21 yrs, in 1980, attempted to run across Canada to raise money for cancer research. Countries around the world stage annual events in support of Terry's dream of finding a cure for cancer. It is non-competitive with no winners or awards.

a necessary platform for mutual cooperation. Those working within the Czech Sports Association retain the independence of their legal status, property, and activities (Czech Sport Association 2009).

At the end of December 2007, there were 85 sports federations and 8,595 sports clubs with 1,305,523 members, enjoying corporate as well as associate membership in the Czech Sports Association. Its conception of activities and organisational structure is in accord with European standards of governmental and non-governmental physical training and sports organisations. The Czech Sports Association is democratic, independent, and non-political, respecting the full autonomy and responsibilities of the associated subjects. It cooperates with a large number of sports organisations (e.g. the Czech Paralympics Committee). Similarly, 77 regional sports unions of the Czech Sports Association are active in all regions of the Czech Republic. In connection with the regional organisation of the Czech Republic, regional unions of the Czech Sports Association were established, starting their activities from 1 July 2001. The primary document of the Czech Sports Association's activities is its Statutes (Czech Sports Association 2009).

From a European perspective, there appears to be a high level of sports participation in the Czech Republic. In 2004, only 35% of the population never exercised or took part in sport, and 62% of young people between the ages of 16 and 24 participated regularly in sport (van Bottenburg 2005, 168). Young people do more sport than older people but men do more than women only in the age group of the 16 to 24 years olds. Women participate more in sports than men, but men do more competitive sport. The most popular club sports in the Czech Republic are soccer and tennis. Ice Hockey as a club sport is also a big part of the sports culture of the country. This sport attracts the same numbers of men and women. In the last 10 years serious membership losses were suffered by handball (-67%) and to a lesser extent tennis (-2%). For men tennis is ranked ninth and for women eighth. Tennis in the Czech Republic is a sport with a long tradition. It was always a sport where people in the former communist era had the chance to travel to other countries to play in tournaments. In the last 20 years and since the fall of communism, the motivation to play tennis has been challenged. Arguably, however, the competitive philosophy regarding tennis is still more extensive in the CR than playing tennis for leisure-time recreation.

3.1.2 Tennis in the Czech Republic

Tennis in the CR has a long history, which goes back to the 1890s where the first lawn tennis club in Prague was founded in 1892. The Czechoslovak Tennis Association was then founded in 1918. Even during Sovietization tennis was more popular in Bohemia and Moravia than in other parts of Central Europe or the Balkans. It is related to different economic development. Before Communism, the Czech Republic was relatively advanced in industrial terms. Around the 1900s it had closer relations with Britain than the neighbouring countries, and a larger bourgeoisie. Tennis was the most popular English sport and the tradition of the sport grew up in Czechoslovakia before the Second World War (Van Bottenburg 2001, 142).

The first important name in the sphere of Czech tennis was Karel Koželuh in the 1920s. Glory for Czech tennis was also ensured by Jaroslav Drobný, who was constantly to be found in the top 10 world tennis rankings between 1947 and 1955 and in 1954 won the Wimbledon tournament. Unfortunately, his fans had to admire him from a distance, as he preferred emigration to the life under totalitarian Czechoslovakia after the communist coup in 1948. Czech tennis reached its peak in the 1970s, when Jan Kodeš won Wimbledon in 1974. World renown was also gained, for example, by Ivan Lendl, who won prestigious world competitions several times, including the 1980 Davis Cup. Among Czech women tennis players, the most famous is Martina Navrátilová, who won every Grand Slam title many times over during the course of her career. Current rising stars of Czech tennis include Radek Stepanek, Nicole Vaidišová and Tomáš Berdych. In addition, Petr Korda, Hana Mandlikova, Helena Sukova, Jana Novotna and Jiri Novak can also be named, among many others. Czech tennis players have been remarkably successful in international competitions.

The Czech Tennis Association (CTA) is divided into 8 regions, in which there are 969 tennis clubs registered, with 5040 courts (Tennis Europe 2009). Each of these regions manages its affiliated tennis clubs. There are about 300 national men's tournaments. There are 907 men's and 937 women's teams competing in the National League, and around 2200 men, 1200 women, and 6000 juniors ranked in the national ranking list (Czech Tennis Association 2008a).

Czech productivity in tennis can be seen in the ranking of the most important organisations the Association of Tennis Players (ATP), the Women's Tennis Association (WTA) and the International Tennis Federation (ITF). In the Top 1000 men's professional ranking (ATP) there are 37 Czechs, and in the Top 100, there are 2 Czech players registered (Association of Tennis Professionals 2008b). In the Top 1000 women's ranking (WTA) there are 34 Czechs, and in the Top 100 there are 7 Czech female players registered (Women's Tennis Association 2009b). In the Top 100 junior ranking for under 18's of the International Tennis Federation (ITF) 1 boy and no girls were registered (International Tennis Federation 2009b). In the Czech Republic today, tennis is a cultural product linked to and associated with society. In the communist era tennis was not very well supported because it was not an Olympic sport, but through the long tradition since the beginning of the last century and the former strong relationship to England, tennis has established itself as a popular, if still high status, sport (van Bottenburg 2001).

3.2 Germany

As Europe's largest economy and most populous nation, with a population size of 82,431,390 (July 2005 est.) (Altmann & Baratta 2006b), Germany remains a key member of the continent's economic, political, and defence organisations. The working class can be divided into three groups: an elite of the best-trained and best-paid workers (12 percent of the population); skilled workers (18 percent), about 5 percent of whom are foreigners; and unskilled workers (15 percent), about 25 percent of whom are foreigners (Geissler 2002). Parts of the group of foreigners live below the poverty line. Farmers and their families make up 6 percent of the population. At the top of this model of the social structure, with 1 percent, is the elite class (Geissler 2002).

3.2.1 Sport in Germany

Sport in Germany is organised in a non-political manner. The main sports organisation in Germany is the DOSB (German Olympic Sport Association), which was founded in 2007 following a merger between the NOC Germany (NOK) and the former 'Deutscher Sport Bund' (DSB). Keeping Germany fit is the aim of the DOSB. Under the motto 'Sport for all' the DOSB has launched several campaigns to increase mass participation, starting in the seventies with the construction of keep-fit trails in parks and woods. Their current campaigns include 'Sport for Health' and 'Properly fit', both of which offer courses and information on how best to use sport to stay fit and healthy (Deutscher Olympischer Sport Bund 2009).

In the DOSB there are more than 90,305 gymnastics and sports clubs with about 27 million members organised – not including those doing sports without being members of a club. The DOSB is organised in 16 regional sports federations, 55 National Sport Governing Bodies, 11 Federations for special purposes, 6 Federations for Science and Education, and 2 Promoting Federations. 2.7 million mostly honorary coaches and staff of sports clubs give 240 million practice hours each year (Deutscher Olympischer Sport Bund 2009a). In the top six sports in Germany we find soccer, tennis and track and field sports alongside typical German sports (van Bottenburg 2001) gymnastics, shooting, and handball. Gymnastics is enormously popular and is Germany's second sport, close behind soccer and before tennis.

Winter sports, too, enjoy great popularity in Germany. The opportunities for alpine and cross-country skiing, snowboarding and downhill skiing make Germany's mountain regions a favourite destination for tourists. Both speed skating and in particular ice hockey are big spectator sports in Germany, like basketball, volleyball, and handball. More than five thousand handball clubs with 838,000 members belong to the German handball association 'Deutscher Handball Bund' (DHB). American football has also become increasingly popular in Germany in the last 15 years.

Over the last decade, some sports trends in Germany have been recognisable. Up to the age of nineteen, the team sports of soccer and basketball are the most popular sports outside the context of competition and matches. After this their popularity decreases very fast. In terms of organised sports, there are two sports in Germany that stand out above all other sports: soccer and gymnastics. These two sports are in the first two positions in the popularity rankings for both sexes. Furthermore, there is a great similarity between the sport preferences of men and women and those of boys and girls (van Bottenburg 2005).

According to the DOSB (2008) 47% of the German population exercised or played sport at least once a month in 2007, 34% (Western Germany) and 27% (Eastern Germany) engaged in sport once a week or more (in 2002), whilst 36% did no sport at all. With respect to intensive physical activity, the German population appears to be more physically active than most other member states of the European Union (van Bottenburg 2005). The large number of members of the DOSB underlines the fact that people doing sports are not a minority; sport is rather a mass phenomenon in Germany. The actual figure may be closer to 18 million German club members (Breuer 2007); however, some sportsmen and sportswomen belong to more than one club, whereas others are merely passive or social members. This figure is even more impressive if we consider the fact that only 29% of German sportsmen and sportswomen do their sports primarily in a club ('der Sportverein') 58% of people regularly participating in sport do not belong to any organisation, – for instance, they cycle or jog – and another 12% use a commercial facility such as a fitness centre or a dance studio. In fact, the number of fitness centres has more than doubled since 1985, rising from 2,800 to 6,500. According to a report commissioned by the Allensbach 'Institut für Demoskopie' (Demographic Institute), 63% of Germans claim to take part in sporting activities, and 34% do so at least once a week (Deutscher Olympischer Sport Bund 2009b).

In the last four years, the German government has become increasingly concerned about the health of the 36% of Germans who do not take part in any sporting activity. Not least for financial reasons – medical research has shown that lack of exercise and physical work is one of the reasons for the increase in cardiovascular diseases, and about 30 per cent of medical costs incurred in Germany result from heart, circulatory or metabolic disorders ('Bundesgesundheitsministerium' = Federal Ministry of Health 2008). This is a major problem in an ageing population, as 52% of 'idle' Germans are aged fifty or over, and only one in ten German adults between the age of 35 and 60 does two hours or more per week of moderate sporting activity. The younger generation is equally threatened by an increasingly sedentary lifestyle characterised by long periods seated in front of a computer or television screen (Deutscher Olympischer Sport Bund 2006).

The correlation between sports participation on the one hand, and age, gender and social class on the other is another characteristic of the German sport situation. The differences in sports participation between men and women and between young and old have significantly decreased in Germany during the past few decades. In Germany the sports played change during people's lives. Team sports and competitive sports are more popular among young people. Health considerations become more important to adults; this is followed by a demand for specific health sport programmes at an older age. The non-profit sports clubs are the major setting for sport activities during youth, while in later ages sport takes place in fitness centres and some informal settings (Breuer 2006).

Today Germany is currently confronted with financial problems at national, federal states' and local levels. For the practice of sports, promotion by the municipalities plays an important part, and is specially endangered at the moment. For this reason the DOSB and its member organisations are strongly advocating a tax reform giving the municipalities (and sport at local level) more planning certainty by assigning specific parts of tax revenues to municipalities for sport purposes (Breuer 2006).

In the popularity ranking order of sports in Germany, according to federation membership and gender in 2008, tennis was ranked in third position (men 4th position, females 3rd position). This is similar to the popularity ranking in Germany among young people under 18, where tennis is also in 3rd position, behind soccer and gymnastics. Interestingly, in this ranking tennis is in the 6th

position for girls (Deutscher Olympischer Sport Bund 2009b). However, tennis has declined in popularity since 1993, at least in its organised form. Van Bottenburg (2005) sees a correlation between the increase in membership in golf and the decrease in tennis membership which is confirmed by the DOSB statistics in the years 2003-2008 (Deutscher Olympischer Sport Bund 2009a). The popularisation of tennis emerged during the 1970s and 1980s in similar ways in different western European countries, and was a result of the increase at that time in the general level of education, income and professional status from which tennis players had always been recruited. People crossed over to the sport where they could feel this atmosphere and feel their status valued (van Bottenburg 2005). In general the tennis boom initiated by the Wimbledon victories of Boris Becker, Steffi Graf and Michael Stich lasted for much of the 1990s, although in recent times the pool of German tennis talent seems to have dried up somewhat.

3.2.2 Tennis in Germany

Gottfried von Cramm, Cilly Aussem, Boris Becker, Michael Stich and Steffi Graf won major tournaments like Wimbledon, US Open, Australian Open and set up successful international careers. After the foundation of the Deutscher Tennis Bund (DTB) in 1902 and some remarkable decades in the 1930s (Gottfried von Cramm), the most successful era started in the 1980s, when as a teenager Becker won the All England Championships in Wimbledon at the age of 17. From the 1970s, membership registrations at tennis clubs increased from 1 million in 1978 to more than 2 million in 1990. Whilst in 2008 membership registrations were down to 1.58 million, the German Tennis Federation (DTB) still has the most members of all tennis federations worldwide.

Table 3.1: Membership development in selected years

Year	Juniors	Adults	Total	Change from the previous year
1973	131,372	369,205	500,577	8.67%
1974	143,369	452,164	595,533	18.97%
1978	257,669	766,490	1,024,159	12.92%
1989	504,853	1,525,918	2,030,771	3.54%
2006	405,668	1,253,135	1,658,803	-3.06%
2007	398,228	1,209,396	1,607,624	-3.09%
2008	397,213	1,189,450	1,586,663	-1.30%

Source: Deutscher Tennis Bund 2008a.

There are 18 autonomous Regional Tennis Federations (Deutscher Tennis Bund 2008c), totalling 1,586,663 registered and 1.06 million non-registered members (Deutscher Olympischer Sport Bund 2009b).

Table 3.2: Membership figures in tennis 2008 by age and gender

Age	7 years		7-14 years		15-18 years		19-26 years		27-40 years	
	Male	Female	Male	Female	Male	Female	Male	Female	Male	Female
members	7,971	6,102	136,137	101,492	81,379	64,133	79,204	55,872	120.577	79,006

Age	41-60 years		Over 60 years		Total		Total
	Male	Female	Male	Female	Male	Female	Male and Female
members	322,836	228,357	198,688	104,909	946,792	639,871	1,586,663

Source: Deutscher Olympischer Sport Bund 2009b.

These registered members play on 44,490 outdoor and 4,602 indoor tennis courts in 9,945 tennis clubs (Deutscher Tennis Bund 2008b). The most talented – elite – players use 18 regional centres, 3 partly national centres and 1 national centre. Around 1000 juniors are supported by 150 coaches in 140 decentralized training centres (Deutscher Tennis Bund 2008d). It is commonly assumed in Germany that the 1980s were the most successful decade for membership development, but the statistics (Table 3.1) tell me that the greatest increase in members in the history of German tennis was between 1971 and 1980, that is, five years before Boris Becker won his first Grand Slam title in Wimbledon. The significant growth of tennis was, however, an international development, which also occurred in many other European countries that did not have players like Boris Becker or Steffi Graf (van Bottenburg 2005, 123). As for mass participation, the important age group of 14-26 years has decreased significantly, whilst juniors aged between 7 and 14 are the leading group amongst players aged under 40 (Deutscher Tennis Bund 2008e). About 55,000 teams from about 44,000 clubs compete in the different leagues. There are some 100,000 juniors regularly competing (League and tournaments) (Deutscher Tennis Bund 2008f). There are around 800 junior, 700 senior, and 285 veterans' tournaments. In addition there are a further 19 international junior tournaments (Deutscher Tennis Bund 2008g).

The productivity of German tennis is shown in the rankings of the most important world organisations, the Association of Men's Tennis Professionals (ATP), the Women's Tennis Association (WTA) and the International Tennis Federation (ITF). In the overall men's professional ranking (ATP) there are 108 German players registered. In the current Top 100 (October 2008) there are 7 German players, in the Top 1000, 56 German players are ranked (Association of Tennis Professionals 2008a). In the overall WTA (women's professionals) 41 German women are ranked. In the Top 100, 2 German women are ranked (Women's Tennis Association 2008a). In the Top 100 ITF junior ranking (U18) 2 boys and 1 girl were registered (International Tennis Federation 2009a). Further, Germany has a higher number of qualified coaches in comparison to other countries (15,000). The DTB invests 1.5 million Euro, or 25% of its whole budget, in elite development (De Bosscher et al. 2003). On the one hand we can sum up by saying that tennis is still a very popular sport for the people – unfortunately solely for watching on TV; by contrast, tennis is predominantly practised by middle and upper middle class people because the membership and coaching fees are too high for the others. This is certainly confirmed by my personal experiences as a professional tennis coach in Stuttgart over 15 years.

3.3 France

The French population has risen to 64,473,140 (January 2008 estimate) living on 547,030 km^2 (108 inhabitants per km^2). About 1.5 million are foreigners from EU countries. Such figures are only of limited significance, though, since citizens of the former colonies and children of foreign parents also born in France have a right to French citizenship (with certain prerequisites). The number of foreigners in the cultural sense is much higher than the official numbers suggest. Most of the foreigners living in France have migrated from Algeria and Morocco. France is a centralised country with around 10.6 million people (17.9%) living in Paris (Ile-de France) (Institut National de la Statistique et des études économiques 2008). The urban population today makes up 72.6% of the total population.

Social inequality, i.e. the unequal distribution of living and working conditions, incomes, and chances of a career in society, has always played a large part in the social and political life of the French people (Lasserre & Schild 1997). France is traditionally marked by a strongly developed division between social strata. Social groups have strongly distinctive class awareness, and social advancement cannot be easily achieved. In connection with this, an ethnically heterogeneous urban lower class has arisen in the French suburbs. The major part of this underqualified population oscillates between unemployment and insecure part-time jobs. Social discrimination and lack of integration has a particularly problematic effect on the younger generation. Thus children and teenagers are confronted with less parental guidance and with frequent conflicts during their socialisation, in families that become impoverished. Many of them leave school without the corresponding certification of education, so that access to the labour market is difficult for them. Some teenagers leave school early and wait for professional qualifying opportunities, with insecure jobs, and drift into criminal activities. Thus the suburbs are not always only areas of discrimination, social isolation and crime, but in some case also the site of the self-organisation of lives and group-specific solidarity (Christadler & Uterwedde 2005; Pierre Bourdieu 1982).

3.3.1 Sport in France

A voluntary union – 'le mouvement sportif' – forms the basis of the sports system in France. There are two major representation structures of the voluntary union, the 'mouvement féderal' and the 'mouvement Olympique'. The 'Comité National Olympique et Sportif Français' (CNOSF) represents 81 sports associations. In 2006, 167,000 'associations sportives' or ‚clubs sportifs' were registered (Ministère des sports 2008).

As in other countries, there are clubs where just one sport is practised (club unisport) and multi-sports clubs (clubs omnisports). Further organisational models are the sports federations (fédérations sportives). The associations are structured democratically. In 2001 there were 109 associations, including 29 Olympic associations, 58 non-Olympic associations and 22 multi-sport associations. In 2001, 74,357 Clubs of Olympic sports were organised and 42,580 of non-Olympic sports. Popular organised sports in France include football (soccer), both codes of rugby, and in certain regions basketball and handball. France has hosted events such as the 1938 and 1998 FIFA World Cup, and hosted the 2007 Rugby Union World Cup. The 'Stade de France' in Paris is the largest stadium in France and was the venue for the 1998 FIFA World Cup final, and hosted the 2007 Rugby World Cup final in October 2007. France also hosts the annual Tour de France, the most famous road cycle race in the world. France is also famous for the 24 hours of Le Mans sports car endurance race, held in the 'Sarthe' department. Several major tennis tournaments take place in France, including the Paris Masters and the French Open, one of the four Grand-Slam tournaments (International Tennis Federation 2008a). Thanks to its geographical situation, some would argue that France offers the ideal conditions for most sports (Digel 2003a).

In the table (3.3) I can see that in the last decades interest in sport (organised and non-organised) in France has increased. Hartmann-Tews (1996) mentions that the development of the 'sports for all' movement (non-competitive sport) has notably increased. Research in 2000 found that around 26 million French people practised a sport once a week (60% of the age group 15-75 years) (Mignon & Truchot 2001).

Table 3.3: Overview of the sport practice of people between the ages of 15 und 75 in the year 2000

Sport Activity	Number (in mill)	Proportion of 15 to 75 years old (in %)	Proportion of Women (in %)	Proportion of 15-29 years old (in %)
Once a week	26,482	60	47	31
In clubs or federations	10,006	23	40	38
Minimum once a year	36,637	83	48	30

Source: Mignon & Truchot 2001, 2.

All Olympic sports have a high prestige in the politics and society of France: sport is subject to regulation by the state. It is remarkable that France never claims to be the sole winner nation in world class sport (Digel 2003a). Sport participation shows that the interest is mainly concentrated on leisure sport activities and traditional sports, and only 23% of 15-75 year-olds are organised in clubs or organisations. The most popular forms of physical exercise in the year 2000 for the French people were walking (20.9m), swimming (14.5m) and cycling (12.8m). Jogging (6.6m) and boules/pétanque (6.1m) were also popular. An overview of the ten most popular sports in France is shown in the next table (3.4).

Table 3.4: The most popular sport activities of the French population in the year 2000

Sport Activity	Number in Mio	Min once a week (in %)	Proportion of women (in %)	Average age	Club or federation (in %)
Trekking	20,933	57	57	45	20
Swimming or bathing	14,548	28	52	34	29
Cycling	12,739	51	41	38	30
Jogging	6,631	61	35	33	40
Boules, Pétanque	6,113	18	27	43	30
Gymnastics	6,052	82	79	41	49
Winter sports	5,314	13	43	35	41
Soccer	4,633	54	8	27	51
Tennis	3,585	35	32	30	53
Fishing	3,047	37	16	44	13

Source: Mignon & Truchot 2001, 3.

Based on sports that are participated in at least once a week, walking, swimming and cycling are the most popular in France. If I look at club-related sport, as in many other European countries, soccer (2,140,133 members) is by far the most popular sport, followed by tennis, with 9067 clubs and 1,064,773 members (Tennis Europe 2008b).

There is no nationally, centrally and systematically directed talent search programme for talented children in sport in general. But the influence of the state in individual and organised sports is tremendous. Members of the DTN of the associations go to the clubs in general to identify and select talents there who have achieved good results in competitions; they decide on financial support, so the support and development of sports talent in France is well established in their federations. The organisation of the federations themselves is basically subject to fiscal regulations; sports receive financial support from the 'fonds national pour le développement du sport' (FNDS). High level sport is based on financial support from the state.

This sports system reflects the political system as a centralised state, in which Paris occupies the dominant position. The sports system is also centralised, like the French economy. The education system is standardised and centralised as well. In tennis, this centralisation is seen as successful in developing top athletes.

3.3.2 Tennis in France

In 1888 the 'l'Union des Sociétés Françaises des Sports Athlétiques' established a 'Commission de Lawn Tennis Club'. The Fédération Française de Tennis (in English: French Tennis Federation), also known as the FFT, as an organisation set up in 1920 that takes charge of the organisation, coordination and promotion of tennis in France. It is recognised by the International Tennis Federation and by the French Ministry of Sport. Its headquarters are at the Roland Garros Stadium in Paris. It was originally founded under the name 'Fédération Française de Lawn Tennis' until it was changed to 'Fédération Française de Tennis' in 1976 (Fédération Française de Tennis 2008). The roles of the FFT include organising tennis competitions in France, most notably the French Open, supporting and co-ordinating tennis clubs, and managing the French tennis teams, including their Davis-Cup and Fed-Cup teams.

The 'Tournoi de Roland-Garros', commonly known as the French Open, is a major tennis tournament held over two weeks between mid-May and early June in Paris, at the 'Stade de Roland Garros'. It is the second of the Grand Slam tournaments on the annual tennis calendar and the premier clay court tennis tournament in the world. It is one of the most prestigious events in tennis, and benefits from the widest worldwide broadcasting and audience of all events in this sport. Because of the slow-playing surface and the five-set men's singles matches without a tie-break in the final set, the event is considered to be the most physically demanding tennis tournament in the world.

The French Tennis Federation (FFT) has around 300,000 registered members, organised in 8,404 clubs. These members have 33,074 outdoor and 2,600 indoor courts to play on (Fédération Française de Tennis 2008). They are supported by approximately 3,700 coaches and more then 10,000 instructors. Around 1,500 clubs are structured for performance practice. Elite players are supported in 8 national centres. Tennis is ranked as the leading women's and individual sport in general in France. Furthermore, the FFT has 1,950,448 registered matches, 10,449 tournaments and 382,000 competitors, and in some popularity scales French tennis ranks $9^{th.}$ (see also Table 3.3) and 2nd for club-related sports. The FFT is centrally organised and monitored by the 'Direction technique nationale' (DTN). The FFT supervises 36 regional Associations (ligues régionales), 85 department committees (comités départementaux), and 1,065,000 licensed players (Fédération Française de Tennis 2008). There are 561,945 licensed junior players aged 18 and under. The total budget in France for the Tennis Association lies at around 100,000,000 € (Euros); 11% of the total budget (€11million) goes into elite tennis. France's status as one of the leading tennis nations is undisputed. 40 French players (22 male, 18 female) were ranked in the top 200 of the world's professional rankings in January 2008. At the time of writing (October 2008) 15 French players were placed in the Top 100 rankings (Association of Tennis Professionals 2008c). In the WTA ladies' ranking, 10 are French female players; in the Top 1000 there are 53 players registered (Women's Tennis Association 2008c). In the Top 100 Junior Ranking of the International Tennis Federation, there are 6 boys and 2 girls registered (International Tennis Federation 2009c). Social stratification in tennis, which was found in Germany and the UK, can also be clearly found in France. Tennis is situated immediately below golf and polo in the French status pyramid (van Bottenburg 2005, 114).

3.4 United Kingdom

In 2007, the UK had around 60.9 million inhabitants (83.4% England; 8.8% Scotland, 5% Wales and 2.8% Northern Ireland). Children aged under 16 represented around one in five of the total population, around the same proportion as those of retirement age (Office for National Statistics 2008). The UK is an economically and socially divided country, which expresses itself in a

North-South divide. This North-South divide has brought the south a population increase. Since many young and better qualified people leave the north, this region is losing its dynamism (Sturm 1997a). But we also have to look at society as a whole to recognise an imbalance in the UK. 3.1% of the adult population belong to the top social layer. This and the upper middle class (17.7%) are financially very well off. 27% of the population form the lower middle class. These are families with small businesses and middle-income employees. 23.6% of the population are skilled workers, and 16.2% workers. Pensioners, widows, casual labourers, and persons receiving supplementary benefit form a residual category of 12.4%. Poverty has increased considerably in Great Britain (Sturm 1997b). The lower 10% of the income pyramid have suffered income losses of 15% within the last 25 years. The richest 10% increased their income by 62%.

Tennis is not only the original English export sport, but also England is seen as the birthplace of sports, because sport events took a distinctive turn in the seventeenth and eighteenth centuries, when for example boxing, running and rowing were standardised and organised at the national level. Reasons for that were the early industrialisation, with the improvement of the infrastructure and a closer contact between the elite and the local population in England, meant that the social elite became more involved with local sports activities than in other countries on the Continent of Europe (van Bottenburg 2001).

3.4.1 Sport in the United Kingdom

The UK has a long history of sports, having figured prominently in their worldwide development. Many sports – for example tennis, golf, association football, rugby, badminton and cricket – originated, or were first popularised, in the UK (van Bottenburg 2001). In the 18th century, British sport was often cultivated by English gentlemen, whilst 'games' were played by the working class. The aristocrats, the dominant social and political power until the 20th century, founded the so-called 'clubs' at that time (Harris 1972). The development of modern sport in the 19th century was given impetus by the universities and

'Public Schools'. Similarly, many organised recreations, such as fishing, camping and canoeing, originated in the UK (van Bottenburg 2001).

Today the structure of UK sport often appears complex and irregular, because each sport has developed in its own individual way, and not as part of a centrally directed plan. Traditionally, sport in the UK has been free of political control at national and local authority level, although the Government does sometimes express views on international matters. Its national aim is to assist with strategies, guidelines, and funding which will help with the development of sport and physical recreation and give support to appropriate national governing and representative bodies of sport.

The overall responsibility for sport at the UK level rests with the Secretary of State for Culture, Media and Sport (who also has an additional responsibility for museums, the BBC, libraries, the national heritage, the Royal estates, etc.), having a sports budget of approximately £66.8 million (except for lottery funding) in 2002 (Digel 2003b). Since the late 1990s each of the devolved government administrations have responsibility for setting their own policies and ensuring that they develop in line with what is wanted in each part of the United Kingdom, with each deciding its own levels of funding for sport. In order to implement these policies, the government earlier set up Home Country Sports Councils and, more recently, a UK Sports Council – UK Sport.

There are five sports councils in the UK (United Kingdom Sport 2008):

- UK Sport (the United Kingdom Sports Council) based in London.
- Sport England (the English Sports Council), based in London, with nine regional offices.
- Sport Scotland (the Scottish Sports Council), based in Edinburgh.
- Sports Council for Wales, based in Cardiff.
- Sports Council for Northern Ireland, based in Belfast and having liaison with the Eire Sports Council.

Many of these bodies are UK (British), although each devolved 'Home Country' usually has its own national governing or representative body for each sport as part of this UK structure. There are some Home Country governing bodies of sport which are not members of a UK organisation – e.g. rugby union, football, cricket, and in the case of Northern Ireland about 35 activities, which cover the whole island of Ireland. This is a particularity of the UK. These sports bodies are independent and mostly voluntary, and – with their clubs – make the major contribution to UK opportunities for participation, competition and training at grass roots level, and progressively upwards to international level for organised sport (Houlihan 1997).

The sports associations based in England can vote in most cases for the Great Britain associations as well. In some sports, sports associations have taken shape for specialized game forms with sets of rules of their own which were organized earlier as game variants under one roof; furthermore, there are separate associations for amateur and professional sport (e.g. the Football Association and the Football League). There are around 10 sports associations in which women and men are separately organised. Furthermore, women are organized in around 30 sports associations.

At the national organisation level there are two central organisations. On the one hand, the Central Council of Recreation Physical Training (CCRPT), founded in 1935 and 1944, changed to the Central Council of Physical Recreation (CCPR). This organisation can be seen as the umbrella organisation of the national sports associations in the UK (Central Council of Physical Recreation 2008). It was estimated that in 2008 eight million participants regularly took part in sport or some form of physical recreation (Central Council of Physical Recreation 2008a). From rugby to country dancing, from motor racing to rambling, the range of sporting and physical endeavours available to the public is enormous. Each of these activities is administered and promoted by a governing or representative body. It is these bodies that make up the membership of the CCPR, namely:

- 280 national governing and representative bodies of sport and recreation
- 150,000 voluntary sports clubs
- 13 million individuals who participate in sport and recreation (Central Council of Physical Recreation 2008b).

The CCPR sees itself as the independent voice of UK Sport and is the umbrella organisation for the national governing and representative bodies of sport and recreation in the UK. Its main objectives are to promote, protect and develop the interests of sport and physical recreation at all levels. It has to be 'at the forefront of sports politics, providing support and services to those who participate in and administer sport and recreation'. The CCPR is independent of any form of Government control, has no responsibility for allocating funds, is strictly non-party, and will support or oppose proposed measures only on the basis of their perceived value to sport and recreation.

On the other hand, there is the British Olympic Association (BOA), which represents the Olympic sports in the International Olympic Committee. The BOA sets out to provide world class services to all who aspire to athletic performance at the Olympic and Olympic Winter Games, to inspire young people to embrace the ideals (British Olympic Association 2009).

Sport plays an important part in the life of the British population. According to information from the European Commission, 23% do exercise or play sport 3 times a week and 45% at least do exercise or play sport once a week (European Commission 2004). Swimming, walking, and the typically British snooker/billiard/pool are the most popular for this group (Sport England 2004). In the UK participation in sport varies according to age, sex, various other demographic factors, social strata and ethnic group membership, as in the other European countries (Sport England 2008).

If we look at the participation level in the most popular sports in the UK, there are unusual features compared with the other three European countries in this study. The most popular sports among the British population (age 16+) in 2002 were walking, swimming and keep fit/yoga (van Bottenburg 2005). Walking is the most popular kind of sport for both men and women. Young women favour walking, physical fitness/yoga and swimming, while men prefer walking, snooker and cycling. Studies by the ONS (Office for National Statistics 2009) have found that men of all age groups are more active in sport than women. Particularly in the age group from 16-24 the difference is considerable; while 50% of men engage in a physical activity on five or more days a week, it is just a fifth with the women. Football ranks fifth in popularity among men, whilst tennis ranks ninth in popularity among women (van Bottenburg 2005). The sports associations with the most members are primarily football, with 7.0 million participants and 5.0 million at school (Football Association 2008), golf, with 800,000 (English Golf Union 2008), gymnastics, with 830,000 members (van Bottenburg 2005) and bowls, with 660,000 members (Professional Bowls Association 2008). Tennis ranks seventh, after cricket and squash, with 286,520 members (van Bottenburg 2005). If we look at the ranking order of the most played sports among the British population (16 years and above, in 2002) according to gender we can note that tennis ranks ninth with the women, with 2% of participants, and men do not see tennis as their sport. If we look at the ranking order of the most popular sports among young people (6-16 years old) in England according to gender, we notice that tennis is a top 4 sport with boys (25%) and in 6th position (20%) with girls. The ranking order according to sports organisations' membership figures in 2002 brought tennis up to 7th place. However, soccer maintains its top position among young people. Van Bottenburg (2001) mentioned the finding that today it is still cheaper to play soccer than other sports, but he also noted that the contrast between 'exclusive' and 'popular' sport is less strongly defined today.

The social stratification of sport plays an important role in England. The General Household Survey from Sport England (2004) shows a clear association between socio-economic status and participation rates in sport and physical activities. Furthermore, sports participation was lower than average among the disabled, ethnic minorities and in deprived areas (Sport England 2004). The statistics from the GHS (2002) Young People Survey stated that very few people in the UK are members of sports clubs. This applies to adults in particular. Whilst around 50% of the age group of 11-16 years old are club members, after school leaving membership drops to 17 % of 16-19 year olds and 13% for 20-24 year olds, then falls further as age increases. English clubs have an over-representation of white, professional males and do not represent many women (4% as against 13% men), semi-skilled or unskilled manual workers (4% versus 16% professionals), Asians, Afro-Caribbean or disabled people. Although more males than females were members of a sport club, more women than men are found in health or fitness clubs. Young people and higher professional groups were over-represented in sports and fitness clubs (van Bottenburg 2005). The UK top ten sports are strongly dominated by those sports whose origins lie in England (van Bottenburg 2005). Tennis-like activities had existed centuries before, at courts and monasteries. In those times, tennis was a game that was played with the hand, where a ball was struck against a wall or against a sloping roof. In the seventeenth century, tennis became a popular form of recreation in courtly circles in England (van Bottenburg 2001).

To summarise this section, we have to mention that the most popular sport for structured games (Guttmann 1978) is football, except in Northern Ireland (where Gaelic games are the most popular sports), and Wales (where rugby union is generally perceived from outside as being the national sport, although there are more registered football clubs than rugby clubs). Cricket is popular in England and Wales, but is less popular in the other home nations. Rugby union and rugby league are the other major team sports, with union generally more popular in the south of England and league traditionally associated with the north. Major individual sports include athletics, golf, motor sport, and horse-racing. Tennis is the highest profile sport for the two weeks of the Wimbledon Championships, but otherwise struggles to hold its own in the country of its birth.

3.4.2 Tennis in the UK

Tennis in Britain as the modern sport can be dated back to two separate inventions. As we noted in chapter two, between 1859 and 1865 Major Harry Gem and Augurio Perera combined elements of the game of rackets and pelota and played it on a croquet lawn in Edgbaston (Gillmeister 1997). Gem and Perera moved to Leamington Spa and in 1872 founded the world's first tennis club (Leamington Tennis Club 2008). The Leamington Spa Courier[2] of 23 July 1884 recorded one of the first tennis tournaments, held at Shrubland Hall (demolished

---

[2] Newspaper 'The Courier in Leamington'

1948), Leamington Spa, England. The rules of tennis varied between amateurs and professionals. The amateur rules were not intended to exclude financial gain – prize money was paid to the winner of the first Wimbledon amateur tournament – it was rather a means of excluding people such as labourers and servants (van Bottenburg 2001). Tennis was the first sport in which women could take part outside of school. Today it is one of the few sports where women and men can participate simultaneously, in mixed doubles for example. In this respect mixed tennis was viewed by some as having an advantage compared with other sports: the tennis club might serve as a good place to find a marriage partner. However, it was not allowed for women to play energetically. Clubs and the game in their first decade was a perfect environment for people from a certain social class, but the standardisation of the rules and the increase in the middle and upper class population made tennis in England and Europe popular as a club sport (van Bottenburg 2001).

Today, the Lawn Tennis Association (LTA), founded in 1888, is the governing body of tennis in the United Kingdom, the Channel Islands and the Isle of Man. Its objects are to promote and develop tennis and to advance and safeguard the interests of the sport and the governing body. Since February 2007 it has been based at the new National Tennis Centre in Roehampton (South West London) having moved from its previous location at the Queen's Club. The LTA had a turnover of £45.8 million for the year ended 30 September 2001 (Houlihan & White 2002) and £43.5 in 2007 (Lawn Tennis Association 2007a).

In 2007 tennis had the following participation rates in England (Tables 3.5 and 3.6):

Table 3.5: Participation rates in tennis

Age	7 years	16-19 years	20-24 years	25-29 years	30-34 years	35-44 years	45-64 years	65+	Total
Participants	14,073	184,000	96,000	61,000	79,000	184,000	201,000	70,000	874,000

Source: Sport England 2008.

Table 3.6: Participation rates in tennis social distinction

Participants	White community	Non white community	Employed	Students	Unemployed	Higher managerial occupations	Lower managerial occupation
Tennis	795,000	79,000	559,000	175,000	35,000	516,000	175,000

Source: Sport England 2008.

In the Lawn Tennis Association and its four regional departments (Wales, England, Scotland and Northern Ireland) there are about 90,000 registered and licensed tennis players. But there are more than 4 million estimated tennis players who are not registered in the tennis associations of the UK. The registered and non-registered players play on 35,200 courts in 2,600 clubs (Tennis Europe 2008a). The best players are supported in one National Centre at Roehampton (Lawn Tennis Association 2008c). All players in the LTA are supported by approximately 6,000 coaches. There are about 3,500 coaches active in LTA affiliated clubs. About 2,900 coaches are licensed by the LTA (Lawn Tennis Association 2006, 8). There are currently (2006) 2600 affiliated clubs. About 830 teams from about 450 clubs compete in the National Club League and some 3,500 teams from about 750 clubs compete in the National Junior Club League (Lawn Tennis Association 2006). There are some 6,000 boys and 2,400 girls regularly competing (at least 6 matches a year). There is no formal organised competitive structure for players under 10 years old. In 2006 the LTA staged 31 weeks of men's events (of which 22 were 'Futures' weeks and 7 were 'Challenger'events) plus 22 weeks of women's events (of which 15 were $10,000 events and 7 were $25,000 events). This placed Great Britain 8th on the men's and 5th on the women's worldwide list in terms of the number of events staged at this level. In terms of ATP and WTA events, the pre-Wimbledon events at Nottingham, Birmingham and Eastbourne are owned and managed by the LTA and Wimbledon, the best-known tournament in the world (Lawn Tennis Association 2006).

The UK, with nearly 50 million Euros, is behind France (100 million) in terms of the total annual budget for tennis, but invests 17% of this in elite performance, including court and facility hire, training camps for elite players (3.5m), funding, coaching and support for elite players (4.6m), and sports science (1.4m). The Grand Slam Tournament held annually at Wimbledon and that at Queen's, staged shortly before it in the tennis calendar, help guarantee this income (Lawn Tennis Association 2005).

At the international level, UK athletes are positioned in all major rankings; however, it is a significant fact that no woman from the UK was ranked in the WTA 100 until 2009. In the Top 1000 ranking, 32 British women are listed (WTA 2008d). In the junior girls' world ranking (ITF under 18), 4 girls are in the top 100, and in the junior boy's ranking (ITF under 18), 7 boys are in the top 100 (International Tennis Federation 2008f). In the men's ranking, 24 players are listed in the top 1000 ranking, whilst only one player was listed in the Top 100 in 2008 (ATP 2008d).

Currently, Andrew Murray is the outstanding performer and the new hope for UK tennis. However, he did not develop his talent under the guidelines of the LTA, since he moved to a Spanish training camp (Sanchez/ Casal Academy) at the age of 15 (Murray 2008).

'Getting the best coaches', 'providing the best technical and sports science support' and 'establishing a straightforward, high quality competitive framework' are three of the visions of the LTA, where the main vision of British tennis is 'winning' (Lawn Tennis Association 2006, 5). First of all, the LTA seeks to increase participation at all levels, from grass-roots up to the highest level of the game. To achieve these goals, the LTA has introduced professional managers throughout the country, including Scotland and Wales. Their main task is improving communication between the clubs and the regional association. This infrastructure development was meant to ensure that in the next three years four out of five people in Britain should be within half an hour's drive of a quality tennis club. Furthermore, the LTA seeks to establish 20 High Performance Centres, allowing more talents 'to develop their abilities.'

The grass roots programmes 2004 (club vision, mini-tennis, city tennis clubs, school tennis) had a participation of around 75,000 children involved in mini-tennis, and saw the implementation of 25 City Tennis Clubs, with the main goal of 'taking tennis to the people' with a low-cost participation opportunity (one pound per session). In 2006 there was also the school sport partnership, with clubs in 222 schools. 148 training courses were attended by 1,750 primary school teachers and 587 secondary school teachers. 475 teams entered the main competition of the national school championship.

In school lessons, athletics (track and field) has consistently been the most popular activity, which most young people have taken part in at least once; 74% in 1994, 77% in 1999 and 76% in 2002. However, participation in two sports has significantly increased since 1994. These sports are tennis and rounders (Sport England 2004). Tennis has witnessed the largest increase in participation in lessons, from 41% in 1994 to 46% in 1999 and 55% in 2002. Participation in rounders has also increased since 1994, from 59% to 71% in 2002. Participation by girls between 4 and 11 during school lessons has increased over the last eight years, and to a greater extent than boys. 58% of the girls participated in tennis in school programmes in 2002 (52% 1994) (Sport England 2004). In its infrastructure development programme, the LTA has increased the number of indoor and outdoor courts, so that more people can play more often. Further, 120 accredited performance tennis clubs, which have structures to identify and develop young talent, are more highly implemented in the development chain of the club vision programme. In sum, in club tennis, a strong organisation and structure from club level up to the regional and national federations correspond with van Bottenburg (2005), who mentions the influence of climate, sports preferences and unequal cost as crucial for the development of tennis. This could be seen as an argument for the LTA to set down this kind of development in their policies.

3.5 Summary: Sport and Tennis in Four European Countries

From a historical point of view Britain and Germany, together with the United States and Japan, are the countries from which most modern standardised sports spread, with the largest numbers of participants internationally (van Bottenburg 2001). Of the four sports that are the most widespread internationally, two (track and field sports, and soccer) come from Britain and two (basketball and volleyball) from the United States; of the next twenty-five, eight are from Britain (tennis, boxing, table tennis, badminton, archery, hockey, bowling, and squash), three from the United States (bodybuilding, triathlon, and softball), two from Japan (judo and karate) and two from Germany (handball and gymnastics) (van Bottenburg 2001, 45). These facts can explain the popularity of sport in general in the European countries selected for this research. Sport in general is very important and well organised in each of the countries reviewed. Central organisations like the DOSB (Germany), CSA (Czech Sports Association), the Sports Council (UK) and the MJS (Ministère des Jeunesse et des Sports) (France) control sporting activities, and all major sports are affiliated to these main organisations. It is obvious that in France the state is directly involved in sport, whilst in the CR, Germany and the UK the organisation of sport is more independent; however, even in these countries sport is financed by the government as well as through membership fees.

The number of non-participants in sport aged 15 and over is similar in all four countries (~39%). Participation in sport in European countries has reached relatively high levels. In a special Eurobarometer survey of the citizens of the European Union and sport participation, 60% of the inhabitants of 25 EU member states stated that they often participated in sport or exercise (European Commission 2004). In this context, the UK and France have the highest participation in sport.

In the UK (2002), men participated in at least one activity. The proportion of adults who had taken part in one activity decreased with age. The social stratification of sport is existent in the UK. At the macro level in the UK, there is a clear association between socio-economic status and participation rates in sports and physical activities. The correlation between sports participation on the one hand, and age, gender and social class on the other hand is also characteristic of German sport. The differences in sports participation between men and women, and between young and old, have decreased in Germany over the last 20 years. From the age of 35 and above, the proportion of women in all age categories who regularly do sport is higher than the proportion of men. In Germany it appears that regular sports participation does not necessarily decrease with age. The participation of women in sport increases after the age of 35 and the number of middle-aged women who take part in sport is higher than the number of men.

In the Czech Republic, young people do more sport than older people and men do more than women. In the age category 16-24, women participate more often than men, although the men in this category do more competitive sport. Women do not take part in competitive sports beyond the age of 18. An increasing percentage of women in the higher age categories can be found among those who regularly do recreational sport. Incidental participation in sport in the CR occurs to more or less the same extent in all age categories. The percentage of sport practitioners increases with a higher level of education. People with higher education also take part in sport more frequently and in a more organised way. The differences, with regard to educational level, are lower in the category with regular sports participation than that with incidental sports participation on the one hand, and intensive sports participation on the other. In France, women take part less in sport than men. There are also some differences if we look at age and educational level. French women aged 35 to 44 years participated in more sport than men of the same age category, and the greatest gender difference can be found among those with a medium educational level. Women in France participate in less club-related and competitive sport. For older people, sport participation declines for both men and women in club-related and competitive contexts. There is a similar development with respect to educational level. There has been a significant growth in regular sports participation among people with a lower occupational training level, although this group has not the same participation level in sports as those with a secondary or higher level of education. Sports participation among the higher income groups also increased. This can be said of sports participation in general for men, but not for women. However, women's participation in club-related and competitive sport is definitely related to their income level. Interestingly, in France there are no discernible differences. People living in big cities or in less urbanised areas seem to approach sport with the same amount of interest. I can suggest many similarities in these societies regarding circumstances of life, standard of living and employment rate. Even in the Czech Republic, a former communist country, the conditions of life come closer to those in the other countries selected.

In all four countries selected, tennis is very popular, well organised and a top 10 sport. The national federations are divided into regional federations and structured down to club level. In all countries competition structures exist and productivity in tennis is shown in tennis rankings and facilities. Here Germany has the most members and facilities. The sport is mainly practised in tennis clubs. In the UK there are many non-registered tennis players, whilst in the other countries most tennis players are registered in their clubs. There has been a decrease in membership in tennis in the last decades, but tennis remains a Top Five club-related sport in all selected countries.

Environmental and societal factors play a key role in tennis in the researched countries. Social stratification can not only be found in sport participation, but also characterises people's preference for different kinds of sport (van Bottenburg 2001). In the countries researched the number of sports participated in increases the higher the socio-professional status becomes. The socio-professional classes choose from a much broader spectrum of sports, and for those from a lower professional background this correlation seems to diminish a little. Some sports have more male than female participants and others vice versa. Tennis activities are equally popular with both genders. A social status hierarchy for sport seems to exist as well. Tennis as a popular sport in the countries researched seems to remain a high status sport, as it was in the past (van Bottenburg 2001). Tennis is played today by people of the middle or upper classes; it seems that there have been few changes in this social status hierarchy over the last few decades. The top social layers remain more attracted to tennis.

In all the countries researched I can note a decline of participation since the 1980s. Van Bottenburg noted in his study (2001) that the increase in membership in the 1970s and 1980s and then the decrease and decline in membership in the 1990s and 2000s could be explained by demographic and occupational changes. A number of social changes since the 1970s can help to explain these trends. The middle-classes grew larger; more university graduates entered the workforce and found employment in the flourishing service organisations, such as health care, social welfare, education, culture, recreation and the environment. On the other hand there was a decline in traditional services with low social status (for example, domestic service). The number of traditional shopkeepers and employees in agriculture and industry also declined (van Bottenburg 2001). Through new trends in sport participation (fitness and health clubs, non-organisational sports) and the change in the value of doing sport in a club, a large decrease in membership has been noted in tennis. Still playing tennis today on a regular basis in the countries researched could be a privilege of people with an adequate income, and it is still not a sport for lower income people. As I mentioned before, the decrease in tennis is less seen in the lack of 'superstars' like Graf or Becker, but is more evident in the fact that people are changing over to golf, especially those over 60 years old. This change to another sport is also identified by van Bottenburg (2005, 122). His research has shown that the status value of the golf club has increased in contrast to that of the tennis club. Something similar appears to have happened in the Czech Republic, France and the UK.

3.6 Conclusion

In this chapter I have analysed European tennis at the macro and meso levels, and identified the influence of different social, historical and cultural contexts in four countries. It is important to understand under what societal and environmental conditions any sport takes place. The expansion of the middle class and upper layers of society are also reasons for an increase in the popularity of tennis, but the decline in tennis popularity over the last 20 years could only be explained by the shift of older people to the more prestigious sport of golf. This has been shown by analysing country-specific surveys in sports participation. An aim of the chapter was to analyse the sport and tennis structures in four European countries (macro and meso level). The message of this chapter is that although the national tennis federations have a well organised administrative and infrastructure in place, tennis is not a sport for all. It is more or less dependent on the social status of the population. In the following chapter I will present a micro level analysis of talent identification and development in sport and in tennis to complement the analyses contained in this chapter.

Chapter 4 Talent Identification and Development in sport and tennis

Introduction

In the previous two chapters I described the development of tennis into a modern sport, the societal background of each selected country, the structural conditions of tennis and the popularisation and institutionalisation of the sport of tennis. This information forms the background knowledge for my research. In the present chapter I alter my focus and provide an overview at a more micro level of research into talent, talent identification and talent development (TID) in sport, and discuss general sports coaching and tennis specific views on this topic. I describe talent detection models in sport in general, and talent identification and development (TID) models in tennis, referring to stages of talent development. Regarding this, I discuss the issue of early specialisation in tennis, the role of the coach in this context, and the importance of the ranking system and the relationship athletes have with parents and coaches.

In the first section I will start by showing that even for scientists who are experts in this field it is not very clear what part talent development should play in the development process of talented children. However, the section can provide information about the TID process, help to understand the complexity of this issue, and underpin any answers to the overall research question of how talent identification and development (TID) programmes in tennis are organised in different European countries. Firstly, I discuss traditional and modern concepts of TID. Secondly, I will show what TID means. Thirdly, I consider how it has been discussed in sport and when it emerged as a concern. Having an understanding of the various TID models and the concerns enables the author to compare these with the practice and theory of the models for the countries researched. The message of this chapter is that talent is not an all-or-nothing phenomenon. It is, rather, a dynamic manifestation that appears to be determined by both innate and environmental factors. As I shall see, extensive and meaningful practice, family support, competent coaches and teachers, and adequate physical resources for playing are significant in the achievement of exceptional performance.

4.1 Talent Development in sport

What is a 'talent'? Talent can be given many definitions, and can be looked on from different points of view: it is a word with many interpretations (Durand-Bush & Salmela, 2000). It is obvious on reading the literature some researchers are still discussing 'talent' with an open mind. Many definitions have been made, but it is still obvious that there are no universally accepted criteria to characterise the concept of talent. As an example, this is how Howe and colleagues (1998) attempted to define talent:

> The talent account has important social implications. A consequence of the belief that innate gifts are a precondition for high achievement is that young people who are not identified as having innate talents in a particular domain are likely to be denied the help and encouragement they would need to attain high levels of competence (Howe et al 1998, 399).

Some scholars are in agreement with their view and others have refuted it. Csikszentmihalyi (1993), for example, indicated that talent involves personal qualities based not only on innate differences, but also on social opportunities, supports, and rewards. Therefore, when using the term 'talent', he implied that there were two dimensions involved: inherited and learned abilities. After analysing the literature, we can mention that there are two main streams in the discussion of the concept of talent in sport. For some, talent is seen as heavily dependent on genetic makeup; for others, athletes become highly successful as a result of environmental factors such as intensive training, rather than innate abilities alone.

4.2 Talent Detection Models and Talent Development in sport: a selective review

Just as the discussion regarding 'talent' offers different approaches, the same is apparent regarding models of detection, identification and development of talents in sport (Wolstencroft 2004). There is one agreement within the discussion of TID: the recruitment of talented young athletes may not be left to chance, if a nation wants to be a leading sport competitor. The early detection and support of talented children and teenagers with the help of a systematic TID programme counts as one of the main tasks for every sport federation. A well-organised programme for talent identification and development ensures the optimum usage of the 'talent pool' (Hoare 2001). It is a fact that most developed countries have a large reservoir of sporting talent. This includes athletes already participating in sport, along with undiscovered talents. There is a need for these talented athletes to be identified and selected more effectively. With careful planning and optimum utilisation of limited resources, a programme can be set in place that will accommodate the different needs of the sport at the present time (Wolstencroft 2004). However, this programme should be refined and improved from time to time in order to readily adapt to relevant social influences and the dynamic environment associated with high level sport (Hoare 2001).

As we have already established in chapter 1, when discussing the concept of Talent Identification and Development programmes, there are several key terms that need to be understood: talent detection, identification, selection and development.

- Talent Detection: this refers to the search for non-participants in tennis, or to absolute beginners.
- Talent Identification: this refers to the process of recognising current participants with the potential to become elite players. It entails predicting performance over time by measuring physical, physiological, psychological and sociological attributes as well as technical abilities, either alone or in combination (Regnier et al. 1993).

- Talent Selection: this refers to choosing those who have a 'chance to make it' and rejecting those who do not have this chance, which is usually done at an early age. Furthermore, talent selection can be used in the short term, for example the selection of a team to compete in a tournament next month (MacCurdy 2006). This approach was typically used by former communist bloc countries. According to Regnier & Salmela (1982), talent selection takes place over a shorter period of time and is focused on choosing individuals who can best carry out the tasks within a specific sport context, for example, the Olympic Games. Talent selection can be viewed as 'very short-term talent detection,' as it is concerned with assessing which athletes will perform best in two months' time, or sometimes even in two weeks (Blahüs 1975; Hay 1969).
- Talent Development: Following the talent identification and/or selection process, the athletes must be provided with an adequate infrastructure to enable them to develop their full potential. This includes the provision of an optimum learning and training environment for the realisation of talent, appropriate coaching, training and competition programmes, along with access to facilities, equipment and support from sports science and sport medicine (Bloom 1985; Côté 1999, Hoare 2001).

As we mentioned at the beginning of this chapter, there is no single model for these things in tennis or in any other sport. Each coach or parent in charge of talent identification and development has an idea about which model can be successful in furthering their talented child, whether they have any background knowledge of talent identification or not.

In sport two main approaches to talent identification and development are quite common – trait and process models referring to the process of talent development. One model was proposed by Bar-Or (1975), who provided a detailed operational procedure for sport talent detection using a five-step approach.

Table 4.1: Sport talent detection using a five-step approach

Step	Operational Procedure
First step	Morphological, physiological and psychological performance variables
Second step	Weigh the results with a 'development index' to account for biological age
Third step	Testing the reaction of potential talents to regular training measures
Fourth step	Family history (e. g. height, sport activities)
Fifth step	Multiple regression analysis model to predict performance from results of the first four steps

Source: Adapted from Bar-Or 1975, 81-85.

First, Bar-Or evaluated children according to a series of morphological, physiological, psychological, and performance variables; in the second step he weighted the results with a 'development index' to account for biological age; thirdly, he tested the children's reaction to training with exposure to a brief training programme; fourthly, he evaluated the family history (e.g. parents' height, involvement in sport, etc.); and finally he used a multiple regression analysis model to predict performance from the results of the first four steps. However, this model was not submitted to any longitudinal study across sport (Durand-Bush & Salmela 2000).

In his research Gimbel (1976) embraced both nature and nurture, and argued that talent should be analysed from three perspectives:

Table 4.2: Talent analysis from three perspectives by Gimbel (1976)

Step	Perspective of talent analysis
First step	Physiological and morphological variables
Second step	Trainability
Third step	Motivation

Source: Gimbel 1976, 159-167.

Talent was divided into internal factors (genetic) and external factors (environment). According to Gimbel (1976), genetic factors are essential in the development of expert performance, but performance is minimized if environmental conditions are not favourable. Gimbel stated that to reach high performance it takes 8-10 years of training, and that this performance level should be achieved at around 18-20 years of age.

Another talent detection model constructed by Harre (1982) was based on the assumption that it is only through training that one can determine whether a child possesses the required attributes to succeed. It was postulated, therefore, that the first step in talent detection is to put as many children as possible through training programmes. They can then be tested during the early years of training to assess their level of performance, rate of improvement, stability of performance, and reaction to training demands (Harre 1982).

These models and procedures have all been questioned. Many scholars have stated that talent, innate or acquired, cannot be used to predict future levels of performance (Abbott 2005; Bartmus et al. 1987; Bloom 1985). Talent perhaps exists, but the interaction between the genetic make-up of athletes and numerous environmental factors makes it very difficult, if not impossible, to determine the longitudinal effects of talent on sports performance.

It is important to note that little research has been done on ways in which elite athletes attain their status in sport (Wolstencroft 2004). One exception is Bloom's (1985) model of talent development (TD). Bloom's model incorporates the development of relationships or attitudes, the achievement of learning. The model was developed through structured interviews with elite sport athletes and non-sport talents. Bloom (1985) was innovative in identifying three critical stages of talent development, and he provided important insights into how Olympic swimmers, world-class tennis players, concert pianists, sculptors, research mathematicians, and research neurologists became exceptional in their chosen fields. For Bloom (1985) one important conclusion was that talent development requires years of commitment to learning, and that the amount and quality of support and instruction children receive from parents, teachers and/or coaches is central to this process. Bloom identified three distinct stages of talent development, not only by chronological age. However, he indicated that these stages are only 'signposts along a long and continuous learning process' (p. 537). The stages provide excellent guidelines for performers who are going through this process, as well as for teachers and parents, who play an important part throughout the career of these performers.

Table 4.3: Talent Development Model modified from Bloom (1985)

Stage	Development
First stage	Early years and stage of initiation
Second stage	Middle years and stage of development
Third stage	Late years and stage of perfection

Source: Bloom 1985.

In the first stage the participants are engaged in fun and playful activities (exciting, special, fun, socially oriented). At this stage parents play a very important part in the development of their children. They should have a positive influence, share excitement, be supportive, and notice their child's talent. Little or no emphasis should be placed on competition. In the second stage, the participants were involved more in serious participation and should show more commitment to the chosen activity. The coaches were usually more technically orientated, respected and with a strong personal interest. Practice time was increased; children become more achievement-oriented and competition becomes a measure of their progress. Parents have to provide both moral and financial support, and should restrict other activities. Competition can be seen as a yardstick for progress. In the final stage, the chosen activity dominates the lives of those concerned. The sport dominates life, with personal responsibility and willingness to dedicate the time and effort required to achieve the highest standards. The coach must be a respected, success-demanding master coach. At this stage, the parents play a less important part in this fine tuning process. Bloom's viewpoint on this process can be best summarised as follows:

> There are many years' increasingly difficult stages of talent development before mature and complex talent will be fully attained. No matter how precocious one is at the age of ten or eleven, if the individual does not stay with the talent development process over many years, he or she will soon be outdistanced by others who do continue. A long-term commitment to the talent field and an increasing passion for talent development are essential if the individual is to attain the highest levels of capability in the field (Bloom 1985).

Bloom's model offers very good data on cognitive, behavioural and social factors important to elite development. The limitations of his work can be seen in that he has dealt only with individual sports (tennis and swimming) in his research. Even the role of the coach in the final stage has been seen very critically (Wolstencroft 2004).

Other TID models have been developed which are similar to or draw on Bloom's model and concentrate more on external factors, especially the influence of the family on the development of talent. For example, Côte (1999) suggested that there are three distinct stages of participation in sport:

Table 4.4: Distinct stages of participation in sport proposed by Côté (1999)

Stage	Participation of sport
First stage	Sampling years
Second stage	Specializing years
Third stage	Investment years

Source: Côté 1999, 395-417.

In the sampling years, parents and coaches are concerned with providing children with opportunities to have fun and develop fundamental skills, positive identities, and motivation. The account of the families of aspiring athletes in Côté's study revealed that play was more predominant than practice or training during this period. In the specialising years, the athletes are focused on one or two sports. They make this choice around 13 years of age and their decision is mainly influenced by coaches and parents. Côté suggested that to avoid early drop-out a mixture of deliberate play and practice should be used. At this stage, parents attributed more importance to school than to sport. The investment years should be achieved at the latest around 15 years of age, and be focused on the development of skills and strategies for competition. The parents show great interest in their children's careers. In summary, skill development and enjoyment were the most important factors keeping children involved in sport. Bloom and Côté demonstrated the important role of environmental factors in the development of talent and expertise.

In their studies of expert performers, Ericsson et al. (1993) observed that even when individuals had access to similar training environments, large differences in performance often occurred. They also found that experience in a domain was a weak predictor of performance. Rather than accepting these facts as evidence of innate differences in ability, they attempted to identify training activities that were most closely related to improvements in performance. They found that '...improvements were generally manifested when performers engaged in well-defined tasks with appropriate difficulty levels, informative feedback, and opportunities for repetition and corrections of error...' Ericsson and colleagues subsequently used the term 'deliberate practice' to characterise these activities. More specifically, they used this term to refer to any highly structured, goal-directed activity aimed exclusively at improving performance (Ericsson et al. 1993).

The amount of 'deliberate practice' does not appear to be constant throughout the career of expert performers. When children start practising, the weekly amount is minimal and slowly increases to maximum levels at later stages of their development. Ericsson et al (1993) argued that it is important to spend at least 10 years, or 10,000 hours, practising before reaching expert status. However, there are many concerns about this idea, since this could not be applied to sport in general. Coaches play a significant part. Salmela (1996) interviewed 22 expert coaches on the topic of expertise development, and found that one of their main goals was to create an environment that was conducive to improving performance. Csikszentmihalyi et al. (1993), among others, note that although enjoyment and fun are part of the process of talent development, there are three most important determinants:

Table 4.5: Most important determinants of talent development

Elements	Determinates
First element	Individual traits
Second elements	Cultural domains
Third element	Social fields

Source: Csikszentmihalyi et al. 1993.

In sum, Csikszentmihalyi et al. (1993) and Abbott (2005), compared with more traditional orientations (Bar-Or 1975, Gimbel 1976), see talent as a more dynamic process that should be developed over a long period of time, rather than a trait that is inherited and remains unchanged for the rest of an individual's life. Hence whether children become top experts in a sport depends on many factors. Some factors are external, such as the society and culture in which they live; these factors affect their access to knowledge, expertise, resources, and support. Other factors are more internal, such as personal qualities. However, Bloom (1985), Côté (1999), Csikszentmihalyi (1993) and Salmela (1996) have influenced most national tennis programmes regarding talent identification and talent development. There are three- or four- stage theories from the research named above which have influenced most tennis-specific TID policies and national publications; most have been published and tailored towards the national needs of the countries.

The review in this section has outlined the principles of talent research and where the national TID programmes developed from. There is a big gap between the theory of the programmes and practice in tennis. The knowledge of TID models and systems in sport in general is very important in order to prepare answers to the research question 'How does TID operate in tennis in the four European countries selected?' I turn to some preliminary answers in the next section.

4.3 Talent Identification and Development (TID) in Tennis

If an experienced coach observes 3 courts, each with 8 children aged 7 to 10 years of age performing exercises (throwing and catching a ball, running, jumping, etc.) it will not take much time to identify on each court one or two children who are much more 'talented' than the others. The word 'talent', which makes people (especially parents) feel so good, is used too often and too soon. Usually, in tennis the term is used to refer to the natural motor skill of one child compared to that of other children. In such a case to use the word 'talent' can be misleading. True talent needs much more than physical skills. It must include such attributes as desire, determination, drive, courage, self-discipline and love for the sport (Brabenec 1996, 10). To recognise these mental attributes is much more important in judging talent; compared with simple 'skill talent', they are very rare.

In tennis, systematic talent identification (TI) programmes started in the early 1990s. Traditionally, tennis has used the process of natural selection (the 'eye of the expert', result-oriented). In recent years, sport-science based tennis projects have seen researchers trying to identify and determine the specific features that tennis requires for young children to become top players (Crespo & McInerney 2006). In 2008, the majority of the developed tennis countries world-wide had TI programmes in place; all having similar fundamental features, including a partial input from sport science. However, it is difficult to differentiate the success of these programmes from the effectiveness of their training and competition system. To identify 'talented' children, physical and physiological features seem much easier to evaluate than internal factors such as mental or technical-tactical skills. Since in tennis skill and decision-making components have an important influence on high-level performance, the prediction level of current TI tests is low. To predict future performance is much more complicated, especially in tennis.

No one can predict that someone can achieve a high level of success in tennis. There are characteristics which can identify some children who can reach higher levels. There are external and internal factors which can be important for any development of talent (Abbott 2005, Bloom 1985, Côté 1999). Internal factors, such as physical and psychological attributes, are very important for the child and have to be carefully developed (Abbott 2005; Hoare 2001). As we have noted, numerous studies have looked into these characteristics in sport generally (Abbott 2005, Bloom 1985, Côté 1999, Csikszentmihalyi 1993, Gabler 1993, Schneider & Bös 1993). Gabler (1993) mentions speed and emotional stability as important factors; Schneider & Bös. (1993), like Ericsson et al. (1993), noted that only 'deliberate practice' or guided training sessions can increase the quality of motor abilities.

Without any doubt internal factors are very important for development, but in this study we are more interested in the external conditions which are important for talent development and which create the platform for internal talent development. Environment, ranking position, parents, coaches and social influences are key points for the development of talent. The purpose of this next section is to show how parents, coaches and athletes interact together in tennis, and how these external influences are important in the development of the talented child.

4.3.1 Existing Applied Models of Talent Development in Tennis

Principally, there are two TI models identified; the natural selection/performance model (where players are introduced to the sport, can develop their skills, become more involved, practice daily and compete in increasingly higher level events, and become professional) or the science-based model (where the emphasis is on several specific sport science areas such as anthropometry, physiology, or psychology). Practice has shown that a combination of the two models works best with respect to identifying and developing talented players (Crespo & McInerney 2006, 2).

A coach and a player and his or her environment are under a lot of pressure to develop talented players over a long period. If coaches are asked how a great tennis player should be developed, there will be different answers. But there are similarities and characteristics seen among tennis players that could help a coach to distinguish the successful from the less successful players. The process of determining what characteristics can be used to predict future high performance is called talent identification (Roetert & Riewald 2003). Developing talented players and athletes is the much bigger challenge for a coach. There are few coaches who have identified talented players at a young age and developed them up to a high level over many years. Financial and psychological pressure can prevent this long-term relationship between the athlete/parent and coach. To develop a child will take at least 10-15 years (Bloom 1985, Abbott 2005). The following section will enable us to understand the complexity of the development of talented tennis players, and will help to provide answers to our research question as to the emergence of the concern and discourse on TID.

There is research into long-term talent development in tennis and how to operationalise this at different stages of the children's development. Scientists have identified three or four stages (Côté 1999; Kalinowski 1985; Lubbers & Gould 2003; Monsaas 1985). Here is an example of the approach of Monsaas:

> The development of a tennis talent is divided into three sections: the early, the middle, and the later years. There are a number of reasons for such a division. It makes the analysis more manageable. It is consistent with the treatment in other talent fields. And, most important, it appears to reflect the changing emphases in terms of family relationships, coaching, the individual's and families' commitment to the talent field, and the dramatically increased time investment by the tennis player (Monsaas 1985, 214).

The following synonyms are widely used:

1. Introduction/Foundation, "sampling years" = 5-12 years of age
2. Refinement/Transitional, "specializing years" = 13-17 years of age
3. World class performance, "investment years" = 17-35 years of age (Monsaas 1985)

The most common international model for the development of talented children in tennis is based on the 'windows model' of Gabler (1983) and influenced by Ericsson's 8-10 years, or 10,000 hours of 'deliberate practice' model. It is no secret that the performance development of a talent increases through permanent practising. It is more interesting if we pursue the question put by Ericsson (1993 and 2003):'is it even possible that the development of elite performance can be fully explained as the result of extensive training?' (Ericsson 2003, 50).

Other researchers underline the act of deliberate practice and conclude that only with a long training process of 15 years can an international career in tennis be possible (Kaminski et al. 1984; Bloom 1985; Ericsson et al. 1993; Bös & Schneider 1997; Conzelmann 2004). In Germany, Gabler & Zein (1983) introduced a model of talent development for children based on four 'windows'. These 'windows' are similar to different development stages of children. They defined the under 10s as the build up stage, the under 14s as the development stage, the under 16/17s as the performance stage, and the professional level as the high performance stage (Gabler & Zein 1983). The International Tennis Federation recommends 5 stages in the development process, which is published as a general framework for the long-term development of a tennis player (International Tennis Federation 1998). Initiation (6-8 years of age), Instruction (9-10 years), Development (11-12 years), Performance (13-15 years) and High Performance (16-18 years) are the key stages for the ITF (see Table 4.6). The countries examined in this thesis (GER, CR, FRA and the UK) have adapted and transformed this long-term development plan into their tennis Talent Development programmes, with more or less minor changes. However, this model incorporates transitions and characterises the stage of development by the completion of certain tasks, relationships or attitudes developed, or learning achieved. But is it as simple as it looks? If I consider the common models in tennis, there are some critical issues.

Table 4.6: Long-term development of a tennis player recommended by the International Tennis Federation

Stage	Appr. Age	Tennis: Non tennis (%)	Training time per week
Initiation	6-8	30:70	2.5 hrs/week
Instructional	9-10	50:50	9 hrs/week
Development	11-12	55:45	11 hrs/week
Performance	13-15	65:35	20 hrs/week
High Performance	16-18	70:30	25 hrs/week

Source: International Tennis Federation 1998, 202.

The Talent Identification and selection procedures recommended by the National Federations are more a task which is concentrated on single testing measurements on one day, which supports a very subjective perspective rather than a fairly dynamic process (Abbott & Collins 2002). To summarise this section I have to understand that the progressive development of a world-class player is a long-term process that, as we showed in the previous section, takes more than 10 years (Ericsson et al. 1993), just as world-class players go through distinct phases of talent development, which is broken down into three stages, and those involved in tennis must understand these stages. Certain skills are emphasised during each stage and it is important that parents and coaches do not try to skip stages in an attempt to make players champions before they are ready. The development of a tennis talent is a fragile process that takes time and quality support from all those involved.

Research tends to indicate that individual features (e.g. genes) and environmental conditions (e.g. parents, training, facilities) closely interact in the player's development process, and even though genetic characteristics play their part the context of player development seems to have a higher relevance. Studies (Balyi & Hamilton 2003) have concluded that exceptional skills shown at a young age do not automatically translate into talent development and performance, and that talent is not always apparent to observation alone.

Most models take a holistic approach to TD, but do not mention the environmental influences on the athlete's development. Most models cannot be representative of the athlete's career; no research is available at this stage. Another issue is that these models are more implemented by chronological age than by certain tasks completed or attitudes developed. However, I know that TD is a long-term process. The fact is that the long-term development path is a complex and continuous process that should involve the identification and selection of talented players at all stages. I have presented several models (Bloom 1985, Gabler 1993, Côté 1999). These models consider different stages of development from the initial exposure of the child to the sport to the retirement of the player. Implicit in many of these models assumptions are made about specialisation at an early age. The next section briefly discusses these assumptions.

4.3.2 Early specialisation

It is true that tennis has its exceptional 'wonder kids' (e.g. Steffi Graf, Jennifer Capriati, Martina Hingis). Probably, these exceptional performers are examples for many coaches, parents and administrators in their federations or clubs, with the consequence that they still believe in the sport-internal identification process for talented children focused on results as a decisive pathway for selection (Joch 1997). In the light of more recent thinking, however, their validity and usefulness are questionable (Durand-Bush & Salmela 2000). In other words, these orientations can be described as a '...measurement of physical and performance variables that are perceived to be a requisite for success within the given sport...' (Abbott & Collins 2002). Researchers have shown that the best age for high performance in tennis is between 22 and 28 (Schwarzer 2007). Thus, to achieve a top 100 ranking in the professional list, it takes more than 10 years of training and 5 years of high performance competition (see Figure 4.1).

Figure 4.1: Correlation between performance development and age in tennis

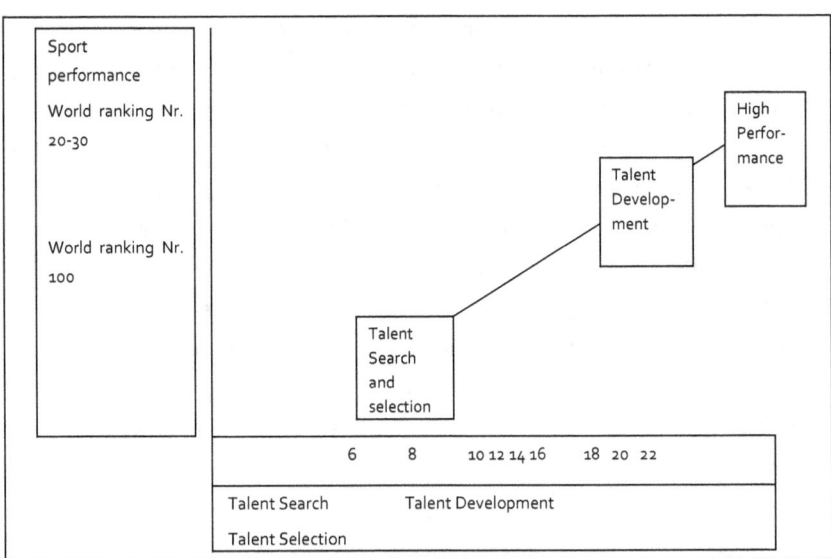

Source: modified from Gabler 1983, 22.

When discussing talent development, it is important to address the question of sport specialisation and when it should occur (Roetert & Riewald 2003, 66). These days (2008) tennis players start to play tennis at an earlier and earlier age, and do not receive fundamental skill development. Researchers have long mentioned that young athletes play a variety of sports, not specializing in one until the early teenage years (Bloom 1985).

Emrich et al. (2005, 114-115) stated that early success and an early beginning of deliberate practice, or a high amount of competition in early years, are not predictors of successful high performance at a senior level. However, any child who starts to train to play tennis around 6/7 years of age fulfils a crucial determinant of successful Talent Development (Monsaas, 1985; Kalinowski, 1985; Ericsson et al. 1993; Bös & Schneider 1997 und 2003; Conzelmann et al. 2004). Bös & Schneider (1997, 2003) state that an early start correlates with better ranking positions. But how young is too young? Today many young talents are seen in academies. Even 6-year-old children (e.g. Jan Silva) have obtained sponsorships in famous academies (in this case the Mouratoglou academy in France). Silva's whole family moved from Canada to France because of the better training conditions. However, this boy was only six, and nobody could predict his future performance. There are too many unknowns when it comes to a 6-year-old boy. It is very difficult to predict any development in physical and mental behaviour (Perrotta 2008a). Conzelmann pointed out that successful German players (national ranking 1-10) started playing tennis at 6.1 years of age, whilst the less successful >25 ranking started at 7.4 years of age. However, real talents show the ability to learn rapidly and well (Bloom 1985; Hohmann & Seidel 2003; Hohmann & Carl 2002). These statistics are fine to read, but when parents stop their lives and pin the family's future on a 5-year-old becoming a high-level tennis player, it puts tremendous demands on the child, and if this is published on personal websites and videos such as 'YouTube' (www.YouTube.com)[3] the pressure on the child will increase very fast (Perrotta 2008a).

4.3.3 Ranking and Achieving Success

In tennis, players are ranked in the national associations or federations (CTS, DTB, FFT, LTA) and as I have seen there are three organisations that rank the top thousand players in the world. The most prestigious rankings are those of the Association of Tennis Professionals (ATP), the men players' professional organisation that ranks only men players, and the Women's Tennis Association (WTA), the women players' organisation that ranks only women players, and the International Tennis Federation (ITF), the junior players' organisation that ranks only junior players (boys and girls). The ranking systems (national and international) are computerised systems that objectively rank players on the basis of the previous fifty-two weeks of play. The ranking, as part of the competition system, is seen as a valid criterion for predicting later success (Bös & Schneider 1997). The high correlation of a good ranking position over a period of 7 years shows individual differences of performance during this time (Schneider & Bös 1993). In women's tennis an early appearance in the professional rankings around the age of 15 years is more possible and necessary (e.g. Steffi Graf, Jennifer Capriati, Martina Hinggis, and Maria Scharapova) to be successful. In his study Carlson (1988) compared the development of Swedish performance players, and found that the successful junior players disappeared from the rankings in later years. Some world-class players achieve their high performance level between 18 and 20 years of age. With this in mind, controlled and organised training should start at the latest around the age of 8. Many Federations are aware of these facts, as can be seen from publications of many workshops of the International Tennis Federation (ITF) or the National Tennis Federations (NTF's).

To find people, including children, who have the necessary skills to achieve this high performance level, should be the main focus of a well-organised and

---

[3] www.tennis.com/wunderkinds

efficient federation. However, examples of rankings at world class level show that more than 80% of junior players of recent years are no longer registered in the senior national rankings. Thus a high junior ranking does not guarantee a successful career in tennis with an appropriate international ranking. Less than 1% of the national ranked players in Germany over the last 10 years have made their way into world-class performance (Top 100 position) within the last year. In the Czech Republic in 2004, 6 out of 22 participants at the National Centre in Perov qualified for the Top 100 seniors ranking in the following year (interview with Richard 2006), but these 22 were already the best players in the former Czechoslovakia and had been selected through competition. The ITF stated in its published comparison of international Junior (ITF) and Senior rankings (WTA/ATP) that 56% of former Top 100 ATP players had been ranked in the international junior ranking (ITF) at a position better than 100. A former No. 1 junior player (since 1994) has a definite chance of becoming a Top 100 player (ATP), but only 24% of the former Top 10 ranked players (ITF junior) are listed for 2005 in the ATP Top 100 ranking. On the other hand, 19% of the players listed in the ATP ranking (2005) were not ranked in the Top 100 (ITF junior), and 25% of the Top 100 (2005) players were not listed in the ITF junior ranking. These numbers show that a good international ranking as a junior does not automatically guarantee a world class ranking in the senior lists (ATP, WTA). I know that a well-placed junior in the ITF ranking needs a large number of training sessions over many years beforehand. And these training sessions increase up to over 20 hours a week for children aged 14-16 years.

Research published by the ITF (Reid & Crespo 2005), which was undertaken on the numbers of ranked junior players over a seven-year period (1992-98), found that a total of 116 boys (from 40 countries) achieved a top 20 ITF junior ranking. As a result, twenty-four players were ranked within the top 20 on more than one occasion.

Table 4.7: Mean highest professional ranking of Top 20 junior boys, and mean age at which it was achieved

ITF Junior Ranking	Total Junior Players	Players to be ranked professionally	Highest ranking (Mean)	Age at highest ranking Mean	Deviation
1-5	32	31	89.2	23.5	1.9
6-10	31	29	142.9	22.8	1.5
11-15	27	24	168.5	23.6	2.1
16-20	26	22	175.3	24.2	2.4
All	116	106	139.7	23.5	2.0

Source: Reid & Crespo 2005, 2.

Table 4.7 shows that 91% (106 / 116) of these top 20 juniors went on to attain a professional men's ranking. Superficially, a comparison within the junior top 20 suggests that higher ranked junior players also tend to achieve higher professional rankings. The mean age at which all top 20 juniors achieved their highest professional ranking was 23.5 ± 2 years. The percentage of top ranked junior players to build on their U/18 successes and reach common ranking goals in the professional game is outlined in Table 4.8.

Table 4.8: Likelihood (in percentage terms) of top 20-ranked juniors reaching a top 100, 50, 20 and/ or 10 professional ranking 2005

ITF Junior Ranking	Professional Ranking			
	Top 100	Top 50	Top 20	Top 10
1-5	56%	44%	34%	5%
6-10	42%	36%	16%	10%
11-15	48%	34%	19%	15%
16-20	31%	19%	19%	8%
All	45%	34%	22%	15%

Source: Reid & Crespo 2005, 2.

Forty-five percent of all top 20-ranked junior players from 1992-98 achieved the professional top 100, while slightly more than one in every third went on to reach the top 50. These figures increase to 56% and 44% respectively if only top 5-ranked juniors are considered. Indeed, one in every four of this group of players reached a top 10 professional ranking. Some similarity exists between the professional ranking progression of the top 6-10 and the top 11-15 ranked juniors, and although fewer top 16-20 juniors reached the professional top 100, their representation in the professional top 20 and 10 compares at a good international level.

The selection of the appropriate means through which to develop the necessary personal, physical and game-based skills for successful, professional tennis performance is a problem that confronts all serious competitive players. Authors from the development department of the ITF in Spain (Valencia) and Australia stated that an achievement of a boys' top 20 junior world ranking should appear to be 'a reasonable yardstick of playing talent and a worthwhile developmental goal for all aspiring male professionals.' (Reid & Crespo 2005, 2)

Table 4.9: Mean age statistics of TOP 100 ATP players

Year	Top 10	Top 50	Top 100	First year pro	Began tennis
2005	27 yrs	25.6 yrs	26.25 yrs	18.1 yrs	6.1 yrs
1996	N.A.	N.A.	24.11 yrs	N.A.	N.A.

Source: Association of Tennis Professionals 2005.

The current top 100 players (2005) have an average age of 26.3 years, whilst this was 24.11 years in 1996 (Table 4.10). The average age in the Top 10 is 27 years (Association of Tennis Professionals 2005). These numbers and facts are regularly published in magazines, journals and at congresses. National Federations include the results in their coaches' education, together with publications and anecdotes of young and successful players (Nicola Vaidisova (CR), Maria Sharapova (RUS), Tatjana Goldovin (FRA), Andrew Murray (SCO) and Anna Lena Groenefeld (GER). The contradiction between an effective long-term development with broad skill development at early ages (U10) on the one hand and an early start with high-level competitive tennis and practice on the other becomes apparent. A successful coach will always be measured by the short-term success of his athletes. Most associations and parents are not really interested in the long-term development process if the child starts young. Public stories, lack of knowledge and time pressure can be named as the key reasons for that.

4.3.4 The role of the parents

The influence of parents plays an important part in the life of top-level sports talents in their high-performance development, particularly in their early career phases (Alfermann et al. 2002; Monsaas 1985; Côté 1999; Würth 2001); both for the initiation of the children into practising the sport, and for the preservation of long-term training measures (Bloom 1985). The emphasis is of course on the sport, but at least recognition and social prestige through the success of their children are acceptable reasons for parents to support their children. Support by the family can be manifested in multiple ways: high esteem, emotional support, praise, comfort and encouragement are components of the support between tennis talents and their families. Emotional support is therefore a central component, an indispensable resource on the way to expertise. An equally important resource, however, is financial support. Considerable costs (especially coaching and tournament journeys) arise mainly in the late development stage or transition phase for the talented to professional tennis, where the association fails to support the player.

It can be frequently observed that parents are not merely 'passive' supporters of their tennis-playing children; they sometimes support them actively as coaches. This occasionally leads to conflicts and coordination problems with other protagonists involved in talent development. Gabler & Zein (1993) confirm that at the beginning of talent development the family represents an important factor, together with training conditions, the ability of the coach, and support by the organisation or association. This confirms the results of a Swedish study: Dahlgren (1984) noted in his research an interesting phenomenon whereby a Swedish district with a low number of club members produced a large number of top players. These results were explained by the circumstance that the top players had learnt that they were strongly motivated by the environment of their organisations, which is explained by a greater social commitment of coaches in rural organisations. Furthermore, Dahlgren noted that the parents of the top players had a very positive attitude regarding the sporting activities of their children (Dahlgren 1984).

Côté (1999) and Delforge (2006) have also pointed out key determinants for positive parental behaviour. It is important to show interest and emotional, financial and material investment, availability, organisation of family life, transport, and nutrition. Knowledge of the competitive sport and tennis world is as important as being a role model. Introducing the child to a variety of sports at the beginning and sharing other activities, giving support, encouragement, comfort and trust are as important as motivation. So too are putting results in perspective, playing down competition and defeat, avoiding a focus on rankings, transmitting values (such as fighting spirit, rigour, attention to detail, respect, hard work, discipline, fair play and good behaviour during matches, etc.). Also important are: establishing a dialogue; decisions must be child driven; maintaining positive communication; being attentive to the child's needs, and paying attention to his fatigue, burnout risks and his experience of competition; setting realistic goals; emphasising the prime importance of play and enjoyment; and the notion of improvement as opposed simply to focusing on results. Parents should develop the child's independence and autonomy. Then there is being present during matches to show support; presence must be neutral, discreet and passive. Finally also important is the parents' relationship with coaches: showing an interest in their feedback; being open to their advice, showing trust and respect, establishing a dialogue, collaborating with them, knowing how to entrust their child and delegate tasks (Sloane 1985).

Jean Côté (1999) determined the influence of the family in the development of the talented athlete. Brown (2001) looked at parental involvement and stated that parental involvement and expectations are associated with success and enjoyment as well as with pressure and stress. Hellstedt (1987) described parents' behaviour on a continuum from under-involved to moderate to over-involved. A moderate level of parental involvement, Hellstedt concluded, is in the best interests of their children. Bloom and colleagues reported in 1985 in their 'landmark publication on this subject' that parents tend to be supportive during the early years of the children's participation, and allow them to decide whether or not to practise (Monsaas 1985). During the middle years, both the athlete and the parents demonstrated a period of increased dedication, and in the later years the parents' role was more restricted, consisting primarily of financial support.

Table 4.10: Characteristics of Talented Athletes, Coaches and Parents

	Early years	Middle years	Later years
Athlete	Joyful Playful Excited	Larger perspective Committed/ linked to sport	Obsessed Responsible Consumed
Coach	Kind Cheerful Focused on progress	Strong leader Knowledgeable Demanding	Successful Respected/ feared Emotionally bonded
Parents	Model work ethic Encouraging Supportive Positive	Make sacrifices Restrict own activities Child-centred	Limit roles Provide financial support

Source: Brown 2001, 61.

Bloom also described the characteristics of athletes, their coaches, and their parents during the three stages (Brown 2001). Table 4.10 presents some of his descriptions. The development of boys and girls will be marked by many misunderstandings on the part of parents. Nick Saviano, director of the USTA tennis player development, suggests creating a master plan. He states that parents who push their children into a 'master plan' too early are setting the child up for failure in the effort to create 'professional' child athletes.

In the same way as that of the children, the role of the parent changes in the long-term development path. Parents have a changing but important role to play at all stages, which continues for many years. No stage can be 'skipped', although there are individual differences as to the chronological age at which a child enters or leaves each stage. The role for many parents is critical during the early years when a child is most dependent. Most children are introduced to tennis as a result of their parents' own interest and encouragement. Following this initiation stage, substantial funds and much time are required from parents to support their children in playing tennis during the specialising and investment years.

To conclude this section, I know that for parents it is very difficult to take the right steps in the development of their children into high performance athletes. The pragmatic experience of parents has been recognised by, amongst others, the International Tennis Federation, which publishes on its website a section headed 'Being a better tennis parent – guidelines to help parents of young tennis players'. However, parents have a significant role to play at all stages of talent development, extending over many years. While a talent development model has been proposed to describe key roles of parents throughout the long path to sporting excellence, it is important to know that parents 'should be parents' and only positive communication with coaches and other responsible people is helpful along the long-term development path of the talented players.

4.3.5 The role of the coach

Tennis has experienced a significant growth in the number of people playing the game world wide. Coaches play a central part in the development of these players at all levels. In view of the spread of tennis and sports more generally, organisations have increased their efforts to provide better education for coaches. This trains the coach to cater for different stages of the development of talented players.

The role of the coach (in competitive sport) enjoys a long tradition in sport science (Alfermann et al. 2002; Bette 1984, Bloom 1985; Cachay & Thiel 1996; Cassidy et al 2004, Franke 1996; Hermann 1996; Hotz 1990; Hug 1991; Killing 2002). Quite recently discussion has centred on two areas: first, the ethical point of view of the coaching profession (Meinberg 2001), and second, the qualification profile of a coach in competitive sport and his or her social competence (Hermann 1996). This competence and qualification change during the various stages of the development of talented athletes. Brown mentions three stages a coach has to fulfil in the development of talented players. In the 'early years' the coach should be kind, cheerful and focused on progress, in the 'middle years' the coach has to be a strong leader, knowledgeable and demanding, and in the 'late years' he should be successful, respected and emotionally bonded (Brown 2001, 61). Studies of the development of expertise have shown that the influence of the coach in the development stages changes (Côté et al. 1999; Kalinowski 1985; Monsaas 1985). Thus Carlson (1988) reports that development was promoted by the construction of a good, long-term relation of the coach to a world class tennis player. Monsaas (1985) summarises in her studies of American top players the part played by coaches in the progress from beginner to expert, that:

> At first instructors did have some important qualities, they were good with children, and they took a special interest in our tennis players, and they spent a great deal of extra time working with them. While the first coaches were frequently lacking the important technical skills of a good coach (e.g. stroke production, strategy), they had interpersonal skills that were very important at this level, that is, they were able to get the child interested and excited about tennis (Monsaas 1985, 234).

In the further stages of development, the 'take off' stage (Schwarzer 2007) and high performance phase, the coaches are perceived as more serious, specialised and qualified (Côté 1999). From the players' perspective, it is important that the coaches are more frequently exchanged if they lack sufficient technical knowledge:

> The change in emphasis during the lessons in the middle years was sometimes accompanied by a change in coaches because it appears that some of the coaches who were good with young children could not teach the more precise skills of the middle years. Even those players who stayed with their first coaches found that they needed to arrange for special instruction with other coaches on particular aspects of their game. (Monsaas 1985, 254).

With rising expertise in tennis, support measures are tailored individually to the athlete. Individual training methodology, goal setting, tournament planning, competition support, communication modalities and motivation help have to be aligned with the individual character. The application of discipline and experiences on the professional tour as tasks or as prerequisites of a successful coach-athlete relation are frequently-mentioned attributes in this context:

> Almost all of the finishing coaches [...] appeared to have one characteristic in common: they were described by the players as rigid disciplinarians. Most of them [...] had coached some of the top players in the world and thus had excellent reputations. Because of this, they had the players' respect, and their authority was accepted by the players (Monsaas, 1985, 263).

Brown (2001) identified several factors which have to be taken in account for a good coach. He stated the importance of establishing a long-term development plan for the athlete. The coach should be a team leader for development; furthermore, a long-term vision is crucial, and to achieve this vision with a strategy the importance of realistic goal-setting is also pointed out by the author. A talented athlete goes through the three stages of development outlined by Côté, Bloom and others; athletes usually need a different coach at each stage (Brown 2001). At the first level the coach makes the sport fun; after this stage the athlete moves on to another coach who is more technical in his approach to the sport. This coach knows the sport and may be a hard disciplinarian. Finally, the third is the level at which a coach takes the athlete to success. This coach has the experience and vision to take the athlete to the highest level. Some coaches are flexible, but most of them are unwilling to let their athletes move to others, with the possible consequence of performance decline. Brown (2001) states the important fact that it does not make sense to rush to change coaches. Athletes who repeatedly bounce from one coach to another in search of a 'secret success' formula may never find it. However, for a coach the development of any athlete can be interesting but also difficult, and identifying and developing talent is in most countries as much a random chain as a well-planned process (Brown 2001, 68). Support is very important, but practice has frequently shown that too much push, interference or wrong goal-setting puts too much pressure on the talented child.

4.4 Conclusions

In this chapter I have provided an overview of TID, and how it has been discussed in the sport science and sport coaching literature. Most of the TID models in sport are built on different development stages, from the young child up to high performance level. The core strategy of these models (Bloom 1985, Côté 1999) has been adopted by many tennis federations and modified to fit their own settings. However, parental influence, the right coach at the right time, the best possible practice environment, and not least a well organised competition system expressed in rankings which are external (Gimbel 1976) are key characteristics for any Talent Development programmes and should be included in any programme. Rankings are the only valid and internationally acknowledged system to compare and measure performance in tennis. But the danger of early specialisation is obvious, because each child and talented athlete likes to move in the rankings as early as possible to show that he/she is talented. Any good Talent Development programme should point out the fact that early specialisation mostly decreases the chances of a successful career in tennis. However, unfortunately, the results promised by many studies of talent identification and development are not achieved by parents, coaches, administrators and players (Digel 2006, 29). Practice has shown that national federations try to put children as early as 5 years on court to take part on competitions (e.g. the 'Play and stay' campaign of the International Tennis Federation).

In Germany (2009) an under-7 tournament appears on the competition calendar: if I pursue the policy of the German tennis federation, at this age fundamental tennis development should only just be commencing, not tournament experience. The International Tennis Federation and many national federations do not allow national rankings for Under 12's, but on the other hand competition series and quantitative coaching bring players to a level even around the age of six where parents think that they have a new 'tennis star' in the family. From personal professional experience, I can state that it is always difficult to argue from the coaches' side with parents about the development process of their children. Most of them like to see their little ones win tournaments even at an early age; this success increases the motivation of the parents to work more on court and plan a professional career for them. As most parents are not themselves involved in the sport, retrospective stories about Federer's or Agassi's families are published and influence communication, as well as the whole master plan of the talented athlete, if there is one.

I argue that it should be the task of any TID programme with a proper guideline on communication with parents, players and coaches to decrease the emphasis on the importance of rankings at an early age and look for broad sporting and physical development. For the coach it also seems to be difficult to follow the theoretical guidelines of the research of Abbott & Collins (2002), Bloom (1985), Côté (1999) and others, because in 99 percent of all cases involving Talent Development the coach is measured by the success of his pupil and not by his long-term development. Most of the time, parents will measure the success of coaching only by weekend competition results. Modern tennis countries like France or Germany hope to avoid this early pressure on children through guidelines. Unfortunately this brings countries into the games which do not care about a broad development of motor skills, or having fun in sport at an early age. They put all their efforts into a tough early specialisation process and finally accept a high drop-out rate, so it will be difficult to follow guidelines from research like that of Brown (2001) and develop the talented athlete. In sum, there is a gap in between the theory of the models and the programmes. Experts like Bloom, Côté, and some others have shown what a model should be like, and what features of talent we, as coaches, have to look for; but unfortunately these models are not executed in practice. So how should a coach or a parent find the right development path in practice from the point where his child has been identified as a talent to his/her becoming a high performance athlete?

The message of this chapter has been that talent is not an all-or-nothing phenomenon. It is a dynamic manifestation which is influenced by internal and environmental factors. The extent to which these different factors influence the development of performance seems irrelevant. We cannot change our genetic makeup, but we can change our environment to make it as conducive as possible to improving performance. Extensive and meaningful practice, family support, competent coaches and teachers, and adequate physical resources were found to play a significant role in the achievement of exceptional performance.

Next I turn to the research I have conducted with organisations and key people involved in European tennis. Here I want to provide a brief summary of what has gone before and what comes next. In chapter 1 I outlined the central aims and the objectives of my research thesis. The message of this chapter was to show how modern sport has been developed into a global communication platform, the circumstances under which tennis has developed into a modern sport, and the difficulties and importance of a TID programme.

Chapter 2 gave insights into the history, system and structures and the socio-structural and socio-cultural background of tennis, and showed that social conditions are closely connected with the success of national tennis federations' talent identification and development. In Chapter 3, the identification of the four countries selected and consideration of certain national, socio-cultural and political-economic characteristics were outlined. It was important to show the structural conditions, the institutionalisation and popularisation of sport in general and of tennis. In Chapter 4, I have sketched various talent development models, and concluded that talent identification and development in general and specifically in tennis is a dynamic process which takes over a decade. A young athlete has to go through many processes of development from the beginning of identification (7-8 years) and development (9-18 years) in one process. Before discussing my research findings in detail, in the following chapter I describe the methodology and research methods I have used to explore the central research questions of this thesis.

Chapter 5 Methodology

Introduction

In the previous three chapters I outlined the background to the talent identification and development programmes (TID) in tennis in four selected European countries. At the outset I discussed the central aims and objectives of the research, the research questions, and some aspects of the research design. In the second chapter I offered a brief overview of the history, system, structures and socio-cultural background to tennis. In Chapter 3, I identified the four countries studied and considered certain national, socio-cultural, social structural and political-economic characteristics. In Chapter 4, I provided a broad overview of research on Talent Development, based upon an extensive survey of the literature in sports science and coaching studies, and discussed general and tennis-specific views on this topic. Various accounts of the multidimensionality and dynamic nature of talent development in tennis were presented.

In this Chapter I will provide critical insight into the research methodologies that underpin this research thesis. First I briefly recapitulate our discussion of the research process and the problem formulation that lead to this thesis. Second I focus attention on the research methods used to accomplish it. Finally I reflect on the challenges and opportunities that I encountered as a professional tennis coach undertaking research into the practise and activities of colleagues, administrators, players and parents operating in the same 'field of play'.

5.1 The research process and problem formulation

All research projects involve to some degree messiness and alterations inevitably occur as a research project develops. The research upon which this thesis is based was no different. Between 2001 and 2004 I was appointed as the General Manager for the OlympAfrica Center in Swaziland, and at the same time I was the national tennis coach for junior and senior players in that country. Additionally I was given responsibility by the National Olympic Committee

(SOCGA) of Swaziland, funded by Olympic Solidarity, to design a talent identification and development programme for tennis. Being asked to develop TID programmes led me to investigate the existing state of knowledge about such initiatives. I soon came to recognise despite official encouragement to develop TID in tennis and many other sports, there was little firm understanding of how exactly such programmes should be developed. When I left Swaziland and returned to Germany to take up the position of head coach with TC Nagold (a private tennis club) in Württemberg, I continued to explore information about TID programmes. I discovered that just as in Swaziland tennis coaches in Germany were pretty much left to their own imitative to develop and implement these programmes. I decided that the search for the 'ideal' TID programme would be a good subject for postgraduate study. This is what I originally planned to undertake at the University of Edinburgh.

As my preliminary investigations developed I realised that I would have to undertake two pieces of research. Firstly I would need to search all relevant published information about TID programmes and their implementation – for example as published by national tennis federations, the ITF and other transnational sports organisations. Secondly I would need to find out from colleagues in the field of tennis coaching, administrators in local, regional and national tennis federations and other key actors in this sport, what their views were about TID. In short I realised that I would have to analyse documents and conduct interviews with a range of people. As I wanted to find out about the situation in more than one country I also decided that the research project would have to become a cross national study comparing written material, views and practises. Fortunately I speak, read and write three European languages – French and English as well as my native tongue German. Hence what I originally thought would be a small part of my attempt to produce the 'perfect' model of TID in tennis has become the main focus of research and this thesis.

As I have already indicated the main research question remains *how are TID programmes in tennis organised and implemented in different European countries?* However I realised that in order to find answers to this main research question, I had to investigate three subsidiary questions: *what is TID, when did it emerge as a concern and how is it discussed in the context of sport?; how does TID operate in tennis in the four European countries selected?;* and *what influence do different social contexts have on the meaning of tennis and especially approaches to TID in tennis?*

In order to do this I undertook research consisting of a review of relevant literature, the analysis of published and unpublished documents, and semi-structured interviews. In the next section I explore each of these research techniques, examine some of their strengths and weaknesses and explain how I conducted the research.

5.2 Research Methods

I decided to employ various research methods, to analyse the available literature, followed by an empirical examination of what kind of TID programme and procedure is currently seen as successful in the selected countries. The analysis of the structure of talent development programmes in each country included an analysis of secondary literature regarding the organisational structure of sport in general and the organisational system of each tennis federation. Some of the detail required was published on the websites of tennis federations, other sources were journals, newspapers and direct contacts with experts. Fortunately I had obtained skills in data searching, data collection and data analysis through a period of study as a master's student at the Institut für Sportwissenschaften, in Tübingen. Online access to university libraries (Tübingen in Germany, and Edinburgh), to the International Olympic Committee research centres (until 2007) and to general databases with sport-relevant literature (SPOLIT, SPODISC), also provided useful sources of information.

Various research studies (Abbott 2005, Bloom 1985, Côté 1999) in theory and practice have shown that key agents in any tennis federation such as administrators, coaches, players and parents have the most influence on the developmental process of talented children in sport; there still seems to be a need for a better involvement of parents and coaches in talent development. Many administrators, coaches, parents, and players do not know much about the talent development of their national programme. Even administrators and coaches, whom we would expect to have the necessary knowledge, do not pass on information about talent development to their players and parents. This has led the International Tennis Federation and several national federations in Europe to publish guidelines of talent development programmes. However, if a father or a mother is not directly involved in tennis, it is difficult for them to understand where to take their children regarding the TD process. This suggested/highlighted the importance to the research of exploring the knowledge and understanding of talent development issues of administrators, coaches, players and parents.

Following the analysis of national and international literature, websites and documents, interviews were conducted with key informants (players, coaches, administrators and parents) in two of the four selected countries – the Czech Republic and Germany. Fortunately between 1998 and 2000 I conducted a world wide survey of school tennis programmes on behalf of the ITF, which developed my skills in designing and implementing questionnaire based surveys. I found this prior experience useful when planning and designing a set of structured questions to be used in interviews. The reasons for including the two countries in the fieldwork were partly practical and partly to enable me to obtain a comparative assessment of TID. Obtaining information about TID for programmes in Germany and the Czech Republic from key informants was made possible through good professional contacts. However, there was no opportunity to get useful first-hand information from the key informants in the French Tennis Federation or the Lawn Tennis Federation. Repeated requests for interviews failed to elicit a response. I sent copies of a questionnaire to senior tennis officials in France and the UK but again they did not reply. So I decided to concentrate on the two tennis federations from the Czech Republic and Germany in my fieldwork and to use secondary sources to compare views of talent identification and development in the UK and France.

Despite my 'insider' status for various reasons it was still quite difficult to get people involved in tennis to answer my questionnaire or participate in interviews. However I was able to get some access to players, parents, coaches and administrators, by using my knowledge of the tennis competition circuit and taking advantage of opportunities to talk to people when they emerged in the course of my professional work. As a result in total, 12 coaches (two national coaches, two regional coaches, one academy coach, and seven talent development coaches), 11 tennis players (six men and women professionals and five upcoming talents), 11 parents of well ranked players and five administrators working for tennis federations were interviewed. Furthermore, I had informal conversations with experts and former national coaches from Croatia, Germany, Brazil and the United Kingdom. See tables 5.2 and 5.3 for the details.

Consistent with research norms and ethical good practice the identities of all respondents have been anonymised. Hence when information derived from interviews is referred to in subsequent chapters (especially chapter 7) fictional names are used to represent these real people. The following table (5.1) identifies all the respondents and the dates of interviews conducted by me in both Germany and the Czech Republic, predominantly in 2006 and 2007.

Table 5.1: Interviews with key actors in Germany and the Czech Republic (names are anonymised)

Players from Germany

Name	Date of Interview
Pascale	18.4.2006/ Questionnaire
Markus	20.11.2006
Stefan	15.6.2006
Eduard	22.7.2006
Fabienne	25.5.2006
Karin	27.5.2006

Players from the Czech Republic

Name	Date of Interview
Milena	1.6.2007
Radana	1.6.2007
Andreas	1.6.2007
Richard	20.4.2006
Daja	25.6.2006

Parents from Germany

Name	Date of Interview
Erich	2.8.2006
Markus	22.6.2006
Thomas	30.7.2006/ Questionnaire
Susanne	30.7.2006 Questionnaire
Ira	20.12.2006
Martina	29.7.2006
Beate	12.12.2006

Parents from the Czech Republic

Name	Date of Interview
Aijka	25.6.2006
Marina	20.4.2006
Martin	19.6.2006
Martin H.	20.4.2006

Administrators from Germany

Name	Date of Interview
Uli	22.5.2006
Carsten	30.5.2006/ Questionnaire
Maria	01.05.2006
Wolf	28.10.2007

Administrator from the Czech Republic

Name	Date of Interview
Miroslav	18.12.2007/ Questionnaire

Coaches from Germany

Name	Date of Interview
Andre	20.11.2006
Boris	20.5.2006
Chris	29.4.2006/ Questionnaire
Darren	29.10.2006
Eric	20.7.2006
Frank	20.7.2006
Gustav	20.12.2006

Coaches from Czech Republic

Name	Date of Interview
Andreas	30.5.2006
Bohdan	25.6.2006
Cyril	25.6.2006
David	7.5.2006
Emil	23.7.2006

The ages of the players ranged from 16 to 36 years of age (average = 24 years). Six of them have achieved an international ranking and five of them a national ranking. During the interviews, eight of the athletes continued to participate in national and international competitions, whilst three of them had retired from international competition in the previous 5 years. All players interviewed were selected because they had been named as talented players. Emphasis was placed on seeking parents whose children had achieved or were trying to achieve an international career. It was important to identify coaches who were working at international level and/or who had a record of developing talented players for high level performance.

Emphasis was placed on getting administrators who were working in key positions in their federations regarding talent identification and development.

Table 5.2: Number of respondents in the research

Players		Coaches		Parents		Administrators		Total	
GER	CR	GER	CR	GER	CR	GER	CR	GER	CR
6	5	7	5	6	5	4	1	23	16

Table 5.3: Characteristics of the respondents of the research

National coaches		Regional coaches		Academy coaches		TD coaches		Total	
GER	CR	GER	CR	GER	CR	CR	CR	GER	CR
2	0	2	4	1	0	2	1	7	5
Professional players wtm		Talented players		Parents of professional players		Parents of talented players		Administrators national/regional	
GER	CR	GER	CR	GER	CR	GER	CR	GER	CR
3	3	3	2	3	3	3	2	4	1

Interviews can be structured or semi-structured. In contrast to the rigidity of the type of structured interview, I decided that it was important to use a form of semi-structured interview in order to produce comparable responses from the four key actors across the two countries. In this respect I followed the advice of the German social researchers Bortz and Döring (1995, 216) concerning the advantages of this method, where I was allowed more flexibility during the interview. Semi-structured interviews provided me with a means to get a greater depth of information and the opportunity to discover the respondents experience and interpretation of their ideas and thoughts in their own words and opinions.

The interviews mainly took place in Germany, Spain and Austria during junior tournaments and performance camps between May 2006 and December 2006. Some of them were conducted at camps of the German Fed-Cup Team in Spain (19.-23 December 2006) and with Czech team players in Austria (15.-20 April 2006). Others were conducted in Nagold, Germany during a national girls' ranking tournament, in Waiblingen, Germany at an international junior tournament (19. July 2006), and in Stuttgart, Germany at the National Tennis Centre (20. June 2006). Finally one interview was conducted by telephone and three took place during a regional district tournament in November 2006. All the participants were assured that the interview and questionnaire data would be treated as strictly confidential.

I used a mixture of sampling techniques to obtain my responses. I used convenience sampling in so far as I sometimes approached people who just happened to be at the same tennis competition as myself. Additionally however because I knew some of the experts whose opinions I wanted to obtain I adopted a form of purposive sampling to reach other informants. Finally I also found that some of my interviewees provided me with the names of others who subsequently took part in the research. In this respect I also adopted a form of snowball sampling.

Altogether I conducted and analysed 33 interviews (and six questionnaires completed by people I could not interview but who agreed to answer my questions in a different format). The interviews and questionnaires contained between 34 and 41 questions about the methods used for talent identification and development, the concept of talent identification and development programmes, their strengths and weaknesses, important characteristics of talented tennis players and their importance, environmental issues and external influences, clear and available guidelines, selection criteria for talented children and some issues related to the tennis culture in their country (see Appendix A for examples of the four different questionnaires). They helped to explore the theory and practice of talent identification and development programmes used in tennis in these countries, and to collect information about what they do, why they do it, and what they think would be best regarding talent identification and development programmes, and especially to achieve more in-depth information about what actually happens in the talent identification and development process in practice. These data enabled me to investigate in more detail any contradictions between theory and practice in the field of talent identification and development in tennis.

The questions were asked in English – English being more or less the official language in the global tennis world and accepted by most of the key informants. Those who could not speak English well were interviewed in German. The face-to-face interviews took between one and two hours and were conducted with a portable laptop computer, on which the answers were directly transferred into a software programme, 'Grafstat'.

I decided to use the German 'Graftstat'[4] software package for the analysis of data for the following reasons. This software was developed by Uwe Diener, with the support of the German Federal Agency for Civic Education. It was very effective for me to create questionnaires and interviews, including online interviews, using this, and provided me with an effective means of carrying out analysis of the data. Time flexibility while conducting interviews was very important; the programme was installed on a laptop computer because most of the interviews were conducted at tennis tournaments. No pre-organisation was required to conduct the computer-assisted personal interview (CAPI); furthermore, it was available and financially affordable. Additionally, its compatibility with Microsoft Excel was an advantage, as any diagram could be represented if necessary using Microsoft Excel. GrafStat also supports all the phases of work in interviews. The construction of questionnaires, an HTML form for Internet interviews, and the recording of data up to and including various evaluation versions, graphic export and HTML documentation were also possible using this package (Diener 2006). In this research we created the questionnaire for the interviews, which were conducted directly from the computer. The analysis of the interviews was also done with the programme. Consistent with the advice of Bortz & Döring (1995, 217-231) the questionnaire included both closed (one response and multiple response) and open ended questions (open response). Those respondents who were not available for face-to-face or telephone interviews were asked to complete the same research questionnaire (Bortz & Döring 1995, 231; De Vaus 2002; Silverman 2000) with closed and open-

---

[4] http://www.grafstat.de

ended questions (see Appendix A). The questionnaires were completed by hand and returned to me.

In order to evaluate the effectiveness of the questionnaire for the key agents the questionnaire was piloted in 2005/2006 in two locations – Germany and Spain. The pilot survey was conducted to find out if the questionnaires were understandable and could be used for research purposes. Firstly I conducted pilot interviews in two German Tennis clubs with key agents (administrators, coaches, parents and players). The reasons for the choice of these clubs for the pilot was that most of the registered players from the German Tennis Federation are members of clubs and further the institutional structure of the clubs in Germany is the same as in the regional and national federations.

Secondly I conducted pilot interviews with key agents from Croatia (two national coaches and two regional coaches, two parents, and two players) from Brazil (two national coaches), Germany (four club administrators and six parents and six players), and from the Czech Republic (two club coaches, two parents and four players). Their responses gave me a sense of how these agents interpreted the questions and how consistent their understanding of TID was. The pilot survey was conducted in English. The main finding of the pilot survey was that the questions were well worded and understandable. In analysing the pilot however I changed the order of the questions and decided to reduce the total number of questions. Additionally it was useful for me to get used to the computer- based interview from the technical point of view.

5.3 Limitations of the Research

A number of challenges were encountered while carrying out the research. One was the variable quality of the primary and secondary data extracted from published and some unpublished documents. The objectivity of the development plans published on the websites of tennis federations was also questionable. Access to foreign libraries was also complicated by the fact that the thesis was conducted part-time whilst I was living and working fulltime in Germany. Other difficulties included coordination problems in meeting experts in each country; translation problems during interviews in the Czech Republic; and differential interview conditions. The position and activity of the interview partners in the respective tennis associations, and the type of interview were also different. As the quality of the written documents varied considerably, some information taken from them has not been able to be thoroughly verified.

To overcome these and other limitations, we often had to accept the informants' opinions without question. Some data could be controlled and analysed through conversations and discussions with other experts. Further difficulties appeared during the evaluation of the answers to the questionnaire. Another was the difficulty in gaining access to key informants in the UK and France. Owing to the lack of a positive response from people in these two countries, it was decided to exclude them from the interview schedule and to evaluate and analyse their programmes purely through available literature via secondary documentary analysis, as we mentioned at the beginning of this section.

Besides the country-specific methodical and organisational problems during data collection and data evaluation, we encountered a number of problems specific to the Czech Republic in obtaining information from administrators. Only private, personal and professional, contacts made access possible. Some relevant documents and important data regarding our research were available only in the Czech language. Translation into German and English increased the time taken for the research. Several questions regarding finance were not answered by administrators for reasons of confidentiality, and the Czech tennis federation does not (yet) publish an annual report including financial details.

One further limitation was the financial resources available for the research. This, and other difficulties, relating to such things as the time involved in travelling to competitions and meetings with tennis experts in other parts of Germany and abroad, were surmounted partly by my professional contacts, my interest in the subject and my linguistic skills. Tennis is an international game and its rules and mechanisms work in the same way in most countries. It would probably be true to say that the language of tennis is English in most countries of the world. Further, all of the countries selected for this study were in the

European Union, so that cultural similarities were more obvious than major cultural contradictions. Through very good contacts between the author and the tennis 'scene' it was possible to identify locations where the various agents would be throughout the tournament season, in 2006 and 2007.

5.4 Conclusion

The study has developed three main research themes which have been designed to explore factors of talent identification and development programmes in tennis from different perspectives (administrators, coaches, parents and players) and the position and knowledge of these people about the TID process in selected European countries. This thesis is based upon a comparative research design (Hantrais 1997). The descriptive method is generally the first stage in any comparative research project, and so published and unpublished secondary material is presented at the beginning of the research – see especially chapters 1-4. I then utilised a mixed method approach (qualitative and quantitative), and used face-to-face interviews, computer-assisted personal interviews (CAPI), semi-structured questionnaires for data collection (Bortz & Döring 1995; Bungard 1979). Data from this research is presented in the next two chapters.

The aim of this chapter has been to provide insight into the methods used in this thesis. I also hope to have demonstrated how I have faced and overcome some of the obstacles inevitable in a piece of social research. I have used my own professional position and 'insider' status in the world of tennis, as well my linguistic abilities, to access relevant data and respondents. In the next chapter, I present the findings of the comparison of the tennis systems, institutionalised in the national tennis federations, in four European countries (the UK, France, the Czech Republic and Germany) which form the empirical focus for this research.

Chapter 6 Tennis and TID in Four National Systems: Major Similarities and Differences

Introduction

The information and research material in this and the following chapter are original and are the result of archival and documentary desk based research conducted in Germany and the UK and interviews conducted in both English and German in two of the four European countries featured in this thesis. In this chapter I present the findings of my research on institutional/organisational factors in the national systems and their specific influence regarding TID programmes in the selected European countries. These findings will lead to a critical discussion about major similarities and contradictions in the execution of the TID programmes in the selected countries, and will help to find answers to the research question about the influence of different social contexts on the meaning of tennis and especially approaches to TID in tennis. Essentially I am looking at the social determinants and processes of sport success in this chapter, and how key actors involved view these determinants and processes in the next chapter.

6.1 Institutional Factors

Productivity Rates in Tennis

Important key factors to be considered in this research are the institutional influences, which includes the productivity of different tennis 'systems'. Under the roof of productivity should be understood the gross rates of finance and investment in elite programmes, the participation rate in tennis, and the number of coaches against the rate of world class players listed in the men's and women's top 100 professional list (ATP and WTA). The question arises whether there is any clear indication of which of the National Tennis Federation (NTF) characteristics are genuinely causative of the world performance achieved? The answer is, of course, complex, with many interactive influences in addition to the straightforward, single factor picture. Such considerations are still useful, however, since pundits and politicians will often present such 'simplistic' solutions (team building, as with the Spanish squad, centralisation, as in France, the 'Kinder- und Jugend Sportschule (KJS)'[5] system of the former German Democratic Republic, and others). Even more worrying, such suggestions may even gain in influence or become policy!

Table 6.1: GDP and budget for the national tennis federation in four European countries

	GDP/ power parity	GDP/ real growth rate	GDP/ per capita	Budget Tennis (est.)
CR	$251 Billion	6.6 %	$24,500	0.5 Million € *
FRA	$2,075 Trillion	2,1 %	$32,600	100 Million €**
GER	$2,807 Trillion	2.5 %	$34,100	6 Million €**
UK	$2,133 Trillion	3.10 %	$35,700	40 Million €**

Source: De Bosscher et al. 2003, Central Intelligence Agency 2008a, b, c, d.
*data provided by tennis administrator 'Miroslav'
**data from De Bosscher et al. 2003

Competitive tennis is dependent on a wide variety of external sources and needs a high budget of the national federation (see table 6.1). For example, the specialist requirements of personnel, spatial and material equipment, coupled with the execution of international competitions, demands extensive financing. Moreover, a sufficient financial base permits the payment of athletes and coaches, once again, crucial components of building an effective high performance structure. Finally, the financial stability of competitive sport increases with the variety of financial resources available. In short, there is a cogent argument that greater finance should equal higher performance, and this should be reflected in the comparative wealth and achievement of National Tennis Federations. Therefore, some 'variable controlled' consideration seems

---

[5] State-organised children and youth sport school for talents

merited, and this is presented in Table 6.2, which is derived from official tennis websites, de Bosscher et al. (2003) and interview data.

Table 6.2: Cross section of the Tennis infrastructure of four European countries

	Budget (est.)	Members	Courts	Clubs	Coaches	TI	ATP/WTA 100	ITF/boys/girls 100
CR	0.5m	0.02m	5040	969	3000	4-5	10	8
FRA	100m	1.07m	33553	8748	19200	6	18	5
GER	6m	1.8m	51271	10274	15000	7/8	9	6
UK	40m	48533	35200	26600	5500	6	2	3

Source: own findings

With respect to the data in table 6.2, we can observe that France shows the highest productivity regarding the infrastructure in its federation. A budget of €100m a year and a large amount of coaches results in the most top 100 players in women's and men's elite tennis (ATP/ WTA rankings). Germany, with the highest number of members, is therefore not that productive. The UK, with the second highest budget and the lowest number of registered members, is not productive at all in terms of world class players. The Czech system, with a low budget and the second highest amount of elite players, seems here to be very productive.

Finance

The German Tennis Federation invests 25% of its annual budget in elite tennis development, the French Tennis Federation invests 11%, but at €11m this is nearly 80% more than the Germans. No precise figures were available from the Czech Tennis Federation, but some informal conversations, as well as interviews (to be discussed in the next chapter) underpin the conclusion that probably more than 70% of their whole budget goes into elite development. In the United Kingdom, between € 6-8m is invested annually the elite programme.

Based on the proportion of top 100 players and the budget for elite development, one could assume that more finance equals more players. Unfortunately for this premise, consideration of the 'cost per player' figures in the table demonstrates the error. In fact, neither gross income nor income controlled for population shows a clear relationship to productivity, at least when this is strictly (but, I would contend, realistically) defined as production of world ranked players. The Czech Republic is by far the most efficient system according to this factor.

France and the United Kingdom are the countries with the highest total budget for tennis. One reason for this wealth could be that these countries run two of the most important tennis tournaments worldwide, the Grand Slams (Wimbledon and Roland Garros), which definitely guarantee a high and certain income. From this considerable income base, the UK re-invests between 17% and 20% of the total budget into its elite programmes for tennis, whilst France supports its elite with 11% of the total budget. By comparison, Germany invests 25% of its whole budget in high level tennis, whilst the Czech Republic has a total budget of just around 500,000 euros to run its whole programme. This budget allows investment in tennis participation country-wide, which should be seen as the bottom of the pyramid of the long-term development of tennis in each country. Together with the reasons explored earlier in this section, more income should result in better performance. This is not the case, however, as money seems not to be the crucial factor in the productivity of a national federation regarding its elite programmes. For example, consider the small budget of the Czech Republic (500,000 euros) against the productivity of their system in regard to rankings (ATP 8, WTA 5) in comparison to the United Kingdom and France, or even Germany. Money by itself does not seem to guarantee successful productivity.

There must be some other mediating factors which act on the apparently obvious cash-performance relationship. Things are further complicated, however, since different factors impact in different ways, even in this small sample of the world game. In France, for example, income from a prestigious tournament is allocated to the promotion of elite performance, with reasonable results. By contrast, the United Kingdom allocates an even greater proportion of its income (albeit a smaller amount of money) with far less benefit in world performance terms.

A different situation appears to exist in Germany, where 50% of the total budget comes from membership fees. As a consequence, mass participation and support for clubs and regional federations is high; the money is quite reasonably spent on things which interest or benefit the people who provide the cash! Despite this pragmatic drive, however, Germany shows the highest percentage (25%) spent on elite programmes, although the absolute amount is much lower than in France and the United Kingdom.

Is the proportion of income per player important in this difference? In other words, does a potential elite player in France receive more support in absolute terms than his/her British counterpart? Not at all! Our research so far has shown that the idea that more finance equals more talented players is an error, and once again the Czech Republic appears by far the most efficient system in terms of this factor.

Participation

To increase the participation rates in tennis is one of the key aims of any tennis federation, and many efforts have been made by national and the international tennis federations to launch specific programmes. Nevertheless it is important for any federation to have a high number of participants, because tennis has first to attract people before talent identification, and later, development into elite players, can take place. In the late 1990s the world-wide School Tennis Initiative (STI) for developing countries was created to bring tennis to primary school (Miranda 2007). In 2002, the International Tennis Federation (ITF) implemented a taskforce to identify how to get more players on to the tennis court. Finally the 'play and stay' campaign was born, which supports an easy start to playing tennis through playing with different balls and different court sizes (Miley 2007). In 2003, the ITF started another campaign to implement the so-called International Tennis Number (ITN) which can be seen as equivalent to the handicap in golf. It was hoped that every tennis player world-wide would have an ITN number (Sharp 2007). In 2005, another programme was launched at the US Open (2005), called Cardio Tennis, a fun and fitness oriented programme for every level (de

Boer 2007). The hope of the ITF and the affiliated member nations to launch this kind of programme was to increase the participation level of tennis world-wide; however, despite the launching of these programmes the decline of interest in tennis and the decrease in members has not been stopped in recent years. Table 6.3 presents estimates for tennis participation at elite and recreational levels in the four countries being researched

Table 6.3: Total Participation

	Registered players	Non-registered players	Total	Courts indoor + outdoor	Tennis clubs (in thd)	Reg. Players per court	Reg and non reg players per court	Elite players
CR	44,513	417,010	461,523	4760	875	9.3	96	60
France	1.07m	3.0m	4.07m	33,553 reg 20,000 non reg	8,748	31,8	74	390
Germany	1.8m	1.06m	2.86m	51,271	10,083	35,1	54	134
UK	275,000	4.3m	4.575m	35,100	2,360	3.3	125	600

Source: Houlihan and White 2002; Deutscher Olympischer Sport Bund 2009b; Czech Tennis Association 2008a; Fédération Française de Tennis 2008.

The people in the countries selected for this study are keen on sport (European Commission 2004; van Bottenburg 1992, 2001). More careful consideration shows, however, that the most popular sports in Germany, France, the Czech Republic and the United Kingdom are not the Olympic and competition sports, but more leisure-oriented sports like Nordic walking, fitness, snooker, fishing and darts (Sport England 2004; Deutscher Olympischer Sport Bund 2009a), or aerobics and netball (CR). In Germany tennis is very popular with most of the young population aged under 16 (Deutscher Tennis Bund 2009a). In the United Kingdom, where the LTA estimated that 4 million people currently play tennis, 1 million people play at least once every two weeks, 57% under the age of 24 and 70% under 35 (Houlihan & White 2002). The participation level of registered members has decreased in recent years (Deutscher Tennis Bund 2008a; Czech Tennis Association 2008a; Fédération Française de Tennis 2008); but tennis is still one of the top 3-5 sports among the population of the countries selected (Czech, Germany Republic, France, United Kingdom). For the decline there have been a number of reasons given.

In the 1980s, before Steffi Graf (GER) and Boris Becker (GER), Yannick Noah (FRA), Martina Navratilova (CR) and Ivan Lendl (CR) entered the international stage, tennis was booming for several reasons, as we have noted (van Bottenburg 1992). In the 1970s, tennis clubs sprang up at an astonishing rate, and this helped create the conditions that fostered such future stars as Graf, Lendl and Noah – and their success in turn helped drive tennis to even greater heights at both high and low level. Mass participation at a low level creates the pool from which high-level sport can recruit its future champions (Digel et al. 2006). In their policies each of the National Tennis Federations which we have selected for this research mentions the objectives of 'developing the game', 'mass participation', the 'increase of registered members' and developing 'performance tennis' as their main mission and vision with the aim of carrying tennis into the future (Lawn Tennis Association 2008a; Deutscher Tennis Bund 2008a; Fédération Française de Tennis 2008).

I can conclude from this section that a country does not essentially need a large number of participants at a low level to produce high-level athletes (CR) (see Table 6.4). The new 'Play and Stay' campaign of the International Tennis Federation, which has been supported very enthusiastically in all the selected countries, and advertised by the International Tennis Federation (International Tennis Federation 2008e), is intended to increase the participation level in this specific age group, in the hope that a future 'star' will be identified as early as possible.

Table 6.4: Members registered with NTFs

	CR	FRA	GER	UK
Members/Gross	20,000	1.07m	1.7m	48,000
Per capita/Pop	0.0002	0.01	0.02	0.0008
WR Player/ members	1/2000	1/60,000	1/188,000	1/24,000
WR Player per member per pop	0.0002	0.001	0.002	0.0004

Source: European Tennis Association 2008

Germany has the largest number of registered players. I can assume that having the most members does not guarantee success. The Czech Republic and the United Kingdom show more productivity in converting members into world class players. In sum, I can mention that participation rates are important for any TID programme, because in all selected countries TI starts at club level with children who are already participating. But participation rates on their own as an important institutional factor cannot be named as the 'only' factor, because CR shows the lowest participation rate, but produces relatively the highest amount of elite players.

Infrastructure

It is undisputed that the right environment and infrastructure, including enough facilities like indoor and outdoor courts, clubs and coaches, are important for tennis, participation and talent identification and development. Perhaps there is a relationship between world class players to the number of courts, clubs and coaches, such that the better the gross rates, the greater the success of the federation? In the following table (6.5) we compare the relationship between tennis courts and world ranked players.

Table 6.5: The relationship of numbers of tennis courts to world ranked players

	CR	FRA	GER	UK
Courts (est.)	5040	33535	50483	35200
Courts/WR Player	504/1	1863/1	5696/1	17600/1

Source: modified from European Tennis Association 2008.

The number of tennis courts and clubs (see Table 6.6), seems however, not to be significant for predicting a successful tennis country. The CR, with around 969 clubs and 5,040 courts (one court for every 4 registered tennis players), seems to be very productive in its elite player development. In the United Kingdom, where 2,600 clubs are affiliated to the LTA, there has been a massive input over the last 15 years, resulting in the number of indoor courts increasing from 67 (1987) to over 1,000 (2004), with approximately 35,200 outdoor courts. Despite this increase, access to indoor facilities, which other authors (for example Houlihan & White 2002) have considered absolutely essential to the development of the game, is still uneven and limited, with just one indoor court for every 58,000 people in Britain. In Germany the relation of indoor courts to members is 1 court to 113 members (in all, 15000 indoor courts to 1.7m members) and in the case of outdoor courts 1 court to 48 members (in all, 35,000 outdoor courts). In France, tennis players practice in 8,748 clubs on 33,535 courts, where we can find 29 registered players per court.

Purely from the statistical point of view, the most courts are available in Germany, where on average 113 registered players have to share a court. Better ratios exist in the UK, where statistically only 2 registered players (in the CR 4) share one court. Concerning the relation of world ranked players to courts, the UK ranks first, Germany second, France third and CR fourth. However, the UK seems not to be the most successful tennis country within the selected countries, and in the world. Germany has the most tennis clubs, but is only ranked third in its probability of producing a world-class player. Analysing the relation of clubs to world ranked players, we have to mention that the probability of producing a world-class player in a club is 1 to 486 in France. In other words, every 486th club can statistically produce a world-class player. In the Czech Republic, the probability of producing a world-class player in a club is 1 to 96, which means statistically, that every 96th club in the CR can produce a world-class player. This seems a very effective ratio.

Table 6.6: Relation clubs to world ranked players

	CR	FRA	GER	UK
Clubs	969	8748	10185	2600
WR Player/ clubs	1/96	1/486	1/1,141	1/1,300

Source: calculated from figures from the European Tennis Association 2008

Analysis of the relation of numbers of coaches and world ranked players (Table 6.7) shows that France has the most coaches in absolute terms, whilst the CR and France have the most coaches per capita (population). The best ratio of coaches per world-ranked player is found in the CR, where only 300 coaches are needed to produce a world-ranked player. In the UK, however, 2750 coaches are needed to produce one single world-ranked player.

Table 6.7: Conversion rate from coach to world-ranked players

	CR	FRA	GER	UK
Coaches	3,000	19,200	15,000	5,500
Coaches per capita / Pop	0.3	0.3	0.2	0.09
WR Player per coach	300	1066	1666	2750

To sum up this section, I can state that the productivity of any country in the tennis world can be measured mostly through financial investment, participation rates, registered members, tennis courts (indoor and outdoor), clubs and coaches. The rankings at international level at least measure the productivity of high performance tennis. For that reason, high performance can be mentioned as a central goal in the policies of the national tennis federations described. In Germany, up to 25% of the whole budget is invested in elite tennis. But this does not guarantee more players in the main ranking lists. The UK has a tremendous budget, but fewer players in the international list than the CR. France, with the highest budget, has a competitive number of players in the rankings, but lacks a real world class player at the moment. Even the relation between tennis courts, clubs, and coaches to world-ranked players has not shown a significant trend towards more courts, coaches and clubs meaning production of more world class players. It is more obvious that small countries with a good infrastructure and, more importantly perhaps a good overview and control of their programmes, like the CR, are more productive in producing world-class players. So there must be other factors that contribute to producing world class athletes! Good coaches are important at each level of the sport pyramid. The importance of such factors as the quality of staff training and the system for developing certified coaches in a country is often underestimated.

Coaches

'Tennis champions are born, not made!' was the opinion until the 1960s; today, both players and experts would say 'tennis champions are both born AND made!', Stojan, an acknowledged international coach in the 1980s and 1990s, stated that a tennis champion needs practice, good organisation, good luck, and talent mixed with development obstacles (Stojan 1996). Without real talent, even the best coach has no chance to develop talented children. Besides practice time and organisation, a future tennis champion needs luck to find the right coach. This coach should be a master coach who has the skills to develop the talented ones. The training of these coaches is the responsibility of the federation, because coaches are part of the development process, together with physiotherapists, experts in biomechanics and sports medicine. They accompany the athletes over several years, supporting the talent development process of the children and guiding them, perhaps over a number of years, to world-class level. The coach represents a minimum prerequisite for the 'production' of top players. Quantity alone, however, is not sufficient with regard to coaches; qualitative aspects like training and acceptance in society play an important part as well. We can observe differences in coaches' education and professional training between the four countries. In Germany, the UK and France it is organised into five levels, whilst in the CR only three levels exist. However, the number of levels does not always relate to the volume of the coaches' training system. There are many differences in the number of hours each course takes in different countries. In Germany, a course to become a professional tennis coach takes 18 months. In the UK, a coach can obtain his first certificate in 12 hours, whilst in Germany it takes 150 hours for the first certificate.

Table 6.8: Coaches' training systems in the countries selected

	Number of qualification levels in coaches' training system organised by the NTF	Lowest level: how many hours?	Highest level: how many hours?	Refresher course/clinics required to keep qualification?
Czech Republic	3			Yes
France	5	75	550	No
Germany	5	150	800 (18 months)	Yes
UK	5	12	200	Yes

Source: De Bosscher et al. 2003.

I can mention that in all selected countries the prerequisite exists for an effective coach's education. A good coach training system can correlate with the productivity and the programmes of the countries described, but in our research there are no significant advantages or disadvantages regarding the education system and the productivity of world class players. The question is rather whether the coaches are interested in guiding the talented in their development process for several years: are they prepared for that task? and, more interestingly, are they interested in doing so? A coach training system in itself cannot guarantee successful player development. A talented player needs the luck to find somebody who identifies him and takes him up to high levels. This is a long-term process, and nothing is achieved by a training system lasting a few weeks in the long-term development process of a player. As I mentioned in this section, the coaches and their education play an important part for any tennis federation that is interested in the development of talented players.

The recruitment and development (in short, the talent identification and development process) of talented young athletes must not be left to chance or to coaches or parents alone. Arguably a TID programme should be a necessity for any tennis federation and even more important coaches are needed to bring this programme into practice.

Talent Identification and Development (TID)

The process of the early detection, identification and development of talented children and teenagers is among the central tasks of the tennis associations, besides mass participation. As Table 6.9 shows, there is not a large gap between the structures of the nations' programmes.

Table 6.9: National Talent Identification and Development programmes

	FRA	UK	GER	CR
Talent Identification	6 years	7-8 years	7-8 years	5-9 years
Fundamental Development 5-10y	2000-3000 'Club avenir" 7-10yrs	Mini tennis 4-11yrs	Mini tennis 6-10y	Mini tennis and Parents 5-9y
Development 10-14y	36 Clubs 'Avenir régionaux" 260 boys/girls	Learning to train	Development 10/11 -12/13 E/ D- Cadre 600 players	National Team 12-14y 5 Players
Performance 12/13 – 16/17	Pôles espoir	Learn to compete	Performance D/ C-Cadre 116 players	National team U14/ U16 5 Players
High Performance 17+	Pôles nationaux	Learn to win	High performance C/ B-Cadre 7 Players	National Team U18 5 Players
Transition	yes		A/B-Cadre 18 players	-

A well-organised system of talent search ensures the optimum use of the 'talent pool'. Corresponding talent support has to be added to it to keep the loss of sporting talents (drop- out rate) as low as possible (Gabler 1993). In France, the fundamental development of talented children starts in selected clubs (clubs Avenir) for children aged 7-10. In Germany, the United Kingdom and the Czech Republic, forms of mini-tennis (with a short tennis court and soft tennis balls) practice and tournaments are common.

In France, at the development stage (10-14 yrs) for talented children around 260 players (boys & girls) have been identified, who are placed in 36 'avenir' clubs at regional level. The British LTA calls this stage 'learning to train'. In Germany, which is more selective in its age separation (10/11-12/13), the cadre system, which is organised regionally, is the main pillar at this stage; around 600-900 players are collected in these regional cadre centres. In the CR, in the age group 12-14 yrs there are only national team players at the national centre. At the performance stage, in France the 'pôles espoir' are implemented to bring the best players together between the ages of 12/13 and 16/17 in regional training groups. In the UK, the main focus is on 'learn to compete' and the achievement of certain results, whilst in Germany, with the cadre system (D/C-cadre), 116 players train together, most of them at regional training centres. The CR continues its system of national squads (U16/U18), for which only 5-7 players, depending on their ranking, have qualified. At high performance level in France, 7 'pôles nationaux' (national training centres) are implemented for professional players or for those who have the potential to achieve a high level. In Germany, at this stage some players (7) are in the cadre system (A/B-cadre) but most of them go their own way, with private coaches.

In the next table (6.10) I show that there are various measures and methods of search for and development of talents in the federations, and the effectiveness and responsibility of organisations (schools, clubs, and tournaments), which is a further interesting point of comparison regarding TID systems.

Table 6.10: Start of Talent Identification

Country	Age of start with TI	Through schools (in %)	Through tennis tournament competition (in %)	Through visiting clubs (in %)	Through initiatives of parents, coaches, clubs or coincidence	Others (in %)
CR	5-9 yrs	0	80	na	90%	
France	6 yrs	0	40	20	10%	Meetings
Germany	7-8 yrs	0	60	0	0	40
UK	7-8 yrs	0	30	30	40%	0
ITF	6 yrs (STI)	30	50	N.A.	N.A.	PTI

Source: own findings

The search for talent varies between the UK, Germany, France and Czech Republic. The clubs are partly responsible for the first talent identification in France and Germany. In Germany most talented children are identified at tournaments and not at clubs. In the Czech Republic, on the other hand, most children start to play with their parents at the beginning of their career, and when they have a certain standard they move on to the clubs. In theory, according to the FFT, LTA, DTB, CTS and ITF, (see chapter 4) talent identification should start between 5 and 9 years of age, through motor tests and 'the eye of the expert' as well as in tournaments. This process is in practice largely based on the results of the players.

The fundamental development of players in Germany and the United Kingdom seems to be important, but on the other hand a full court playing standard around the age of 8 is a criterion for getting more support (practice lessons, financial support) from the NF. In the development process of a junior aged 14 there are some differences between the countries described. In France (membership in the 'Club Avenir' and results) and the CR (TOP 5 Ranking) there are clear criteria on how to get support from the NF. In Germany there is the cadre system, which allows the identified children to be invited into cadres (A-E), but again only results are counted and without an adequate ranking the player cannot qualify for these cadres. Unfortunately, selected players (e.g, players from the D-Cadre U13 DTB Ranking Top 10) do not know exactly what benefits they have and how they can use this selection for progress in their development process. Additionally in Germany, the selection for regional squads starts at the age of 9, which requires training practice of 4-6 hours a week during the preceding 2 years, and further a tournament increase from the age group of the under 7s is to be noticed.

France has clearly centralised structures. To be identified as talents in France, children should already have started to play tennis 'somewhere'. If these children play in tournaments at an early age, they have a chance of being detected for the 'Clubs avenir' and 'Pôles'. In the long term, rankings and tournament success are the main criteria for being supported by the Direction Technique Nationale (DTN) in Paris. The UK has prepared some tournament series for different age groups such as 'Road to Wimbledon' and 'Robinsons Ace'. A development framework document *How to get to be a Wimbledon champion*, was divided into four steps, 'mini tennis, learn to train, train to compete, and train to win'. But the LTA did not have (in 2005 at least) the structural features of the other countries such as cadres, national training teams or performance clubs, even at the regional level.

Training/ Practice

We know that qualitatively demanding training based on the latest scientific knowledge with qualified coaches has positive effects on the development of the level of the game (Monsaas 1985, 240). In the preparation for competitions a variety of factors play an important part, e.g. the composition of the training groups, the type of training methods including planning, the existence of special training facilities, and also possibly training camps. The total quantity of training within the federation has the same key role as the overall weekly/monthly training plan of the player.

Table 6.11: Total hours of training within the federation

	Age U8	Age U10	Age U12	Age U14	Age U16	Age U18
CR	10hrs	10hrs	12hrs	14hrs	22hrs	26hrs
FRA	4hrs	8hrs	12hrs	16hrs	21hrs	21hrs
UK	5.5hrs	12hrs	18hrs	22hrs	27hrs	30hrs
GER	7hrs	9hrs	11hrs	12hrs	13hrs	16hrs
ITF	9hrs	11hrs	13hrs	13hrs	17.5hrs	

Table 6.11 gives an overview of the total hours of training that the best players (identified talents) in each country can participate in within the programme of the federation. There are big differences between the countries described. For example, a talented and identified tennis player in the UK has the highest amount of training and participation level at age U18, while a talented and identified player in the CR has the highest amount of training at age U8. But in 'productivity' the UK is far behind smaller countries like the CR.

To conclude this section with findings: we have shown that it is an error to assume that more money equals more talented players, as is the assumption that a good infrastructure guarantees better productivity of the system regarding high performance players (top 100). The coaches' training appears crucial; there are no major differences, but to include in the education of the coaches more detailed talent identification and development programmes is very important from a practical point of view, but not well executed in the selected countries. Schools do not play an important part in TID. In the CR, detection of the talents takes place mostly at tournaments, while in Germany the club system is also important for detection. In France, the centralisation of the TID programme can be named as an advantage over against the other countries, as is also the direct influence of the government on this programme. The disadvantage of the system is the problem of financing this programme, without a large income through a 'Grand Slam' Tournament (e.g. the French Open), this would be very hard to imagine. In contrast to France, the UK also has a large amount of money available, but does not by far have the same success.

In the next section, we will look at TID within the development systems of the four European national tennis federations.

6.2 Development Systems in Four European National Tennis Federations (NTF's)

Within the tennis federations selected, there are consistent guidelines with a number of minor, systemic, contradictions. Crucially for the topic of this thesis, all the federations attach great importance to fundamental basic development up to the age of 10/11 years. Until this 'threshold' age, all tennis competitions are proposed as child-oriented and carried out as 'mini-tennis' competitions. Notwithstanding minor variations in this threshold age, the picture is pretty uniform in its child-oriented nature. In short, all the NTF's aim to provide a gentle introduction before increasing competitive pressure.

Table 6.12: Progressive Development in four national tennis federations

	FRA	CR	GER	UK
Talent Identification	6	5/6	7/8	6
Talent Development	10 <	10 <	10 <	10 <
Performance	13/14 <	13/14 <	13/14 <	n/a
High Performance	15 <	15 <	15 <	15 <

Source: own findings

There is one major contradiction, however, so substantial that it challenges the premise underpinning all the NTF systems considered. In their policies, the NTFs employ a long-term player development pathway which takes about 10 years of training; in short, all have adopted the Ericsson 10,000 hours rule, as discussed in chapter 4, albeit often uncritically. Unfortunately for the child-friendly picture presented, if a player were to adhere to the described development concepts, he would hardly be able as 17 years-old (girls 15 yrs) to be ranked in the Top 100 at the ITF Junior Rankings, which run from 14 to 18 years of age. Nevertheless, under current conditions (and I will consider this point in a lot more detail later in the thesis), the position a 16/17 years-old male player (or a girl of 15 years) must normally achieve if s/he is later to be ranked in the Top 100 professional (ATP/WTA) rankings is as follows: a training volume of a minimum of 20 hours/week and tournament participation at international tournaments of at least 60 (GER) or even up to 80 (FRA) matches a year, for a period of 5-10 years. This is completely at odds with the more easy-going, child-centred approach.

As an example, take a young player and make sure he receives the prescribed fundamental development until 11 years of age (GER/ UK). Perhaps his skills will develop and he will become a good player, but crucially it will be very hard for him to get into regional or later national support and squads. As a consequence, he can develop his game and performance only by chance and in the end without any official financial support. This early specialisation route is exemplified by the admission of 12/13 years old players, in Germany to D/C-Cadres, in the Czech Republic National Ranking and in France 'Avenir National', who are selected for national performance cadres. In France, for example, the regional squads are open to 10 years old children, although only a total of 260 places are available nationally for all players up to the age of 18. Such procedures necessitate early identification. For example, regarding Talent Identification (TI) in Germany the system requires that children should be identified mainly at club level at the age of 6-8 years. The clubs then register the 8/9 year old children for the district talent identification day. In France the main objective of the identification process is to build up a broad base of competitors in their so-called 'Avenir Club' with children aged 7-10 yrs. Thus, despite its stated emphasis on early fundamentals, the French Tennis Federation stresses the role of this club in 'building competitors' and developing young competitors at the bottom of the pyramid of high performance (original: 'développer un large vivier de jeunes compétiteurs à la base de la pyramide au haut niveau") (Fédération Française de Tennis 2008a).

In the UK, the basic message for 'tomorrow's champions' is also to develop their fundamental skills like agility, balance and coordination up to the age of 11. So far so good, but at what age and where exactly the identification process should take place in the UK is not clear. Further, only the statement (Lawn Tennis Association 2004) that in the second development stage ('learn to train') the basic shape of the tennis strokes should be established shows that, in the same way as in the German concept, the children have to play tennis too!

From my reading of the various publications of tennis federations, mini-tennis seems to be an important tool in all the selected countries. However, all this does is transfer the Talent Identification process from full tennis competition to a mini-format. In short, since play can start earlier, talent identification can take place earlier! However, this hard edge does seem to be 'disguised' within a very child-friendly format of fundamental work. Unfortunately, this child-centred approach may not be enough to generate a Wimbledon champion, and most NTFs demand a more focused and tennis-centred style from their coaches. For example, the district coach (elite qualification) in Germany is required to develop the ability of the children to play on full court even at a young age (interview with the High Performance Coaches 'Darren' and 'Eric' of the National Tennis Federation of Germany). This position is confirmed by the ad hoc (i.e. organisational) publications of the NTFs; for example, the promotional material for the bi-annual district identification tournaments in GER states clearly 'Grossfeldspielfähigkeit wird vorausgesetzt' (in translation: Ability to play full court is required) for the age group under 8/9. This situation is also clearly apparent in the Czech Republic, supported by both interviews and publications (Württembergischer Tennis Bund 2004).

Further pressure for early success is apparent in the 'expectations' of coaches, and the ways in which they gain recognition. The districts in Germany and the coaches in CR are always measured by their short-term success. The various district and regional squads compete against each other, and the more successful a district or regional squad is, the more support and acknowledgement it gets from the national association. This could be one reason why a child will be selected mainly through his/her results in the identification tournament, which includes mini-tennis and full-court play. This tournament emphasis continues throughout the system in the selected countries.

At the next level, there is a regional identification tournament (in Germany held twice a year) which is organised by the regional associations. At the age of 9-10, identification takes place at a tournament on full court, together with some motor skill tests. However, interviews with and reports from coaches in this system, together with my own experience as a coach, have shown that the results of the motor test from district to regional level are without meaning. Those players ranked successful in regional and national rankings are supported at national level. In summary, the ability to play full court as a 10 years-old child is a prerequisite of the federation.

There is one other strand to this dichotomous system. In theory, the school systems are important for talent identification within the countries described (De Bosscher et al. 2003). A completely different picture is seen in practice, however, there is no conclusive concept either in the countries compared. All measures within schools can take place only on the basis of individual initiative, because tennis is not compulsory in the curriculum. As such, this stated 'important component' is entirely up to the networking skills of the individual coach!

All selected countries have introduced and manifested a progressive system regarding the development into world class players. Similar to a pyramid approach with a broad base, this process should end with a large number of world top ranked players. But in each of the countries selected, there are major internal contradictions. The national talent identification and development policies support the broad development of fundamental skills at an early age, but in practice parents and coaches follow the 'method' of early specialisation and early success measured through results. It seems that they are more interested in short-term success than in the long-term development of the children; the possibility of dropping-out from the sport seems very remote to parents and many coaches.

For the purposes of this thesis, two major points emerge from this section. Firstly, that despite an apparent and consistent logic in the talent identification and development systems proposed, the practice is extremely different from what is prescribed. Secondly, and I suggest, as a consequence of the circumstances and choices which predominate in each national environment, the 'productivity' of the systems as generators of world class players varies greatly.

6.3 TID in the Four European Countries

Talent Identification and Development in Tennis in the Czech Republic

Tennis has a very long tradition in the Czech Republic. For decades the system has been producing very good international top players (Jan Kodes, Ivan Lendl, Jana Novotna, Martina Navratilova, Tomas Smid...). In this section we describe how the Czech Tennis Federation (CTS) pursues TID in practice. The system of Talent Identification and Development in the Czech Republic can be described as centrally organised. As its main pillar, the ranking list has to be mentioned, with 7,584 registered tournament players; this represents a third of the 20,208 registered players. Every player down to the age group U12 is registered in this list after an official game, no matter whether he/she has won or lost (Czech Tennis Association 2008b). Second, the full coverage of national and international level tournaments has to be mentioned. This guarantees a high degree of competition experience at an early age. This tournament platform is supported and accompanied by a competitive league system which also seems to be a pillar for the competition ability of the CR players (Czech Tennis Association 2008b).

It is notable that the CR has 3 tennis committees which have different tasks. The first committee of the Czech Tennis Association (CTS) consists of four persons who are responsible for the department of tournament and league tennis. The second committee has to visit, watch and discuss the work of other international tennis associations and their strengths in the area of tennis sport. The third committee, which consists of three persons, has to control the talent search and development programme; further, it fixes the criteria for admission to the National cadre U15, and the procedures are continuously evaluated and if necessary improved. A published catalogue of anthropometric and physical criteria, like endurance, speed, movement, agility, and motivation rounds off the work of the committee.

The introduction of these projects is an important milestone in the Czech Tennis Association. It is worth mentioning a mini-tennis project which was published and has been organised nationally since October 2004. This serves as the basis for a new support concept. This mini-tennis project primarily appeals to schools and sports instructors. In 2005, 8 national tournaments and a national championship were organised. An important point in this policy is that full court game ability is presupposed as well as the acquisition of mini-court game ability for children aged around 8 years. An interesting point is the fact that the full court game is not formally allowed below 8 years of age. The mini-tennis programme for 'under 10s' also has to be seen in the Czech Tennis Association as the environment where talented children can be identified by coaches (Czech Tennis Federation 2009). The league competition series and the Junior National Team can be seen as the next important development steps in the policy of the Czech Tennis Federation (see Figure 6.1).

Each year the Czech Tennis Association has to name a single national team which is divided into the age groups U18/U16/U14/U12 and which recruits the best 5 players from the national ranking list. If a player loses this top 5 position, he loses his place in the national team, and the training facilities too. The example of former Czech Under 14 &16 National Champion 'Richard' in the development process of a junior from 6 to 16 is useful . Most players in the CR learn tennis from their parents (70% of Top 100 ATP). 'Richard' started to play tennis 4 times a week with his father from 5 to 9 years of age. He participated in around 25 tournaments a year. 'Richard' went to Prerov, a national performance centre, at 9 years of age. The tournament numbers in which he participated in the CR alone remained similarly high. He qualified for the National Team at U12, U14 and U16 levels. For the U18 National Team he did not qualify because of his ranking (no. 7). After the age of 18, 'Richard' dropped out because of health problems. In comparison to 'Richard', two compatriots (Jiri Novak and Bohdan Ulhirach) have qualified for the world ranking (ATP) and top 10 at senior level (Novak). Yet these players did not belong to the U16 National Team. 'Richard' himself left performance tennis in 1994. He stated that one of the biggest disadvantages in his career was the high pressure to win as a junior. Another problem from his point of view was the fluctuation of coaches in his development process. Today he is working as a performance coach in Germany.

Figure 6.1: Progressive development stages in the Czech Tennis Federation (modified from an interview with the Czech Administrator 'Miroslav' 2008)

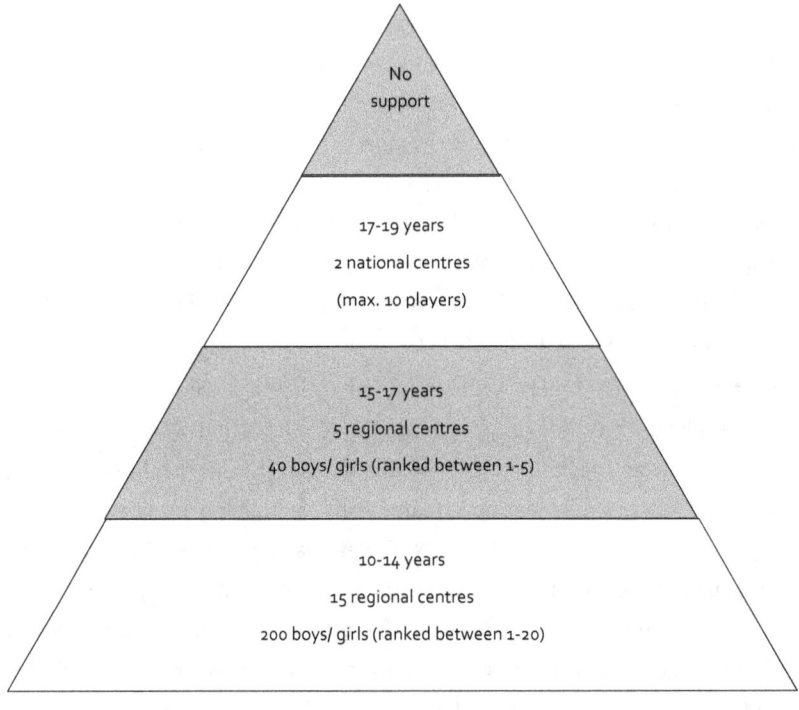

The Czech Tennis Federation favours a well-organised ranking and tournament system for its athletes[6]. For Talent Identification (TI) it uses simple physical tests which are in use for different age groups, in which values like the Body Mass Index (BMI) also influence the judgement. To follow a fundamental development

---

[6] The information in this paragraph is derived from an interview with a Czech professional tennis coach conducted in June 2006.

in line with the other countries in this study seems almost impossible in the Czech Republic's Tennis Association, as long as the results achieved are the most important selection criteria. The competition standard even for young ages is very high, and the parents as the first mentors for their children are focused on improving the level of play in competition: "...*they (parents) don't care about a dynamic development process*" (Bohdan).

The Czech commission for talent search has tried to develop the Mini-Tennis project mainly at school level. In the future, countries like the Czech Republic will have to run more programmes for mass participation to increase participation at the grass roots level. Through the positive advantage of the central orientation it should not be difficult to implement and improve programmes for the development of talented young children. Motivation to travel and to earn money still seems one of the most important factors in starting a tennis career (Interview Bohdan in 2006). Clubs are interested in good players' development, because it is through them that they acquire their reputation, acknowledgement and sponsorship in the public domain. The most talented player has always received the most support from the clubs. The fact that the coaches have been paid by the club supports this procedure. However, these days the practice is changing. Through the economic changes in the CR, the clubs are also struggling financially and are looking for financially independent parents who can pay for their children's lessons. The talented, perhaps with a less strong financial background, will be left behind. (Interview Bohdan in 2006)

Even during the communist era, the sport of tennis in the Czech Republic was successful in producing high-level players and developing an infrastructure for tennis which was comparable with that of western countries like Germany or France. From the population and geographical aspects, France is much bigger than the Czech Republic, but in the 1980s and 1990s French players were not as successful in world tennis as Czech players. However, in the last 10 years the modified and newly structured Talent Development system of the French Tennis Federation (FFT) has brought results and made France one of the world's leading tennis nations. In the next section we explore the French system.

Talent Identification and Development in Tennis in France

The main objectives and mission of the FFT are to promote, organise, and develop tennis in France and unite the affiliations of the clubs, to encourage and support their efforts and to coordinate their activities. Furthermore the FFT seeks to increase their numbers in the best hundred players (ATP/ WTA ranking), to facilitate the transition from junior to senior level, and to create real professional athletes. The general performance concept is based on 5 pillars. The following figure shows the development process from club level to elite level:

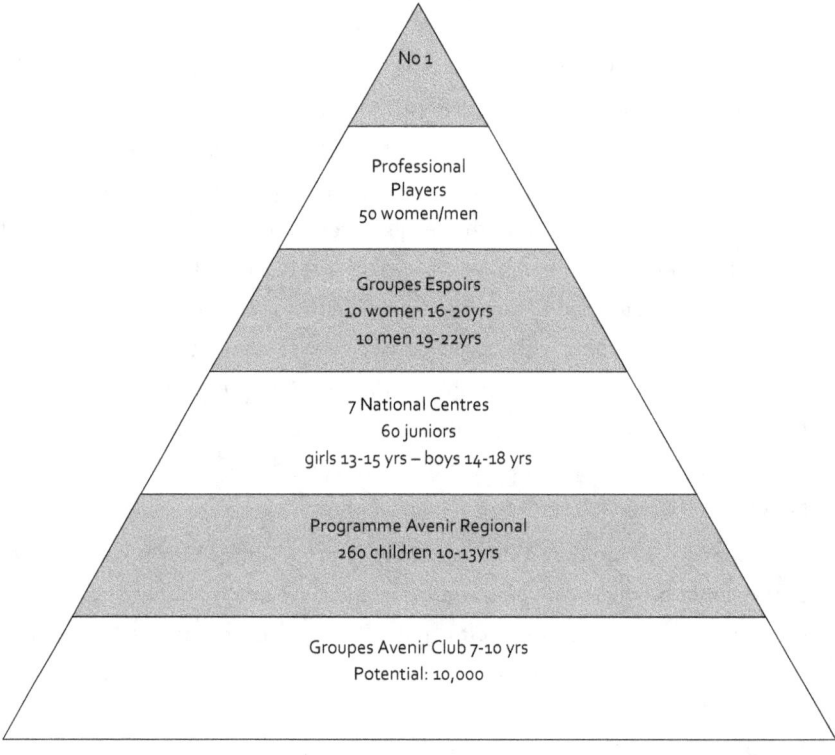

Figure 6.2 : Progressive development stages in the French Tennis Federation «La Pyramide Du Haut Niveau» (modified from Fédération Française de Tennis 2008c)

Table 6.13: Elite player participation

	Professional	Groupes Espoirs	7 National Centres	Avenir régional	Avenir club
Age		girls 16-20 boys 19-22	girls 13-15 boys 14-18	10-13	7-10
participants	50 women/men	10 women 10 men	60	260	10,000

Source: modified from Fédération Française de Tennis 2008c.

There are 2,000 – 3,000 'Avenir' clubs with 10,000 participants around France with the objective of developing a large number of competition players at the base of the pyramid and improving the talent detection process at an early age. In the tennis academy integrated into each club, there are 3-5 selected players (with a minimum of one girl). This group trains and travels together to small tournaments. As a main goal for groups of this kind we can mention that these juniors have to learn how to train in groups, how to prepare themselves by physical fitness, and travel to competitions. They are able to get individual coaching. Around 2,500 clubs participate in this programme, in which around 10,000 children are organised. The best performers in this 'Avenir' programme can join the 'Groupe avenir régional' at the minimum age of 10-11 years (Fédération Française de Tennis 2008c). There are 260 boys and girls in 36 'Groupes avenir régionaux'. The objective of these groups is to prepare the players for and integrate them into the National Centres ('Pôles France') and to increase the number of young children and players who are interested in getting professional development. These players have to improve their technique, tactics, physical fitness and mental toughness, and maintain their enthusiasm and spirit and develop their sense of fun and ambition to play competitively. The regional association proposes to the 'Direction Technique Nationale' (DTN) a 'Groupe Avenir Régional" (36) which is supposed to include 4-12 players. The main criterion is the potential to become a future top player among these selected players. Under the supervision and financial support of the DTN, the squads compete against the other 36 'Groupes Avenir regionaux' For training purposes the players return to their regional centres and practise there (Fédération Française de Tennis 2008b).

The FFT maintains 11 decentralised centres in France. These 'pôles' (centres) are the responsibility of the regional league (Association) but with a national coordinator. These centres are interregional for training and recruitment. There are two groups: the juniors of the Groupe Avenir Programme Régional (aged 10-13 years), and the better regional players (aged 14-18) who are not integrated into the national centres (Pôles France). The objective of these 'Pôles Espoir' is to give the players a chance to join the national centres and to improve the regional level of play. The age categories can be between 10 and 18 years. The coach should accompany the athletes to tournaments.

The FFT maintains 7 national centres for 13-15 years (girls) and 14-18 years (boys) with the objective of training the juniors to international level and regrouping the better players at this level to support the development process to the next level for each athlete. These centres are to prepare the athletes for international tasks and create a healthy attitude in their behaviour. The minimum age for girls is 12 and 13 for boys to be integrated into these centres (*Pôles*). The recruitment is the responsibility of the DTN too. The players stay and practise in these centres for around 2-3 years. If these athletes show potential for an international career they move to one of the two largest centres, based in Grenoble and Paris.

The FFT maintain 6 Performance Groups (Groupes Espoir) for 16-20 years (girls) and 19-22 years (boys). Each year the DTN nominates 3-4 groups of boys and girls. They travel together to tournaments and train in Paris or Grenoble under the supervision of a national coach. The amount of training with the federation increases significantly from the age of 8 (4 hours a week) to 21 hours a week at the age of 16. This shows that children aged 8 already get the opportunity to train with the federation. The FFT encourage international tournament participation from 10 years of age (Fédération Française de Tennis 2008b).

In France the Director of Coaches' training (Directeur Formation et Enseignement) for the DTN (Jean-Claude Massias) controls the whole programme in cooperation with his assistant directors for boys/men and girls/women (Fédération Francaise de Tennis 2008c). The Director is at the top of the central system. The fundamental feature of this system is the 'ligues' (departments). In each of the 36 regional departments there are two full-time employees. One is an administrator paid by the government and one a regional coach or coordinator employed by the FFT. The regional coaches have to report to and get their orders from J.-C. Massias at two annual meetings. The full-time administrators also take their orders from Massias. The regional coach is responsible for each talent identification measure at district and club level. He has to report very closely to the DTN in Paris. The FFT supports the identified youngsters (7-10yrs) financially in their clubs. This gives the DTN an overview of each identified talent in the country. The amount of 3000 talented children decreases to 160 at 10-12 years, whilst the influence of the DTN on their daily development process increases. For the children the age of 12 seems to be crucial, because around this age they may be selected for one of the 6 'Groupes espoir'. They have to leave their homes for boarding houses at the National Centres. The move to the centres can be seen as the most important fact in the development process of the selected children. The athletes, parents and coaches are willing and prepared to leave their home surroundings and move to competitive and professional environments in the NC. Another advantage is the flexibility of the system. Sébastian Grosjean (ranked 49 in February 2008), for example, was not identified at the age of 8, but at 19, through good tournament successes, he entered the FFT training environment.

There are two full-time coaches who control and monitor talent measurement in France, mainly through visiting clubs without previous appointment. The coaches in the clubs have to follow the frame guidelines of the FFT for Talent Development. For example, each Talent Identification test is conducted together with the regional coaches, where the best 6/7 years-old will be selected for the programme 'Avenir club' (club programme for Talent Development). At this stage, the children, now 7/10 years-old, will be supported financially at their clubs. This money supports the most talented in their clubs with additional practice lessons. In 2006, 3000 children participated in the programme. To develop to the next stage, the regional coach again selects the most talented for another training group. At this stage the 3000 children supported have been reduced to 160 athletes. The demand for tennis-specific skills and greater responsibility for the 10/12 years-old increase. Each week they have to work 4-6 hours on court, do 2 hours fitness training and play many matches per week against the other best players of the region. A practice book is an absolute must (Massias 2006). Two coaches control the clubs and the progress of the programme the year round. Around 12 years of age there is a difficult step in the development of the juniors. If they are good enough, measured by results, they have the chance to train at the 'Pôles France'. There are six of these in France. This costs the parents only 300 euros per month.

The DTN invests around 11 million Euros in around 200 coaches and administrators. The FFT is aware of the fact that without their Grand Slam tournament (Roland Garros) this concept would not be affordable. The FFT has not produced a Top 10 player in the past 10 years (2005). Some former French top players, like Guy Forget, suggest that the French system needs a Top 10 player in the near future; if none appears they will be facing problems in the recruitment of future athletes (Massias 2006). However, while this thesis was being written (from 2004-2008), France developed into one of the leading tennis nations in Europe in terms of its production of world class players.

Talent Identification and Development in Tennis in Germany

The support of the German Tennis Federation extends to many areas: mass participation, school tennis programmes, leisure sport, youth programmes, veterans' tennis, talent development programmes, coaches' training, and women in tennis. The development of junior world class players plays a key part in the policy of the German Tennis Federation (Deutscher Tennis Bund 2008). It is important for the German Tennis Federation to have a common policy with regard to the development of young tennis players. This development system is very progressive (adopting the 'pyramid' approach) with an early start (play and stay programme and mini-tennis programmes) and a high participation rate during the long-term development process towards world class standard. The

DTB summarises these long-term development goals according to five stages. These stages are recommendations of the DTB for coaches and clubs to set up a guideline for the development process of children.

Figure 6.3: Progressive development stages and cadre selection in German tennis (modified from Deutscher Tennis Bund 2008)

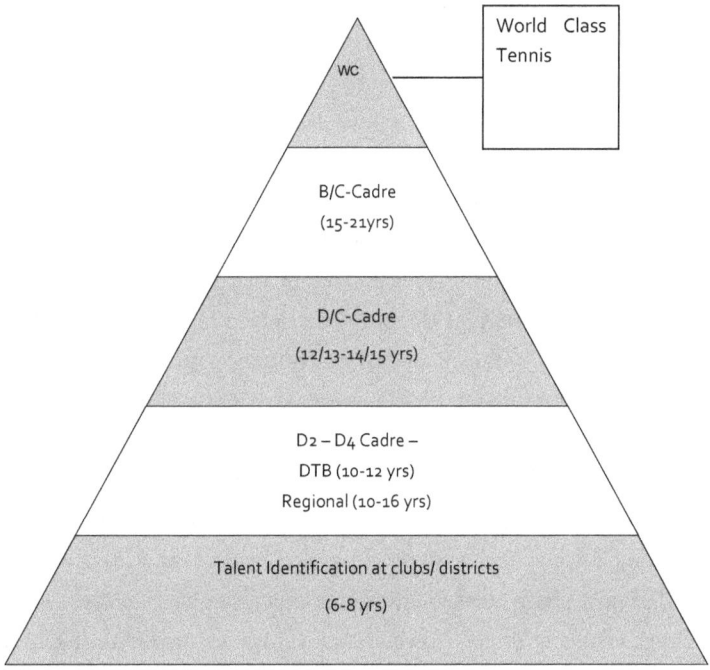

The DTB has divided up the different performance categories into so-called cadres (see Figure 6.3). The cadres run from A-cadre (high level, high performance stage) down to E-cadre (talented children, development stage). The A-, B- and C-cadres are organised and monitored nationally by the DTB and their coaches, whilst the E and D cadres are organised and led by the regional federations. To become a member of one of these cadres, an athlete has to fulfil several criteria. Here ranking lists and results at regional and national championships are important. In October 2005, for example, 137 elite players were selected for cadres A-D. In the E-cadres, approximately 1200 children were selected. (Deutscher Tennis Bund 2005).

According to a National Coach at U14 level, Hans–Peter Born, the reality of this talent selection and development is also at odds with the suggested policy (Born et al. 2002). To run the best possible development process, identification has to be completed at the clubs with children who are no older than 8 years. The next identification takes place at around 9 years, is completed at district level, and runs twice a year under the guidance of the 18 regional federations in Germany. These children have first to be nominated by a club. The regional identification process includes full court playing standard and is designed for children around 10 years. At national level, criteria for selection include tournament performance and performance diagnostics. The most talented are selected for the D/ C-cadre[7]. The national association supports regional associations with this developmental programme (Born et al. 2002)[8]. If selected for one of the cadres the children train with the national coach for a certain number of hours (4-8 hours) a week, including motor skills development. An under-8 player even takes part 7 hours a week; this increases to 12 to 13 hours a week for players aged 11 to 12 years. After they have followed the training programme for approximately one year, the regional coach will select the next step through the district and regional U10 championship. The amount of training might then increase to 12 hours a week. The next phase is the identification process at national level. With good tournament results at regional level the player will be invited to the U12/ U13 national championship. With good results, the talented child will be selected for the D/ C-cadre. If everything goes well, the above mentioned performance factors will be supported throughout the development process. Unfortunately, the DTB is now undergoing a phase of radical change. Through sport policy, a critical evaluation of the past decade in tennis and changes in competences at the executive board, as well as a decrease in registered members and in the

---

[7] D/C Cadre: Performance groups for different ages (12-15 years) and levels, here up to the regional level

[8] A/B/C Cadre: High Performance groups up to the international level

participation level nationwide, new concepts from certain universities (e.g. Cologne, Saarbrücken or Leipzig) with the main goal of taking tennis in Germany into the next decade have been introduced. There is an impression that all the organisations involved (DTB, RF[9], universities, experts) are not working homogeneously. This possibly explains the weak appearance of the DTB in questions of competitive sport and talent development.

The German Tennis Federation runs two official identification tests, one for the age group 6-11, which is called the general sports motor skill test (Allgemein Sportmotorischer Test, AST) and the Physical Fitness test (Konditionstest, KKT) for 11-18 year olds. This test was developed by the University of Heidelberg (GER) in cooperation with the German Tennis Federation between the years 1983 and 1986 on the basis of 1000 volunteers. The various tests in the KKT represent relevant physical characteristics in tennis (speed, strength and endurance). The AST (6-11 years old) is based on the testing of motor skills in tennis. The AST represents the factors agility, speed, hand-eye coordination and endurance. These two tests have been used by all regional federations up to now as a tool to identify important characteristics for tennis players. At the end of each test the coach can evaluate the results in a standardised table to derive recommendations for the players (Deutscher Tennis Bund 1987). For any talent identification in Germany, the programme 'Balltalente 2000' has been used to identify children at schools. This test contains 5 single tests and is used at primary schools for 7-8 old children. This test includes speed, agility, and strength (throwing), endurance and hand-eye coordination. The regional federation has also supported this test financially. All of these named tests are executed more or less within a time range of two or three hours. Other factors, such as day performance or environment, are taken into account for the children whether they fail or pass this kind of talent test, so it is questionable whether they are as successful as they should be. Practice has shown that the best results do not guarantee finding a talented tennis player. Each country included in this research thesis tested the necessary and requisite skills for a talented athlete.

---

[9] RF – Regional Federations

At first sight, the talent identification and development programme of the German Tennis Federation (DTB) appears to be educationally sound. Reflecting tennis-specific research, often commissioned by the DTB itself, sensible limits are placed on the balance between generic and specific development for young players. Most particularly, the level of competition is also limited, with a maximum of 30-50 matches up to the ages of 12 and 11 (male/female respectively).

Unfortunately this 'ethical and empirically based procedure' seems to disappear in practice. More and early tournament participation for children aged under 10 (e.g. Mini–Tennis, and Talent Team selection) and a tournament concentration of more than 70 singles/year as well as selection for squads, which includes financial benefits, reveal a contradiction between practice and policy. Indeed, it is questionable whether the system could ever be applied if top flight performance were a genuine aim. For example, 5 of the current top 10 under 18s (female) on the ITF World rankings are aged 15 (International Tennis Federation 2009). It would seem impossible to move players to aspire to the next level of performance if only generic motor skills development, as is mentioned by the DTB in its manuals, predominated up to the age of 10/11.

The strategy of recruiting talents through the standardised traditional competition system of the organisations and associations is common. The result orientation in the competition seems to be the main selection criterion. This form of talent recruitment has been described by Bernhard (1987) 'as the natural (primitive) selection system which is simple to understand for parents and players' and therefore this selection system seems to be effective and economical (Bernhard 1987). The high plausibility of this recruitment strategy is obvious. The problem is not so much the application of this result-orientated process as the monopolisation of this application. Every club, district and federation uses at least the results and rankings to select the athletes for their cadres and squads. This seems logical: how is a coach to justify the appointment of children ranked number 10 instead of the number 1 to regional training measurement? If played simply by results however, the development of the game can be impeded. A twelve-year old can become a regional champion without being able to play a volley. Creativity and variability are stunted for a player to achieve more results as a junior. A variable game, however, is demanded later. In other words, if a coach were to follow the letter of the talent identification policy law, s/he would end up with players who were not selected for the next levels of training (and crucially, funding) unless the young players were very special talents. Financial support can be crucial for these athletes too, because travel expenses and hospitality are very expensive and amount to figures of more than 6,000 Euro/ year[10], which are often not affordable for parents with an average income of 2,391 Euro a month (Central Intelligence Agency 2008c).

Talent Identification and Development in Tennis in the United Kingdom

Junior Talent Identification in the UK is done by tournaments and special County talent ID days, regional assessments and national performance 'road shows'. Tennis skills, co-ordination and athletic ability are important features. At this stage the talented players should play a minimum of three to four times a week (Lawn Tennis Association 2008a).

The LTA supports the development from talented youngsters to world class players by different measures. The LTA calls this the National Performance Programme, which has been seen as a strategy for identifying and developing tennis talent. To realise its vision, the LTA focuses on three pillars: the best coach, technical and sports science support and advice and competition. The LTA has decentralised its national training to work more at club level and in the High Performance Centres. There are currently 19 HPC's (2008). The players in the HPC's are between 10 and 16 years old. A performance pathway defines the milestones that line the route to world-class tennis. They have developed a talent identification system that should be easy to apply on a consistent national basis. Talent Scouts should be part of this national network system (Lawn Tennis Association 2008a).

---

[10] 7000 USD is the average investment for a 12-year-old athlete per year (ITF 2002)

Figure 6.4: Progressive development stages in the Lawn Tennis Association (modified from Lawn Tennis Association 2008b)

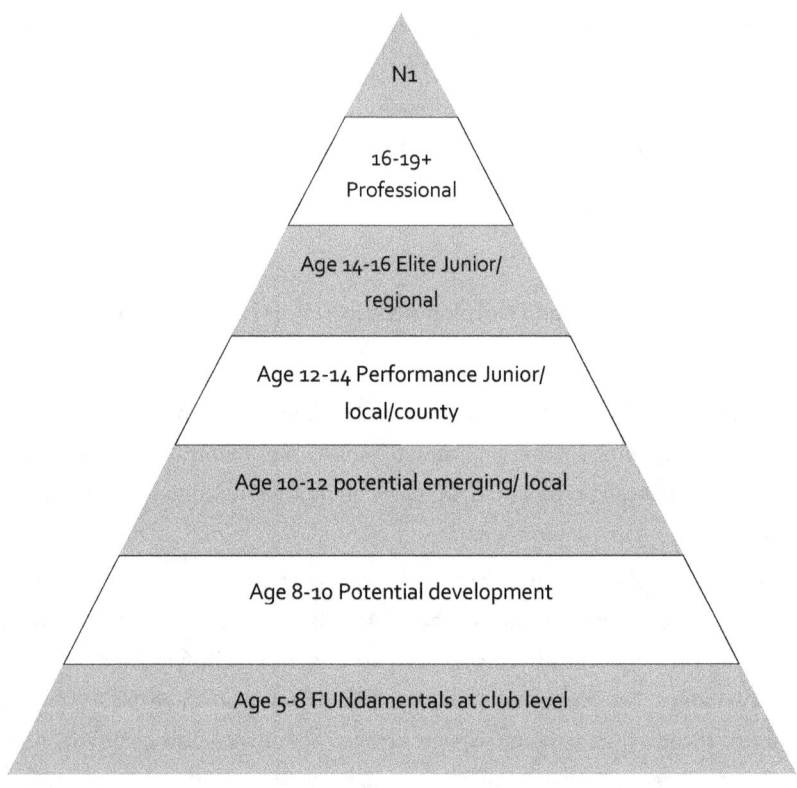

The LTA uses statistical data on the ranking history of ATP and WTA top 100 players to evaluate whether young players are on the right path to a professional career. For women a WTA ranking around 300, and an ATP men's ranking of around 100, are important milestones for development into professional players. The LTA has developed a system of categorising its players based on rankings and where they are in relation to national and international standards (Lawn Tennis Association 2008b).

The LTA provides and has implemented a National Tournament Structure. 800 club teams are registered. At junior level 25,000 children compete in the national junior league. At the top of the bottom level, the LTA supports 600 players between the ages of 9 and 22 with year-round support including access to the official winter training base in Spain (La Manga). In the UK a performance player can practise in one of the 19 High Performance Centres, which are strategically located.

The LTA shows commitment to creating the right environments and training structures to help Britain's most talented young players to reach their full potential and perhaps participation in Wimbledon. This programme is called - WINNING- and is based on 4 pillars: 'Learn Fundamentals' (Mini-Tennis) (5-8 years), then 'Potential Developing" (8-10 years), followed by 'Potential Emerging' (10-12 years), and 'Performance Junior' (11-14 years), and 'Elite Junior' (13-16years), and 'Apprentice Professional' (15-19 years), and finally 'Professional' (17+ years) on track to the Top 100 world class ranking (Lawn Tennis Association 2008b).

In the first stage (fundamental development) the children, aged between 5 and 11, aim to improve coordination in general, hit tennis balls, learn to score, and get into their first competition at Mini-Tennis level (see Figure 6.4). The basic shape of tennis strokes should be established by the age of 10 for boys and 9 for girls. In Scotland, for example, seven Mini Tennis Coaches have been appointed to deliver and promote programmes at club and county level, in addition to inter- and intraclub competitions.

In the next step, 'Learning to train' the LTA aims to develop the physical skills and begin to develop strength, stamina, speed, and stability from the age of 9 or 10. Furthermore, all the basic strokes should be consistent and will naturally be made with increased racket head speed. The recommended time for physical activity (including 5 hours of tennis) in a training week should be 12 hours at the age of 11. Until the age of 12 the focus is on putting the basic tennis skills in place and 'learning how to compete'. From the age of 12, young players should work on their shot selection and tactics. The LTA states that young players should keep working on flexibility, speed, and strength and core stability at this stage, with coordination well established, but endurance becomes most important as the 'future champions' begin to play longer and more intense matches. Technically, players should be well established by this age, but will now start to increase the range and power of shots, adding spin, and angles, mixed with rallies. The players need to become more aggressive in their game. Match strategy and tactics on different surfaces becomes increasingly important as talented players meet opponents who have trained in different climates and on different surfaces.

By the age of 19, players will need to be fully self-sufficient and ready for touring, so academy players should begin to plan for themselves. This includes goal setting, being self-disciplined on and off the court, from tennis specific training to eating the right food. In general, players should now take responsibility and pride in their performance and act like professionals. Players will now need to play about 70 individual matches each year, an increase from 40. These will range from representing local clubs to national competition, and mean a balance between confidence building and extending the comfort zone to challenge the player. To maximise the benefits of training, this should be done in 3 blocks, broken up between 3 blocks of competition. Each week of the training block will include 14 hours, with 12 hours of tennis.

There are now Under 10 (Ariel Mini Tennis) and Under 12 events for both boys' and girls' age groups, and players compete over a series of one-day local, county and regional tournaments to produce 36 finalists UK wide (in the Robinsons Ace competition). In previous years the winners were invited to the 'Wimbledon Experience' to meet and play with Tim Henman and have a guided tour of the All England Club.

'The Road to Wimbledon' is a new Under 14 singles competition for both boys and girls. Winners of club level singles progress to a County final, normally staged in June-July. County winners then progress to a National final, to be held on the grass courts at Wimbledon around August. For players aged 16 or 17 the priority is winning; the main focus in this development stage is 'train to win'.

Physical thresholds are pushed in training in preparation for tough 5-set matches (in the case of boys). Training from 16 or 17 should begin to prepare a player for performing technically, tactically and physically throughout a tough match. Training should allow for early and late maturing players, but to start with the LTA look at an average 17-year-old. Tactical and technical skills should be developed in the game situation. A maximum of 90 individual matches, divided into 3 blocks, should be played per year. Players must want to play and to win. The LTA supports the children aged around 8 with 5.5 hours per week of training, which increases to 22 hours a week for a 14 & under player. Besides this, the amount of international tournaments to participate in per year, increases from 10 (age 12) to 20 (age 14). The Talent Identification process in the UK thus takes several forms. With the LTA, this TI starts at six years of age. It is interesting that 40% of the identified children are identified or supported by their parents or relatives, in clubs or by coaches. The schools are not involved. 30% of talented children are identified at tournaments (de Bosscher et al. 2003).

The LTA has decentralised its national training, wishing to give clubs more responsibility and support. This seems to be the reason for the LTA creating High Performance Centres (HPCs) and linked Satellites (county accredited) clubs. The players are based there. Long travelling times to training sessions must be avoided; talented players should have no more than a 30 minute drive to or from a performance environment. In practice, however, there are often car journeys of more than an hour from home to the training environment. In summary, talent camps have to be organised for players from 8 to 14 years. Satellite clubs are to act as feeders for talented children to the HPC, particularly for 10 and under and the HPC's for young players aged 10-16. Finally, there are the National Tennis Centres (NTC), which the LTA calls its 'hub for British Tennis." In short, in the UK, funding guidance or any selection criteria are mainly based on rankings and results. The LTA gives guidelines as to what to do at the different age stages, but which players are finally identified through which kind of process seems to be unclear. The responsibility for the real search for talent lies with the LTA. It seems to be complicated for the LTA, as the national association, to support and implement a national talent identification programme for Scotland, Wales and

Northern Ireland. The basic ideas in theory of decentralisation and the development of HPC'S are very progressive. In general, the LTA has set up a reasonable programme which covers players' development, infrastructure development and coaches' training. This gives an athlete the opportunity to develop his/her skills in a long development process. The 4 main pillars from Mini-Tennis to High Performance standard and their explanations give a clear indication of what to do on court. There are also some tournament series which give the children the opportunity to compete and qualify for the next levels.

6.4 Conclusion

After the evaluation of secondary data about institutional/ organisational factors in the national tennis system, and additionally some informal interviews with experts, several tendencies have been identified in the structure of the four European tennis federations. Tennis in the Czech Republic (CR) is characterised by a mixture of centralisation/ decentralisation and a strong tournament and ranking system. The Czech Tennis Association (CTS) is responsible for the national teams, where gifted players are supported. Furthermore, the amount of international tournaments from Under 12 to Satellite and Futures for professionals is similar or higher. A clear structure of long-term development and programmes is still under construction.

Tennis in France is characterised by two essential features. On the one hand, a comprehensive connection to state politics is distinctive and on the other hand, the tendency toward centralisation that is perhaps a characteristic feature of French society in general. The state intrudes in sport not only by regulating it; it also sees itself as having the duty to support sports activities wherever possible. This explains the centralising orientation of the French Tennis Federation. The FFT receives a large amount of financial support from the 'Ministère de la jeunesse et des sports' (MJS). In addition, the MJS provides the tennis associations with a large number of its own employees, who take over special areas in their high-level and competitive programmes. One expression of the strong state influence is that the training of coaches is organised by the MJS and not by the FFT itself, and furthermore there is special training for the area of public sports administration which is also located within the responsibility of the MJS (professeur de sports). Besides the MJS, the Ministry of Education contributes considerably to the success of competitive sport in France. This supports the top athletes in their education at school. They can get their education at school or even directly at their training place. In contrast to the FFT, the German Tennis Federation (DTB) is more federally constructed. The regional federations and even the district federations are very powerful in their long-term decisions (Interview with 'Darren' 2006). The selection of talented children for cadres (A-E) at regional and national level is mainly controlled by the Regional Federations (RF). This leads to some communication problems and a lack of competences, which influences the execution of programmes. One of the latest pieces of research is critical of the existing system (Conzelmann 2004). The outcomes of the existing system certainly do not correlate well with the number of players and the amount of money which has been invested in elite tennis. Tennis in the UK is also characterised by a mixture of centralisation and decentralisation. The Lawn Tennis Association's annual budget ranks second after France. Its selection criteria and funding for talent development are based on rankings and results at tournaments. Yet similar to France, until the end of 2008, the UK had also failed to produce one top three player or a large number in the top hundred.

The message of this chapter has been that in all four countries the framing conditions in their development system for talented players are more or less similar, but differences in the productivity of world class players are obvious. Money for development does not seem to be the only decisive factor; coach training is also similar in each of the countries selected. The infrastructure for tennis is definitely better developed in Germany, the UK and France than in the Czech Republic, but the CR is more productive of top 100 players. Are there some other social factors that can explain this? Are the motivations and interests of players in performance tennis higher in the CR or France than in the UK and Germany? To answer these questions, I will look in the next chapter at the findings from my interviews with the key agents involved: players, parents, coaches and administrators.

Chapter 7 Comparing Views of TID in European Tennis

Introduction

In this chapter I will report on and describe the results obtained from primary research into the TID systems in the four countries and interviews with administrators, parents, coaches and tennis players in two of them. The previous chapter has outlined the importance of a TID programme for a tennis federation. However, to include such a programme in a national federation's written policy is the easier part, while to set up this programme in practice is more difficult. It is obvious that often the key stake holders of talented children like parents, coaches and also administrators are very uncertain about how best to organise a long-term development plan for their young athletes.

This chapter will show what has happened in the selected national tennis federations and describe their experience in the long-term talent development process of athletes. Focussing especially on two contrasting nations (the Czech Republic and Germany), I carried out interviews with emerging elite players, parents, coaches and development administrators. i collected information about what they do, why they do it, and what they think would be best regarding Talent Identification and Development (TID) programmes in tennis. This data enables me to investigate in more detail the contradiction between theory and practice in the field of TID in tennis identified in the previous chapter. The primary data is complemented by secondary information – from the print media, magazines, journals and websites – and information about practices in the other countries, France and the UK. I begin the chapter by briefly commenting on key factors influencing sport and talent identification and development in the selected countries.

7.1 Talent Identification in its socio-economic context

In the context of Talent Identification and Development, the society has to be named as an important resource for any talent identification and development system. For the countries examined it can be stated that they all are politically stable. A centralist orientation of the political organs of a country and the possibilities of clear hierarchies, central control, specific task assignments and strategic planning can have a positive effect on sports. For France, it has to be assumed that its centralist political structure makes an important advantage possible in the purposeful and systematic search for talent and support.

This can only succeed if the organisational structures of the federation also have a centralist construction. The problem of the centralist orientation is, however, the concentration on well-developed infrastructural regions, while the less well-developed will be neglected. A better distribution of any measures is carried out to all regions in a federalist system, since the regional administrations are responsible there. This can be judged positively for Germany and the United Kingdom. Furthermore, the individual regions can develop individual interests and distinguish themselves by their successes. On the other hand, a federal structure can also be negative; as such a state construction can cause greater difficulties in developing uniform programmes beyond regional borders.

The economy also has to be recognised as an important resource for talent support. The income of the private households decides mostly whether money can be 'invested' in the children and in sports talent. A majority live in relative prosperity, particularly in the 'established' industrial countries, like France, Germany and the United Kingdom. But unemployment and economic crises lead to fewer and fewer people being able to invest in sports.

For the parent organisations of the sport, the National Olympic Committees (NOC) shares their responsibility for sports with state organisations. All the NOCs in the countries examined have honorary executive committees. The tennis associations have only one leadership organ, but they are subdivided into different committees, which can take independent decisions. If we look at the number of employees, we find that there are only approximately 15 full-time positions in the Czech tennis federation, and 30 in Germany, while there are more than 200 in France (Deutscher Tennis Bund 2009, Massias 2006).

To safeguard the continuance of tennis, it is necessary to recruit young people for the sport who are ready to make a long-term career as top athletes. If one wants to belong to a leading tennis nation, then early identification and good talent development are absolutely necessary. On the one hand, it is important to discover as many talents as possible; on the other hand, it is necessary to optimise this search for talents by selection procedures.

For the countries examined, various characteristics of their search for talents can be recognised. In the Czech Republic, it is the state that is responsible for the search for talents, cooperating with the tennis federations. The Czech Ministry of Culture and Sports is responsible (Czech Tennis Association 2008). In France, Germany and the United Kingdom, the tennis federations are exclusively responsible for the search for talent (Lawn Tennis Association 2006, Fédération Française de Tennis 2008c, Deutscher Tennis Bund 2009b).

Differences also exist as to the question which staffs are responsible for the search for talents. In the United Kingdom, the sports instructors try to take over this task directly. Thus sports teachers can have two days per week off working as school sport coordinators to build up a network of municipalities, schools, sports clubs and sports associations for their talent search. This programme is financed by the lottery funds of the Sports Council (Gratton & Taylor 2000; United Kingdom Sport 2008a). Of course, the coaches are another group of talent seekers. In France, the UK and Germany, these are the club coaches, in the Czech Republic the coaches of the sports schools. In France, the experts of the DTN have to be mentioned as exemplary.

Table 7.1: Organisation of Talent Detection in the different countries, and people Involved

	Organisation	Personnel/ "Talent searcher"
FRA	Fédération de tennis (FFT)	Experts of the DTN, Sports teacher, Coach
GER	Deutscher Tennis Bund (DTB)	(Club-) Coach, Sports teacher
CR	Czech Tennis (CTS)	Experienced coach of Academy, Sports Scientist
UK	Lawn Tennis Association (LTA)	Regional performance manager supported by coach and teacher

Source: modified after Digel et al. 2006

In the Czech Republic, a targeted search for talents in tennis is carried out in sports schools or clubs. As a rule, systematic tests are used to recognize talented children early. Besides training observations by experienced coaches, motor, anthropometric and physiological methods of testing are used. At higher performance stages, competition performance, control tests and psychological tests are applied as criteria for selection (Zháněl 2004). A specific search for and choice of children with the aim of winning these for the competitive sport are carried out in the CR.

The search for talents is less systematically carried out in France than in the CR. Although the sports instructors are responsible for the search for talents, there is no systematic search for talents there. Only when the children are already in a club and have drawn attention to them by competition results do the experts of the DTN intervene. The children and teenagers identified by these experts due to their competition performance are sent to the regional sports centres, the 'pôles espoir', where they are supported comprehensively.

Similar observations can be made in Germany about the search for talents, which can only to a limited extent be described as a systematic search. Sports lessons are not effective places for the search for talents. In the former German Democratic Republic (GDR), the search for talents had fundamental significance for the outstanding successes of the system. After the unification of the Federal Republic of Germany (FRG) and the GDR in 1990, however, it was not achieved to transfer this system to the new system of the Federal Republic. Furthermore, the search for talents seems rather to be left to chance. There are some efforts ('Jugend trainiert für Olympia, Sichtungsmassnahmen der Vereine'), but one cannot speak of a systematic search.

In the UK, since the end of the 1990s there have been attempts to improve the unsystematic search for talents by sport instructors and coaches by means of various programmes (world class start, world class performance). The Active programmes of Sport England are different programmes which do not only increase the leisure sport programme, but discover talents additionally through the three areas of Active Communities, Active Sports and Active Schools by the

World Class Start Programme, and promote them through the World Class Potential Programme. The schools also play an important part with their teaching and out-of-school sports programmes in the search for talents, in which the sports instructor takes on the role of the talent searcher. However, talent search and talent development in the UK is still the responsibility of the federations.

Another distinction arises, depending on the target group, as to whether the talent is sought in schools or in the clubs. The question as to the geographical location is of importance here, too in the search for talents. Furthermore, it is important whether the search for talents is carried out in terms of the specific sport (tennis) or generally.

First it has to be said that in countries like France, the UK and Germany, in which sports clubs exist as a basic sports structure, talents are sought in these clubs. A search for talents is also carried out in the schools, but this search is unsystematic, as I have mentioned already. In principle, the search for talents in the Czech Republic is carried out generally (not sport-specifically), with the focus clearly on the popular Olympic sports.

There is cooperation in France between the tennis association and the schools. The task of sending talented children to the clubs is that of the sports instructors. In principle, the rule of the tennis association is that the young talents first do their training in the clubs and then draw attention to themselves by competition results. Talent searchers of the tennis association attend competitions at schools in the UK. In addition, the association carries out Talent Identification Days, which take place near High Performance Centres.

In Germany the competition 'young people are practising for Olympic Games' (translated: Jugend trainiert für Olympia) is used for the search for talents. Only players who are already playing tennis take part in the tennis competitions. Due to a centrally controlled system and a search for general sports talents, the tennis associations depend on their own actions. As a rule, cooperation is dependent on the experience of the coach, whether he initiates an action, or how far he can and would like to recognize the talent and promote it. In France, Germany and the UK, there is a tennis- specific search.

In the CR, an outstanding part is played by specific sports schools; there the children are observed during training and repeatedly tested (Czech Tennis Association 2005).

Geography also plays a central part in the search for talents in the different countries. In Germany, the regional federations ('Landesverbände') are responsible for the search for talents. There is a similar situation in the CR. Nationwide activities are carried out in France, while in the UK the talent search is concentrated on regions where the infrastructure is available for development (High Performance Centres).

Table 7.2: Target groups for talent search in tennis

Search area	CR	FRA	GER	UK
Sports Club	no	yes	yes	yes
School	yes	sometimes	sometimes	sometimes
Other	sports school	-	-	youth club
Geographical	national	national	regional	regional

Source: Digel et al. 2006.

7.2 The Financing of Talent Development

Of course it is as important to support talents as to search for talents. This is mainly the case in the training-specific and financial areas. In principle, a general sports structure and a specific sport cadre structure can be found in the countries examined. In June 2001, about 6,000 French athletes were registered on the national 'liste des athlètes de haut niveau' (Digel 2003a). Also in Germany, the athletes are divided up nationally uniformly into A, B, C, D/C and S cadres. A-cadre athletes are usually international top-class sportsmen. In the competition year, approximately 120 athletes were registered in the cadres of the DTB. Less distinction is made in the CR. A national team exists for each of the different age groups. French athletes of the 'liste haut niveau' get personal support (aides personnalisés) if they apply to the responsible DTN. In the UK athletes can get financial support from UK Sports (Gratton & Taylor 2000). Participation in world class performance programmes is a prerequisite here, though. In Germany, there is the 'Deutsche Sporthilfe', a central organ for financing athletes (Deutsche Sporthilfe 2008). Sponsoring starts on the application of the federation from membership in the C-cadres for 1800 athletes (Deutsche Sporthilfe 2008a). In the CR, athletes can receive financial support from the regional sports administrations. The tennis associations support their athletes separately by fee-reduced training or a financial contribution for travelling to competitions. The following table gives a survey of institutions which grant financial support.

Table 7.3: Financial support

	Institution	Average amount in € per year/ athlete	Criteria		Notes
			Min.	Amount	
France	Ministre de la Jeunesse, des Sports et de vie Associative (Aides personnalisés)	3,200 (Olympic sport) 1,350 (non-Olympic sport)	Liste des sportifs de haut niveau	Performance level of specific sport	
Germany	Deutsche Sporthilfe	Not known		C-Cadre	Performance level, social importance	No single calculation possible
CR	Regional sports community	Not known	Not known	Not known	No published criteria
UK	UK sport (athlete personal awards)	17,000		Category C	Performance level, other income	Only for sports of the WCP Programme

Source: Digel et al. 2006, 312.

Each country examined has specific training centres. In the CR, the talents do their training in academies and private sports schools. The training of the French top players in tennis takes place almost exclusively in the 'pôles'. In 2004, 132 'poles' were established. So the DTN of the association has a network of "pôles" (filières du sport de haut niveau). The network of the 'pôles' is financed by the MJS. In Paris, the INSEP plays a central role in talent development. 35 different sports are integrated there (including tennis). 550 qualified employees, paid by the state, work at INSEP.

In Germany, the concept of the National Centres ('Bundesstützpunkte') as a basis for the 'Bundesleistungszentren' has a long tradition. These training bases of the leading federations, to which the tennis federation also belongs, are staffed by coaches and can be used by cadre athletes. The 20 Olympic Centres 'Olympiastützpunkte' established since 1985 in Germany form the highest structure element in Germany. They are not used by the tennis federations, however. They have their own decentralised bases (Deutscher Olympischer Sport Bund 2008d). There is a similarly decentralised network of training centres (high performance centres) in the United Kingdom. The next table gives a summary of the national training facilities of the selected countries from a comparative perspective.

Table 7.4: National Centres

	Centres	Stay and support
FRA	"Pôles" France	Permanent
GER	National performance Centre National training centre Olympic training centre	Not permanent Not permanent Sometimes permanent
CR	Sports schools Olympic training centres	Permanent Permanent before competition
UK	Network UK Sports Institute	Not permanent

Source: own findings

7.3 Tennis and TID in the Czech Republic, Germany, France and the UK

The following section outlines tennis and TID in the four European countries, drawing on both archive material derived from documents and interviews.

7.3.1 Tennis and TID in the Czech Republic

In the Czech Republic (CR), with nearly 1,000 tennis clubs (in contrast to Germany with its 10,000), tennis is a very traditional and competition-oriented sport. The CR consists of 8 regions, in which 969 tennis clubs with 5,040 courts are registered. Each of these regions manages its affiliated tennis clubs. They represent 20,208 registered players.

The system of Talent Identification and Development (TID) in the CR can be described as both centrally organised and decentralised. One of its main pillars is the ranking list of 7,584 registered tournament players. This represents a third of the total of 20,208 registered players. Every player down to the U12 age group is registered in this list after an official game, no matter whether he/she has won or lost. The Czech Tennis Federation is affiliated to the Czech Sports Association (CSA). In their programmes, it favours a well-organised ranking and tournament system for its athletes. One of the main criteria is the cadre structure. During communist rule, the cadre structures were more or less a classification system which controlled the performance progress and selection of talented athletes for specific support measures, from a broad base to a small top (pyramidal system). An athlete starts at the bottom and with good development he will go through all the levels in this system until he has approached the top of the pyramid. Each stage of the performance pyramid contains different systematic training and competition, for a period of 8 to 10 years. The start of tennis practice lies at around 7 years of age, and specialisation starts after 3 years' development of fundamental skills.

In the CR, the parents are those mainly interested in the development of their children in the sport of tennis. If they start to play tennis at around 5, there is always the hope of achieving a good international playing standard. Interviews with parents of talented players have shown that their main goal in the CR is to achieve national level as tennis players.

For Talent Identification (TI) the regional and national federation offers simple physical tests for different age groups, in which values like the Body Mass Index (BMI) influence the evaluation. To pursue a fundamental development of talented players, as recommended by the International Tennis Federation (ITF) in its publications (International Tennis Federation 1998), seems almost impossible in the Czech Republic's Tennis Federation, as long as the results achieved are the most important selection criteria. The competition standard is very high even for young ages, and parents, as the first mentors of their children, are highly focused on improving the level of play in competition. They do not appear concerned about creating a dynamic development process more focused on the individual development of the players in the different stages of the long-term development process.

To play tennis in the CR is always seen as a potential means to achieve professional status. Recreational tennis, as played in the UK or in Germany, is not very popular. This can be seen in the virtually non-existent recreational participation in tennis. In CR there exists a high degree of competition experience, even for the Under 12's. To build up a competitive league system and a ranking system is the main aim for the Czech Tennis Federation, in order to develop future champions. The only criterion they use in the development and identification process is ranking. If a player, no matter whether from U12 or U18, does not achieve a Top 6 position in tennis in the country's rankings, she/ he will lose financial support. However, tennis in the CR is still regarded as a means to get international acknowledgement, and this is the main motivation for many young players to train hard.

Recently, through the implementation of several commissions, the Czech Tennis Federation has tried to professionalize its administrative work. A commission for talent search has tried to develop the Mini-Tennis Project (for Under 10's) mainly at school level, to get more children into the sport. In the future the Czech Republic will run more programmes for mass participation, to increase participation at grass roots level. Through the positive advantage of the centralised system, it should not be difficult to implement and improve programmes for the development of talented young children. Again, motivation to travel and to earn money still seems one of the most important factors influencing those who seek a tennis career. Clubs are interested in good players' development because through them they can enhance their reputation, gain public acknowledgement and sponsorship. The most talented players have always achieved the most support from their clubs. The fact that the coaches have been paid by the club supports this procedure. However, these days the practice is changing. Following economic changes in the CR, the clubs are also struggling financially and are looking for financially independent parents who can pay for their children's lessons. The talented that may come from poorer financial backgrounds will be left behind.

7.3.2 Tennis and TID in Germany

The German Tennis Federation (DTB) has the most registered members worldwide in its 18 regional federations, with 1,710,145 members. In Germany, there are 10,024 registered tennis clubs with 49,109 tennis courts available. There are 18 regional performance centres, three semi-national centres and one national centre. In these centres, there are around 120 players, divided into cadres from A to D. In the A-cadre are the professionals (approx. 15), in the B-cadre the semi-professionals (approx. 50), and in the C/ D Cadre the 13-/14-year-old players (approx. 1,200).

The central goal of the talent development programmes of the DTB is to guide the talented juniors and seniors to international level tennis. The goal of the DTB is to establish a programme which starts at club level and ends in the D/C cadre for talented juniors (Born et al. 2002). Germany identifies its talents mostly in clubs; the clubs are responsible for getting children on to the court. Parents are primarily interested in supporting their children in an attractive sport. The main characteristics of their children in playing tennis are motivation, interest and performance. Most of the children have been identified by coaches as talented, but it is the parents who have had the main influence on the children to start playing tennis. The main goal for the parents is that their children achieve at least national level in tennis.

Interestingly, around 70% of the children have not been placed in a development group for talented children. During external coaching, the parents mentioned interest in the sport and hard and good training as very important for their children. Together with parents, coaches play the most important part in the development process of the children, whilst the national or regional federation seems not to play a key part. However, the parents recognise a development programme organised by the national or regional federations. Regarding financial or equipment support, 60% of the talented children have not received any support (Markus). Asked about the involvement in other sports, as many as 60% of the parents mentioned that their children have not participated in other sports which do not conform with the programmes of the national federations, which support fundamental development at an early age (Thomas)[11].

Asked about rankings, as many as 60% of under 12's have had top regional rankings better than position 30 (Gpa-1). Annual planning seems to be very important for the parents, but has not been very professional to date. The reason for this could be lack of knowledge or interest on the part of coaches or administrators.

In short, parents are not well informed about tennis in general. Fundamental training and developing a broad base at an early age (U10) is not done in practice. Ranking is very important and parents tend to see only the short-term success of their children as measured in results and rankings. In addition, the national or regional federations do not play any key part in the development of their children – or the parents think they do not. There are many negative judgements of the system of support and most of the parents complain that this support could be done much better.

---

[11] Information in this and the following paragraph were derived from interviews with parents of German tennis players.

One of my main findings has been that there is a big contradiction between what is prescribed and what is actually done in practice in the Talent Identification process. Tennis is still an expensive sport, so each Talent Identification programme is as good as the social standard of the parents. In other words, 61% of tennis players are from the middle class. So before any TID programme takes place in practice, a coach or an institution should first confirm the financial status of the family. This seems ridiculous, but TID takes a long time, and support is just available for those who have achieved good results in the past. To get these results, much money has to be invested in the development of the children, and this will be a challenge for parents from a poor background. In short, the social background seems to be an underestimated but really decisive factor in Talent Identification.

Because of the tremendous financial investment required, the top level of world-class players remains very selective, and many talents without money are lost to the sport. However, at first sight, the German Tennis policy for TID appears to be educationally sound. Unfortunately, this 'ethical and empirically based procedure' seems to disappear in practice. More and early tournament participation for children aged Under 10 (Mini–Tennis, Talent Team selection) and a tournament concentration of more than 70 singles/year (i.e Yannik Offermanns an U12 German Top Player) as well as selection for squads which includes financial benefits reveal a contradiction between practice and policy. Indeed, it is questionable whether the system could ever be applied if top flight performance was a genuine aim. It would seem impossible to move players to aspire to the next level of performance if only generic motor skills development, as is mentioned by the DTB in their manuals, predominated up to the age of 10/11.

The strategy of recruiting talents through the standardised traditional competition system of the organisations and associations is common. Orientation by results in the competition seems to be the main selection criterion. This form of talent recruitment has been described by Bernhard (1987) as 'the natural (primitive) selection system which still is practised for lack of theory escorted action concepts because it seems to reflect' the discipline-specific feature complexity most validly and therefore to be effective and economical (Bernhard 1987). The high plausibility of this recruitment strategy is obvious. The problem is not so much the application of this result-orientated process as the monopolisation of this application. Every club, district and federation finally uses results and rankings to select the athletes for their cadres and squads. This seems logical: how is a coach to justify the assignment of a child ranked number 10 rather than number 1 to a regional training measure? If played simply by results, the development of the game may be impeded. A twelve-year old can become a regional champion without being able to play a volley. Creativity and variability are stunted in order to achieve more results as a junior. A variable game, however, is demanded later. Financial support is crucial for these athletes, too, because travel expenses and accommodation are very expensive and amount to more than 6000 Euro/year[12], which is often not affordable for parents with an average income of 2,391 euros per month (Statistisches Bundesamt Deutschland 2009, Central Intelligence Agency 2008c).

The selection and progress of a talented player are dominated by tournament success. This was confirmed by the opinions of the experts who were interviewed for this research. In other words, if a coach were to follow the letter of the policy law for the TID programme, s/he would end up with players who were not selected for the next level of training (and, crucially, funding) unless the young players were very special talents.

The productivity of the German system is not very high, however; if we compare the number of German tennis players and the top ranked players in the world rankings, we have to conclude that something goes wrong in the planning and development process. Here it seems that the decentralised structures of the Federation are a disadvantage.

German tennis policy, with its philosophy of TD (Talent Development), appears to be educationally sound. The level of competition is limited to young ages (the under 12s). This theoretical procedure, however, seems to disappear in practice.

---

[12] 7000 USD is the average investment for a 12-year-old athlete per year (ITF 2002).

Early tournament participation for children aged under 10 and tournament concentration of more than 70 singles matches a year reveals the contradiction between the policy and the practice of the German talent development programme. A strategy of identifying the talented players mainly through results is most common. Most coaches do not look for potential regarding tennis-specific skills; instead they look for results, because every institution in tennis from club level to the federation uses results and rankings as the main criteria for the selection of children for squads and supporting them with money and other resources.

7.3.3 Tennis and TID in France

The FFT (French Tennis Federation) has around 300,000 registered members, organised in 8,404 clubs. Its members have 33,074 outdoor and 2,600 indoor courts to play on. The members are supported by approximately 3,700 coaches and more then 10,000 instructors. Around 1,500 clubs are structured for performance practice. At 8 National Centres, the elite players are supported. Tennis is ranked as the no. 1 women's and individual sport in general. Furthermore, the FFT has 2.0 million registered matches, 10,872 tournaments, and 391,000 competitors, and in the popularity scales French tennis ranks first as an individual sport (Fédération Française de Tennis 2008).

In France, the responsibility for the search for and selection of talented children is with the clubs. They get support from sport teachers in schools, who will send possibly talented children directly to clubs. Through agreements with school sport associations (UNSS and UGSEL), the schools have to cooperate with the clubs. However, at least the clubs are still responsible for the talent search. They go to competitions and try to detect talent on court. Additionally, the Direction Technique Nationale of the specific sport association sends out a person in charge of talent identification. More specific programmes for talent identification do not exist (Digel 2003). But if talented young children are integrated into the clubs and performing well, the 'cadres techniques' take care of the talents. The development of these talents starts mainly at the regional centres ('Pôles espoir') (Teuber 1990; Fédération Française de Tennis (2008c). These central sports centres show the typically French centralistic orientation to talent development, and underpin the centralistic structures.

The 36 'Ligues' at basic level are organised centrally from Paris. Even at club level, the French Tennis Federation (FFT) financially supports 3,000 children between the ages of 7 and 10 years with additional training sessions. 160 of them are selected for league level for further training measures. Two National Coaches support the selected clubs. Jean Claude Massias (Director of the Direction Technique Nationale, DTN) sets out the annual plan and it is necessary to follow that. Around 12 years of age tennis players will be concentrated in their 'pôles'. The criteria have to be very strict, but if a player has to leave the 'pôles' he will always have the chance to come back. The FFT has built up an infrastructure with regional and national centres and their coaches. However, the differences are the centralisation of their organisation and the controlling of the measures in the TID process.

7.3.4 Tennis and TID in the UK

In the Lawn Tennis Association and its four regional departments, there are 48,533 licensed and 4.3 million non-registered tennis players. They play on 35,200 courts in 2,600 clubs (Lawn Tennis Association 2006); the best players are supported at three national centres, ten International High Performance Clubs and 40 to 50 High Performance Clubs (Lawn Tennis Association 2006). All players are supported by approx. 5,550 coaches. The activities of the regional federation are coordinated by the LTA. The LTA is the governing body of tennis in the throughout the United Kingdom, but these regions are looking for more independence in their decision- makings.

The UK, with GBP 45 million, is behind France (100 million Euro) in terms of the total budget for tennis, and invests 17% of this in elite performance, with aspects like court and facility hire, training camps for elite players (GBP 3.5m), funding, coaching and support for elite players (GBP 4.6m) and sports science (GBP 1.4m). The Talent Identification process occurs in several forms. In the LTA this

TI starts at six years of age. It is interesting that 40% of the children are identified by their parents or relatives, in clubs or by coaches. 30% of talented children are identified at tournaments (De Bosscher et al. 2003). The schools are not involved.

The LTA has decentralised its national training, wishing to give clubs more responsibility and support. This seems to be the reason for the LTA's creating High Performance Centres (HPCs) and linked Satellites (county accredited) clubs, where the players are based. Long travelling times to training sessions should be avoided; talented players should have no more than a 30-minute drive from a performance environment. In summary, talent camps are organised for players from 8 to 14, Satellite clubs should act as a feeder for talented children to the HPC, particularly for 10 and under, and the HPC's for young players aged 10-16. Finally, there are the National Tennis Centres (NTC), which the LTA calls its '...a focal point for Britain's top players...' (Lawn Tennis Association 2008c).

7.3.5 Summary

To summarise, I have found that centralisation of the organisational structures in a tennis federation appears to be an advantage and can have positive effects for TID. In France the federation is organised centrally, in contrast to Germany or the UK; in the CR it is a mixture. The infrastructure of tennis is well-developed in all selected countries. A cadre structure for different levels in all countries is evident and is similar to TD models, as I have shown in chapter 4. There are differences in the social contexts in the selected countries. It appears that only people from a certain social environment can participate in tennis and thus automatically in talent identification and development programmes, with the consequence that perhaps the real 'talent' is never identified. Interestingly, a good programme, enough money or the best infrastructure cannot close the gap between the theory of TID programmes and the practice.

In the next section I hear the different views of key agents (players, coaches, parents and administrators) regarding talent identification and the development of talented children and the programmes which are implemented in the selected tennis federations. These views, which have emerged from interviews and questionnaires (see chapter 5), will provide a better understanding of TID from a practical point of view, and I hope to identify and confirm my findings from secondary data and literature from the last sections. Players play the central part in talent development, and the TD programmes are centred on the different development stages of the players. Coaches are the key to understanding that TD is a dynamic process and how to implement programmes in the players' annual schedule. Parents are the main supporters for a number of years, and administrators implement the programmes in the policies of any tennis federation.

7.4 Views of Players, Coaches, Parents and Administrators

The following section derives from interviews conducted in Germany and the Czech Republic in 2006 and 2007. The interviews were conducted in both German and English and were translated by me after the interview. The data in this section supplements the information reported in the previous chapter. The interviews therefore support the purpose of confirming the objective data collected through documentary analysis.

7.4.1 Views of Players in Tennis in Germany and the Czech Republic

As there is a federal structure in Germany, it is very difficult to centralise tennis. The 18 independent regional federations develop their own programmes. Players from the different federations cannot train together in a national centre. Talents between the ages of 9 and 18 can compete nationally but train only regionally. As early specialisation is a must, at mini-tennis level forms of competition exist for seven-year-old children regionally.

In the Czech Republic, the national federation has started to introduce many programmes. At the present moment it is obvious that high performance sport is in need of development. The practical implication of the system in the CR is that more programmes have been introduced in the clubs. Through the political changes in the 1990s, the living standard has risen and yet the number of people who play tennis is decreasing. Having more money, players believe in more individual coaching. In earlier times, many players worked with one coach, so they had the opportunity to train under very competitive structures.

Following semi-structured interviews with German and Czech coaches, players, parents and administrators, we present the findings as to what they think about their national Talent Identification and Development programmes in the next section[13]. In Germany, the players interviewed had not noticed any Talent Development programme for themselves during their 'middle years' (Monsaas 1985, 235). It became obvious that the German Tennis Federation had not effectively transmitted information about its role in the Talent Development Programme to the players. Most of the players interviewed (8 out 11) started tennis through the involvement of their parents between the ages of three (5/ 11) and five (3/ 11). The personal goal of the players was to achieve international level playing standard (7/ 11) with an approximate ranking of better than 100 (ATP/ WTA). Seven have been identified as talented players, but equally seven of the players asked about their talent development did not know that they had been part of a talent development programme, so they believed that the national tennis federation was not necessary for their career.

Discussion about money and training facilities has always been an issue. Asked about the strength of their Talent Identification and Development programme, one player noted: "*I was able to stay in an academy that was a good advantage and my former coaches have been very good*" (Pascale). "*Parental support*" was mentioned as crucial for the career of another (Eduard). A third player (Stefan) stated that to practise in an academy from the beginning of his 'middle age' (Monsaas 1985) was the best thing he could do. Other players (Fabienne and Karin) mentioned that the German system was good for each age group; everything seemed to be well organised.

As a main weakness of the Talent Development system in Germany, the players noted the lack of enough training time and facilities: "...*I know that I should train*

---

[13] More information can be found in the appendix

more and start earlier to train hard to achieve international rankings,..., 2-4 hours during or just before puberty were not enough..." (Pascale). For some players the biggest weakness of the programme was what one called the "*trial and error*" mentality of the federation. The interviewee felt that the instruction they received had not been very systematic (Markus). Some of the respondents mentioned the system itself as the weakest link in their development process:

"...*It is the system itself: if you do not achieve results, there will be no support from the federation any more or never. So you have to start as early as possible to train and to compete and forget about fun at an early age. That was a big problem in my time and I guess until now nothing has changed...*" (Eduard).

Another player suggested to me that the talent identification of the federation was a farce. At the beginning of playing tennis: "...*everybody is on his own, there is weak communication between the coaches and the players*" (Markus).

"*In Germany many players think that if they have achieved a number 1 position in the national ranking as a junior, they are the best, but at the end during the transition time from junior to professional level, players like me have to learn that at professional level nobody takes care of us, so we are left alone; that was the point where I failed...*" (Eduard).

As in Germany, the players from the Czech Republic started tennis largely because of the involvement of their parents or relatives. The difference from the German players was the goal setting of the Czech players, reaching high positions at international level. One sought to achieve a top 50 position, whilst two were trying to achieve a top 20 position at international level. Four had been identified as 'talented', but a similar proportion of Czech players as Germans did not recognise themselves to be part of a talent development programme. Three of the Czech players felt that support from the federation was not necessary for their career development. Four thought that they could achieve international success without the support of the federation.

The strength of the talent development system in the Czech Republic has to be seen as the good competition level, even for young juniors. As one player remarked:

"*In my country (CR) there is a good standard of play even at junior level, so we can compete at a very high level... we have good international players and if we see how they play, we know what standard we have to achieve... I think this is an advantage... furthermore; the Czech Republic is not a big country, so we can travel to tournaments quite easily.*" (Daria)

Some other players confirmed that "*in the CR we have good competition and tournaments*" (Ondrej). In the Czech Republic there are very strict and simple criteria for selection to the national squad. This was seen as an advantage in the development process by one male player so "*everybody was aware about what he should achieve*" (Richard).

Another (female) player mentioned that "*...in our country the strengths are the clear criteria. Everybody knows that the ranking position is the decisive factor.....you get better support and certainly it is easier to win first or second round matches...every other point is not relevant; it is just your performance.*" (Radana)

One weakness of the Talent Identification and Development system in the Czech Republic was the "*pressure to get the right performance...the federation is not really taking care of us so we are left alone...nobody tells us if we are on the right track...*" (Milena). Another weakness of the federation regarding their talent development system is the lack of financial resources, and no financial support until players have achieved international level. "*It is always a money problem; we waste time travelling to other countries to play in a league for money... so we cannot qualify for better rankings at the relevant tournaments.*" (Ondrej) A very high drop-out rate was mentioned as a result of this pressure: "*There are many drop-outs throughout our system, even if it is too much dependent on the financial resources of each person.*" (Radana)

7.4.2 Views of Coaches in Germany and the Czech Republic

If the athletes want to achieve top performances, they are dependent on personnel support. The coach plays an important part here. The quality of the training has, however, to be looked at. In all the countries examined, there is a division between coaches who are trained for different levels. In Germany, part of the content of the coaches' training is also talent development; this, however, takes up only a small portion of the training period in comparison with other training components. This was similar in the Czech Republic.

In Germany we interviewed seven coaches ranging from club to professional level. Only two coaches recognised the priority of Talent Development, and only one saw his main task in the identification of talented children. Asked about their knowledge about coaching, three mentioned experience as their most important tool. Their personal reasons for coaching were mainly to help players to develop physically, psychologically, and socially. The majority of the coaches practise social tennis ('Breitensport').

A Talent Identification programme appears to be very important for them, but the approach taken to it was different for each of the selected coaches. One mentioned the "*pyramid approach, from mini-tennis to full court play... to bring players to competition level*" (Andre). Another said "*one day testing is an important part of the identification programmes*" (Darren) as well as the "*expert's eye*" (Darren). Another coach mentioned that he had "*no specific programme. In my academy there are many different types of players of all age groups, so the plans have to be made very individually*" (Gustavo). Many coaches (3/12) stated "*experience*" as the main reason to run their programme, and two used the guidelines from the federation.

The German Talent Identification and Development programme was seen as "*very strict and bureaucratic*" (Andre), but there is a programme a "*coach can follow*" (Eric). For the coaches this programme was not very effective – only one saw the programme as effective. Some coaches (3) were influenced by anecdotes and stories about world-class players, but most of them did not try to actually model their athletes on the careers of world-class players. In the opinion of three of the coaches', it was thought that were better paths by which to develop young people to a high performance level. The ranking system was important or very important to them but also less important for coaches than a talent development programme. Results were considered the most valid criteria for several of the coaches to support a player. The strengths of the national talent identification and development programme were seen as being "*very organised and structured*" (Andre) and a "*good programme*" (Andre; Boris; Eric) although two felt that "*there are no strengths*" (Chris; Frank).

The main weakness of the programme, according to the coaches, was "*too much paperwork*" (Andre) and the fact that "*too few highly qualified coaches are working in the field of tennis*" (Boris). The high number of tennis clubs and places where people can play was seen as a big weakness; and their loss of control over the development of each identified player was also considered a big disadvantage. The federation cannot oversee all the programmes running in a single tennis club (Darren). The coaches (5) from the Czech Republic had registered no specific programme for Talent Development measures. Here there was a different philosophy for coaches. They select good players, in the 'early years' (Monsaas 1985, 215), in which the coaches believe they can reach a high level in the 'later years' (Monsaas 1985, 254). Parents have to find a coach "*who could be in charge for them*" (Cyril). In the Czech Republic there is a strong "*...In the CR is a strong selection system ... mainly through results...*"*so everybody knows exactly when he gets support or not...*"*(Bohdan).* Any player can obtain national support; he and the coach know the criteria. A player has to be ranked in the top 5 national junior ranking to go to the national centres in Perov and Prostjov. If he loses his ranking for more than 6 months, he has to "*leave the national centres*" (David). This could be hard for the coach and the player.

In the Czech Republic, the clubs do not offer any talent selection; if a child is to be identified as a talent, the parents should first take him/her to the court to be given a lesson. The coach decides whether he will train the child or not. Mostly the children have been trained by their parents before, and the parents have decided whether the child is talented or not. Social tennis ('just for fun') in the Czech Republic is not very popular (David).

7.4.3 Views of Parents in Germany and the Czech Republic

Parents' interest and participation in their child's learning contributes enormously to his or her achievement in tennis. It is difficult to imagine how these children could have got good coaches, learned to practise regularly, and developed a high commitment in tennis without a great deal of parental guidance and support. The role of the parents in supporting the long process of talent development is only a piece of the talent development puzzle, but it is a crucial one (Sloane 1985, 476).

The parents selected for this research had children who were training and competing in the 'early' and 'middle years'. The parents did not play tennis at competition level. Their children had been identified as talented by coaches (4) and parents (1). Some parents stated the proximity of the club and the availability of good coaches as motivations to bring the children to the tennis club. Even in the early years they believed that the goals for the children should be to achieve national level playing standard. The children practised between 6 and 10 hours a week. Only one of the children was selected for a talent development group, and two were not selected for a regional squad. Asked about the support they received for their children, the parents stated the coach's and their own support as crucial.

Regarding the Talent Development programme they were more controversial. One said "*there seems to be too much concentration on the player who is already integrated into the tennis system, like squads and support measures. For so-called 'late flowering' talents it is very difficult to receive support in any way*". (Erich). Other parents had "*no idea about the programmes and thought they are not available for their children*" (Markus and Thomas) or it seemed "*not very clear*" to them (Susanne). The support from the federation was not very highly valued; there was no (4) or very little (2) support for the children. Tennis was, however, very important for two of the selected families. The aspiration for the child's future in tennis was "*to have fun and play at the best level she can reach*" (Erich) and to be a "*good player*" at national level (Ira).

In the Czech Republic, one opinion about the Talent Development programme was as follows; "*It is okay if the child is selected, but the initiatives of the parents are more important. There are certainly many children with potential not identified because of lack of knowledge on the part of the parents*" (Aijka).

For some other parents in the CR, the system was considered useless; *"no support, no information regarding the development stages for the future or of what to do and how; there are many parents who do not even know the sport of tennis, so how could they have knowledge of talent development programmes?"* (Marina). The support from the federation was mentioned as not very important, because there was hardly any support. Three had knowledge about an existing Talent Development programme. For the parents in the Czech Republic it was *"difficult to go the whole way. At the beginning of tennis we had no idea how difficult and expensive it could be to become a professional player"* (Martin). They mentioned the lack of information as crucial at the beginning of the child's career (Martina). Regarding the lack of information about Talent Development, they were influenced by anecdotes and stories about world-class players. In the Czech Republic, too, tennis played an important role in families and they hoped that their children would achieve a professional level one day (Cpa-1). However, the parents were also realistic: *"It is very hard, and I think it needs a lot of power to go through the whole development from the beginning"* (Martin).

7.4.4 Views of Administrators in Germany and the Czech Republic

Administrators play a key role in the national federations. The German and Czech Tennis Federations are well structured and each field has its own administrator. The clubs are organised in the same manner. Especially relevant for this research were the administrators who organise and implement the youth programmes of the federations.

In Germany these are called the 'Verbandsjugendwarte' (translated: regional youth coordinators) and their staff. Each of the 18 regional federations had its own youth coordinator. The selected administrators have to organise and run participation programmes and organise the junior tour in their regional federation. In their opinion, the recruitment of talented players should take part in clubs; later they should be able to get lessons. The talent searching programme was also seen as the responsibility of the clubs or individuals. One administrator stated that there was a regular evaluation about those identified as talented children twice a year. They showed a good knowledge of important characteristics of talented children. Asked about the ideal environment, one administrator mentioned "*ours*" (Uli), "*all in one, something like a boarding school*" (Carsten), or where "*school, friends, coaches and courts are in one place (centralised)*" (Maria and Wolf). Some administrators stated that the talented children should look for private sponsors or go to an academy. They stated the importance of financial resources during the development process of the player. They mentioned the ranking system as very important, mainly to select players. Asked about the social position of the sport, I was told that "*everybody can play but to achieve a certain level, money or financial backing is essential*" (Uli), and it is becoming a more exclusive sport (Carsten). This confirmed (according to Wolf) that "*in Germany not everybody can play tennis; coaching and membership are much more expensive than memberships for other sports like soccer or handball*" (Wolf).

The strengths of the Talent Development programme were seen in the "*good infrastructure, enough courts (outdoor, indoor), good coaches, and a good competition system*" (Carsten). The main weaknesses were seen as the "*lack of coaches in the club to identify children, too many small clubs, where no scouts come to identify talented children, and too much bureaucracy in the regional and district federations*" (Maria and Wolf). The suggestions regarding talent identification and development in Germany were to identify clubs where coaches were doing a good job, and "*implementing more talent scouts*" (Wolf).

In the Czech Republic, administrators are also of importance within the national tennis federation (CTS) and its 8 regional federations. But TID in the CR is rather restrictive, with few talents involved in the Czech development system. The one interviewed administrator (Miroslav) stated that boys aged 10-14 years, ranked numbers 1-20 in the national junior ranking, altogether about 200 boys, are trained at 15 training centres. 40 Boys aged 15-17 years ranked number 1-5, trained altogether in 5 training centres, while 10 boys aged 17-19 years, the top players, trained in the two national centres. So there is no involvement of Czech administrators in social tennis, nor is there a youth coordinator. The administrator (Miroslav) said that only two officials from the Czech Tennis Federation (CTS) controlled Talent Development (TD). This TD is financed 60%

by the Czech government and 40% by sponsors. The administrator (Miroslav) also admits that money is a big problem in the CR too, so either the parents finance the training of their child completely or if the child is within the system the parents still have to make a relatively high financial contribution. In any case the CTS never finance a player completely; there is always additional sponsorship needed. The exception is for the 10 top players aged 17-19 years training at the national centres. The strengths of the CR Talent Development programme can be seen in its clear structure, its transparency, and its successful reward orientation. The main weaknesses were seen in the *"lack of funds, also due to the economic crisis, increasing lack of interest in professional tennis, and a high number of non-registered members"* (Miroslav).

7.5 Conclusion

This chapter has addressed two of the main research questions of this thesis: first, I know how TID operates in tennis in the four European countries selected, and second the influence of different social contexts on the meaning of tennis (especially to TID). The analysis of the secondary data and literature has shown that, as we mentioned before, a certain centralisation can have a positive influence on TID programmes, as in France, but this is very expensive for the federation.

In sum, regarding talent identification and development, I can say that there is a big contradiction between that which is published by the federations in theory and that which is mentioned in practice by key informants such as parents, players and coaches. I have seen that the administrators interviewed support the official opinion of the federations. All these key informants complain about receiving less support in all areas of the talent development of their federations. The importance of the federation is not seen by the players as very great, with the consequence that most players have sought their own way to achieve international performance level. The financial background of the parents is crucial and the federations cannot give the talented players much support. This has been seen by all key informants as the biggest issue regarding long-term development. A more in-depth analysis of these findings will be given in the next chapter.

Chapter 8   Discussion and Critical Analysis

This thesis was designed to find answers to one main research question, 'how talent identification and development (TID) programmes in tennis is organised in different European cultures'. In the previous chapter I presented results obtained through primary research, by interviewing players, coaches, parents and administrators in the Czech Republic and Germany on talent identification and development in their countries and by analysing secondary literature on talent identification and development there and in the UK and France, to find answers to this main research question. I have investigated three subsidiary research questions as follows:

1. What is TID, when did it emerge as a concern and how is it discussed in sport?
2. How does TID operate in tennis in the four European countries selected?
3. What influence do different social contexts have on the meaning of tennis and especially approaches to TID in tennis?

The first subsidiary research question was answered in chapter 4, which took into account the emergence of the concern with and discourse on TID. The conclusion of that chapter was in fact that talent is not a phenomenon which can be identified in one day or at some isolated testing events. Talent development is rather a dynamic process which is dependent on the influence of parents, coaches and administrators and the environment in which the TD takes place. On the other hand, internal factors like behaviour, motivation and much more have a great influence on the development of the child. The task of the federation in TID is very important here, because nobody can change his genetic makeup, but the federation can change our environment, to make it as conducive as possible to improving performance. The models (Bloom 1985) which have been suggested by researchers have been mostly implemented by national federations, but they seem to be achievable only by an exclusive circle of children or players who are helped mostly by the financial support of their parents on their way to national talent support.

The second subsidiary research question was answered partly in chapter 3, and partly in chapters 6 and 7. To answer this question we provided a background to the organisation of sport and especially tennis in the four countries using historical, sociological and sport specific data sources in chapter 3, and then more detailed accounts of the organisation and implementation of TID (chapter 6) and critical reflections from key agents involved in two of the countries (chapter 7).

I have identified the strong influence of social, historical and cultural contexts. I understand the importance of societal and environmental conditions for any sport to take place. The popularity of tennis increased in proportion with the increase of the middle and upper classes of society in the 1970s and 1980s, but the decline in membership in all the European tennis nations selected can only be explained by older people changing from tennis to the sport of golf, which is more exclusive. Tennis is no longer – and perhaps never was – a sport for all; it is more or less dependent on the social status of the population. However, it is undisputed that people from a wealthy background can only take part at the talent development programmes of the federations selected. Guidelines such as coaches' education or practice time for talented players are similar in the selected countries, but they do not seem to have much influence from a practical point of view in the selected countries regarding TD. The productivity of the Czech Republic system in contrast to the other countries (Germany, France and the UK) is obvious; interestingly, it does not have a budget like that of countries like the UK and France, where the Grand Slams guarantee a high yearly income. In the CR the tradition, the cultural implementation of tennis, the social motivation to earn a living income by playing professional tennis and also the competition level in their own country, which makes expensive travel unnecessary, make the small Czech tennis federation (in contrast to the others) very successful in producing world-class players. But even in the CR, regarding talent identification and development in the same way as in the other countries selected, we find a big contradiction between the theory and practice of TID. The reason is clear: to implement and construct a programme with the aid of specialists, or to implement it via websites, means a lot of work, but to spread this programme to coaches, clubs and parents, or even to make them understand how to work with it, is almost impossible. Such a programme can only support the key agents by providing them with information, but tennis players, no matter what age, are individuals, and each has a different approach to achieving the top level. Again, the financial and social background of the parents and relatives is crucial, and the federations cannot give much support to the talented players. If a regional federation in Germany (WTB) identify just 4 ten-year-old players out of thousands who can attend the regional federations' training measures, the whole talent selection and development system is questionable. This has been seen by all key informants as the biggest issue regarding long-term development.

The third subsidiary research question was addressed in chapters 2,3,6,7 and the present chapter. First, children in Germany, France and the United Kingdom begin to play tennis under completely different conditions – including motivations and aims – from those in the Czech Republic. While tennis in the CR is aimed at a professional career, and defined as such at an early age, in France, the UK and Germany, tennis – in fact the whole TD process of a talented child – takes place parallel to school, with the aim of reaching 'GCSE' or 'A' levels and maybe (as in the case of a German mother I interviewed) achieving a good national level in tennis. France is an exception here, as it centralises tennis talents at an early stage of the TID process in boarding schools. The consequence seems to be that during development into a professional player there is always a conflict between an individual's school career and tennis career. Practice has shown that most parents in Germany, and recently also in the CR, will put school education before tennis practice. Unfortunately the prestige of being a top athlete and having a future as a professional is very low in Germany. On the one hand, in society gold medals are applauded with pleasure and many spectators in front of their TVs even wear national colours or put their country's flag out of the window; national medal statistics during world-championships are published in newspapers, tennis champions get their headlines in the main channels. But on the other hand if personal success becomes individualised, key agents like parents do not believe in the hardships of long-term development as a sport professional, and shy away. This is also supported by the fact that there is a big decrease in participation in tennis after the age of 14 in Germany. Pressure at school gets higher and more difficult; and there are further reasons such as the onset of puberty, changes of coach, infrastructural problems, or other interests which have more influence on juniors at this stage. Under these conditions it is not easy to maintain the performance standard of the sport and to work hard on court. We know from practice that the amount of training significantly increases in proportion to the level of play and age. This correlates with the investment in travel, coaches, and equipment for the sport. To show the investment of parents in their children, which is definitely adaptable for any player in any of these countries, the example of a 12 years-old girl (ranked No. 5 in the WTB (German Regional Federation) and No. 20 in the National Federation) in Germany is described in Table 8.1 below[14].

Table 8.1: An Under 12 Player's annual expenses for tennis

2004	Tournament	Travel	Coaching	equipment	Total
Activity	29	5,500 km	4 x a week for 40 weeks	Clothes, racket, shoes	
Expenses	750 €	550 €	4,000 €	600 €	5,900 €

Source: own findings and Lawn Tennis Federation 2006

Altogether, the parents of this girl spend around 6,000 Euros per year on the development of their daughter, and this is a low calculation, because at this age a child has to play at national tournaments, which means more travelling, more accommodation expenses, and finally more coaching and practice, all of which combine to increase costs. Even an under 9 years-old child who is already identified as a talent costs his/ her parents' money (400 Euros per month). Compared with the GDP in Germany (2,250 Euros/month/per capita), this is around 20% of the monthly average income (CIA 2008c). As a consequence, we can conclude that only parents with higher salaries can afford such a budget for their son or daughter. Further, travel expenses to international tournaments are

---

[14] This table has been calculated by adding all the typical expenses involved in tournament participation, travel and equipment purchases, derived from a real case.

not included, and this is reckoned to be an essential feature in the long-term development of a junior player (Reid & Crespo 2005). In France and the UK, with a similar GDP per capita, this financial pressure is the same for the parents; in the CR it is even higher. As a consequence, the girl's development, even before she is detected by the NF for their programme, will cost, if we take the 'Ericsson 10-15 yrs' approach, around 100,000 Euros (the LTA calculated £250,000). We know that the average age of a Top 100 player (ATP men's professional ranking) is 24.7 years (Reid & Crespo 2005). The calculation is simple: to start tennis practice around the age of 6/7 years, then train for 10 years, and then start the most difficult and expensive period, the transition to professionalism, will finally cost the parents or possible sponsors (who are mostly not interested), after a progressive increase in monthly costs, around 200,000 Euros. The Lawn Tennis Federation calculated costs '...about GBP 250,000 to develop a winning player from age 5 to age 18...' (Lawn Tennis Federation 2006). The players have to travel, need accommodation and coaching. Boris Becker will confirm this amount of money; we know from him that until his tremendous victory at Wimbledon aged 17 in 1985, his parents invested the equivalent of nearly 500,000 Euros in his development (Bosch 1990). We can find similar conditions for Goran Ivanisevic from Croatia, one of the best tennis players the world saw in the 1990s, and former Wimbledon champion. Goran Ivanisevic practised hard as a junior and played well in the former Yugoslavia. In the long transition from junior to senior level to becoming a professional, his father ran out of money. So the father sold his house in Split (in Croatia) and travelled to an international tournament with the objective that his son had to win or, if he lost, they would have to cancel his international career.

If I now consider the whole development process of a German, Czech, French or British (UK) talent, and take into account how early and how successfully the tennis system (the NFs with all their apparatus) gets involved in the TD process, taking over not only TD itself but also releasing the talent's parents from financial pressure, then we would be tempted to say that the Czechs and the French are in a relatively good position, and the Germans and the talents from the United Kingdom in a relatively bad position. But, as we have seen in Chapter

7, even the Czech players complain of a lack of support from the federation and state that parental financial support was needed for their career. Even worse, dropping out of the national squad meant the end of financial support. Thus, financial backing by the player's parents is of central importance. If this is not given, a player's long-term development seems impossible. Under these circumstances, it would be impossible for a player in the CR to achieve international playing standard level without the support of sponsors or the NF (De Bosscher 2003).

The example of Jan Silva illustrates the hard and insecure path to top level tennis. Jan Silva trained at the Mouratoglou Tennis Academy in France. Each morning, he practised for about an hour with his mother, and than he went to school. After school and lunch supervised by a nutritionist, he played tennis for another hour. At 3 p.m. he visited his physical trainer. Later on he might train again for another hour if he likes. In 2007 Jan celebrated his sixth birthday. If Jan and his family stayed at the Academy until Jan became a professional player, the owner of the academy would have invested between 2 and 3 million US$ in Jan's career, from coaching to equipment to regular visits by a physician. No child of this age has yet received a full scholarship to a major academy (Perrotta 2008b). Jan Silva's family sold their house in the USA and moved to France. But whether he succeeds or not, he illustrates the fact that the pressure on him and his family is as hard as the serves, forehands and backhands in the game. As the tennis world expands, coaches note that top-level instruction at an early age becomes increasingly important. The conclusion seems clear for children whose parents do not have the financial background to pay for this long-term (10-12 years) development or are not exceptional 'wonder-kids', most of them start playing tennis at social level around 7 years of age; and perhaps they have been identified as talented.

Professional training like Jan Silva's is more and more difficult to get. Nick Bollettieri, the founder of the Bollettieri Academy in Florida (USA), which has been producing world-class players for two decades, has stated that it is impossible for him to predict the future performance of a 5-year-old boy or girl. However, parents are now more willing to spend money on the 'insecure' career of their children, but have to accept that this early start and training will not produce results as quickly as it once did. It is a fact that to be the no. 8 in the world ranking at the age of 14 (as Jennifer Capriati from the United States was in 1990) is virtually impossible today (Perrotta 2008b). So where does this lead to? If money is such an important argument for TD, do we now need investors with a gambling mentality who will invest between 500,000 Euros and 3 million US$ in a 5-year-old talent without any guarantee that it will develop within the next 13 years into a 'cash-cow'? Or are all our future top ten players' children of the upper classes of the richer nations of the world whose fathers or relatives have 'invested' their pocket-money in the TD of their children?

I have to mention again that these social differences have a large influence on the approaches to TID in tennis. The recruitment of talent – or rather 'children who are interested in tennis' – still takes place in the clubs in Germany. Maintaining these training facilities costs members a lot of money; this means that players can be financed only by families with larger incomes. Unfortunately, these days the children of poorer families are not represented in the tennis clubs at all. This social distinction has changed over the last two decades. Tennis is now, again, a sport for the wealthy.

However, this situation is not only represented in the social structure of the European tennis federation, which I have selected for this research; there are numerous examples of individual players throughout the tennis world, and I show an analogous example of a player from Zimbabwe (Africa). He[15] achieved world top ranking as a junior (ITF ranking 66) in 1999 and has been a national and continental under-18 champion. He received a scholarship for one year in Spain and had the opportunity to travel to the United States as a college player, but now he cannot continue his career due to his financial situation, so he has failed to achieve a breakthrough internationally.

Regarding this social issue, in the interviews and questionnaires, coaches, parents and players mentioned finance as one of the most important influences

---

[15] I came to know this player when I worked as a sports expert for the International Olympic Committee in Swaziland between 2001 and 2004.

in their long-term development of a professional player. Even if I look into the history of famous tennis players, I note that most of the players came from a rich background, e.g. René Lacoste (FRA), whose father was an industrialist. Susanne Lenglen (FRA) is another example, as she grew up in a palace near Cannes with her own tennis courts. Among the more modern tennis players is Boris Becker (GER), whose father was an architect, who also built the National Tennis Centre at Leimen. Becker stands for a typical German tennis player, whose family itself played tennis and brought him to the sport, whilst Ivan Lendl's (CR) parents, too, were powerful people in the former communist CSSR.

I know that talent identification and its programmes in Germany, the Czech Republic, the UK and France featured in this thesis are the starting point in players' development. In this, the national federations have included coaches, clubs and school programmes as well as courts and equipment, competition and training support. Most of the policies of the countries selected include school tennis programmes to identify this talent. However, the International Tennis Federation (ITF) introduced a world-wide school tennis initiative called School Tennis Initiative (STI), which is mainly to select talented children and develop the game world-wide. If I take the statements of the ITF, thousands of pupils, mainly in primary schools, follow these programmes. A survey in 2000 showed that most affiliated members of the ITF have run school tennis programmes for years. However, the identification cannot be the central aim; there are some recommendations as to what to test and how, and Germany and the Czech Republic run some of these procedures. More important is the development from a selected talent into a professional tennis player. The federations of Germany and the Czech Republic give some recommendations about what to do in this long-term development process, but in practice coaches, players and parents have mostly no idea how to implement a long-term programme for a player; they are failing to plan training on a annual basis. This would signify a big difference between theory and practice, as well as system and empiricism. Whether this is the case for France and the UK, too, I cannot say.

My research shows that there is a big contradiction in the development of tennis talent. The parents all mentioned financial, environmental and communicational barriers as the main problems in the development of their child. Players themselves mentioned the non-systematic approach to their development. Many of those interviewed stated that if they could turn back the clock, they would do many things in their tennis development differently. Some of them criticised their coaches because of their lack of knowledge. Some complained about the travelling time needed to go to national centres, and feelings of lack of confidence when there. Competition pressures (even on 12 years-olds and younger) are enormous, so how could they build up important psychological characteristics (e.g. self-confidence) and a broad motor skill base, if they are entered for competitions as early as possible? Remember that the Tennis Europe ranking starts for players aged 12. There are even unofficial world championships for U12s ('Orange Bowl') and the U10s (in Croatia). To compete there costs a lot of money, and to win some matches (not even the tournament) takes 3-4 years of intense preparation on court for 15-20 hours a week.

Klaus Hofsäss (the former Fed-Cup captain in Germany) noted the low performance level in women's tennis. More coaches or former players should be involved in the development process of young talents. The federal system of the DTB, with its 18 regional federations, is not really working effectively. The problem is the result-oriented thinking of parents, administrators and coaches at junior level, but this is not a predictor for future performance (Hofsäss 2008). More worrying is the fact that even the regional federations in Germany do not adopt the national TD system. As an example, the Bavarian tennis federation (BTV, the biggest in Germany in terms of membership) has implemented a totally new approach in its performance concept, beginning with level one (out of four). A talent has to run through these four development stages from district level to regional level. If they are finally good enough, measured by ranking, they can join the boarding house and use the advantages of short distance and full support 24 hours a day. This concept does not seem to be very new in its structure, but the positive thing is that the administrators set clear criteria for each level. However, this will not change the social make-up of the individual players, because to get into this stage parents and others have to invest a lot of money to achieve the main criteria (results at tournaments).

Another interesting finding involved an interview with the mother (Martina) of a former no. 1 listed player at the Under 14 level in Germany in 2007. His mother mentioned the unorganised information about the development process of her son. If she had not pushed her son towards tennis, he would have never ended up with the success he has today. She complained about the lack of interest of many coaches at regional and national level. For her, a straight practical development process did not exist. The system was self-perpetuating. He had competed in some TE (Tennis Europe) tournaments and mentioned the advantage of the players from Eastern European countries, who were competing better because they had left school and tried to become professional players around 11/12 years of age. Some of them travel with personal coaches; some of them do not even have anything to eat during tournaments. However, the social motivation to be a well-known professional player and the hope of earning a lot of money is evidently very important for achieving a successful career.

The biggest institutional differences and topic of discussion between the programmes of different countries is the question of centralisation and decentralisation. France has a high degree of centralisation, and Germany is decentrally organised, although there are attempts to organise the programmes more centrally. The Czech Republic is more centrally organised, but there are private academies involved in the system of Talent Development. However, there are similarities in the structures of the Talent Identification and Development programmes and procedures in tennis. In most of them, whether in Germany or France, the framework of Talent Identification and Development is very similar to programmes introduced by the International Tennis Federation (ITF) and based on the work of sport scientists and educational psychologists (Bloom 1985, Gimbel 1997, Gabler & Zein 1983, International Tennis Federation 1998). It all starts with Talent Identification around 4-7/8 years of age; then through age-specific training measures, the next step should be achieved around the age of 10/12-12/14 years. Further, at around this stage the children or young athletes should be selected for cadres (Germany) or listed in high positions in rankings (CR) to get more support from the federation. Around age 16/17-18/20 the world standard of tennis should be achieved.

Further, successful countries show more productivity in world class players (De Bosscher et al. 2003). Precisely this productivity shows that many registered members, as in Germany, are not an indicator of successful programmes or a guarantee of producing many international top players. Here the productivity of the Czech Republic is far better, with far fewer members and its infrastructure for tennis. Another factor is the financial situation of a federation. Whilst the 4 Grand Slam nations (Australia, France, USA, and United Kingdom) are far better established than the CR, there are more Czech players listed in international rankings.

In each of the countries selected for this research project I find similar problems regarding Talent Identification, drop-out rates and early sport-specific specialisation. As I mentioned above, sports scientists criticise performance in sport taking place too early. A high drop-out rate around 15 years of age may be one reason. On the other hand, many examples of world-class players' development (Roger Federer, Andre Aggassi, Pete Sampras, Boris Becker and many from Eastern European countries, e.g. Russia and the CR) give experts like coaches, administrators and sports scientists the impression that it is important to start as early as possible with specific and deliberate practice. This correlates with the fact that in international academies 5- and 6-year-old children get a full scholarship for the academies, and even whole families change countries in order to live near the academies (e.g. Jan Silva, 6 years; Tristan Boyer, 6 years; Zachary Svajda, 5 years – see Perrotta 2008). This seems to them to be the only way to achieve a good level. In the CR, age 9-10 seems to be the borderline for being discovered by the National Association or a similar international academy like the Bollettieri, Casal, Sanchez, or Ferrero Academies in Spain or in the United States, as in the cases of Maria Sharapova, Petrowa, Marat and Dinara Safin, and many more; this costs a tremendous amount of money and is not affordable without sponsorship. In Germany average players from a good financial background attend international academies (e.g Kim Twelker, 12 years). In the eastern European countries and in most academies the opinion is common that a large amount of tennis practice is the decisive factor for international success. For example, in the CR the opinion is apparent that an 18-year-old athlete should have hit around 3.6 million balls to achieve world class performance. A lack of technical and tactical ability later on in the player's career is accepted by the parents and coaches.

In an interview in 2005, Jurij Judkin, the former coach of Maria Sharapova, who was the first Russian woman to win the All England Championships at Wimbledon, aged 18, and achieved the number one ranking in 2004, stated that Sharapova started to work with him on a daily basis for 3-4 hours at 4 years of age. Further, Judkin stated that the first deliberate practice should actually start around 3 or 4 years of age and last more than 6 hours a week. As another example, a talented girl named Lisa, aged 6 years, had started playing at the age of 5 years. Her training plan contained 90 minutes of deliberate practice each day, as well as 3 hours of hitting tennis balls against a wall. Additionally, she has to improve her fitness three days a week (Reitschuster 2005).

Judkin stated that on the way to the top a 12-year-old girl has to invest around 80,000 Euros a year in her performance development, including travelling to tournaments (Judkin 2005). To afford this amount of money, a good performance at an early age is required to get sponsors or to get the support of the federation. Under this financial pressure, it seems logical for parents and coaches to start early, no matter what consequences there will be for the child. If we look into TID practice, we know that results on tennis courts and at tournaments alone are not enough to identify children as talented. But results and rankings lists are transparent for everybody, and if regularly updated these are an indicator of the performance level of any player, no matter whether junior or adult. For that reason Talent Identification, and still more Talent Development, are linked to the rankings lists.

However, if I analyse experts' opinion in contrast to the practical situation we have to state that talent identification in tennis is practically 'unresearched' (Unierzyski 2006 and 2003). Bartmus et al. (1987) reported in a symposium the results of a longitudinal study of 100 tennis players. Their conclusion was that 'no uniform tennis performance ability exists: deficiencies in one area of performance can be compensated for by a high level in others' (Bartmus et al.

1987). The fact is that talent identification is usually based on results at tournaments which have been achieved at an early age. This makes sense for them because federations and sponsors do not want to invest in players without good results on court; however the consequence is that many talented players who do not achieve good results at an early stage are lost. In addition to that, much research (Bloom 1985, Côté 1999, Schönborn 1993, Gabler & Zein 1983) has shown that various factors determine performance level in the early stages of a tennis career rather than at a professional level. Therefore on-court results before puberty cannot be used as "predictors" of the future performance level; unfortunately in practice they are used as a predictor.

Normally, any process of talent identification and development should detect the level of factors affecting performance in tennis, and cannot be based purely on performance results. The fact is that talented players cannot have big deficits in any important ability or a factor limiting performance, even at the age of 10-12. A slow player can be a champion at the age of 12, but never at the age of 20. Since it is almost impossible to develop all predispositions to a maximum level (e.g. speed versus endurance), a talented player ought to have at his/her disposal all the major abilities (so-called limiting factors) at a good level (e.g. around average or better). There are many issues and concerns about talent identification and development, and all these findings are valid for all countries. I think that a national federation can only provide its institutions, the clubs, coaches, parents and players with frameworks regarding talent identification and development.

Summary

This chapter has critically discussed the findings of our research, which enabled us to offer some provisional answers to our research questions. We are now in a position to recognise differences between the theories of what is published (secondary literature analysis) and the practice (primary research with key informants) regarding talent identification and development in tennis. The theory mention a broad development until the age of 12/13, but the practice shows that a 12 years-old needs a complete game to achieve regional or national support, which is important if we see increasing financial investment during the development stages. Talent development is a dynamic process and is dependent on many factors, as we have mentioned in the previous chapters. In all the countries studied, TID programmes are implemented; unfortunately these programmes are for players who are already involved in the tennis system. Furthermore, in practice, the financial situation is of major importance for the key agents, and is one of the main reasons to stop playing tennis, no matter whether the children are talented or not.

The next, final, chapter provides interpretations of and overall conclusions to our findings. It also offers some personal reflections on the processes we have looked at from the point of view of myself as a professional tennis coach.

Chapter 9   Interpretation and conclusions

Throughout this thesis, the major emphasis has been on the TID programmes of four different countries and their actual success in practice. From each of these countries we selected secondary information about the structure of society, the sports system, the tennis federation and its talent identification and development programme. Part of the research involved interviews with players, parents, coaches, and administrators from Germany and the Czech Republic, to provide a view from key agents involved in talent development and identification. In Chapter 2, we discussed aspects of the socio-cultural development of tennis as well as how modern tennis is organised worldwide. In Chapter 3 we gave an insight into the structure of four European countries and the position of sport in general, and how tennis in particular was organised in these selected countries. We then discussed the literature on Talent Identification and Development in general and described some common talent models in tennis in Chapter 4. Chapter 5 outlined the methodological issues encountered in this comparative and multidisciplinary study. Chapter 6 introduced findings from the study of TID in the four national tennis systems and identified some important similarities, differences and contradictions regarding talent identification and development in tennis in the selected countries. In Chapter 7 we presented our research findings both from a literature search and from interviews conducted with key agents in tennis from the Czech Republic and Germany. In Chapter 8 we discussed and analysed the results of the research.

In this final chapter, features of TID programmes are described, and the limitations of the current research are considered. Future research needs are identified. Finally, some generalisations from my position as a professional tennis coach are offered.

We have shown that talent development is a complex subject which requires a multidisciplinary approach to begin to understand it. This thesis compared national TID programmes, not the individual success of talented players and athletes. To deal with the whole field of talent identification and development from different perspectives in sport science was not the aim of this thesis. Instead the social and cultural environment of the talented players, the published TID programmes, and the broader social and economic context in which people in the different countries live have been treated as of central importance.

Related to our main research question, we can state that the successful search for a talented player is one of the most important goals for any tennis nation, system and federation. Without talented players, the continuance of competitive tennis is not conceivable. The search for sports talents and their identification is carried out in all the countries examined. However, all the countries examined provide evidence of a not very thorough search for sport talents. Programmes exist in cooperation with schools which are aimed at enlarging the group of people to be identified beyond the clubs. The search for talent in tennis is built up similarly in the CR, where the identification of talent takes place in clubs too. The identification of talent is mainly dependent on a well-trained coach or administrator, who has the necessary skills. Specialised coaches and full-time active personnel or special talent seekers can only be found in France, where the coaches of the clubs are responsible for the selection of talent. Where talent is identified and selected, the administrators of the 'Direction Technique Nationale' (DTN) will test and select the children from tennis clubs again. Here it has to be noted that the specific search for talent only starts at a late stage, because of this staff constellation. In Germany and the UK, in contrast, it is school teachers and coaches in the clubs that have the responsibility. In the UK there are development coaches or development coordinators who coordinate talent activities. This can only be assessed as relatively positive.

With the talents finally identified, the most difficult and important part of their careers begins: Talent Development. We find cadre structures in France and the Czech Republic as well as in the UK and Germany. They have the advantage that financial support can also be applied to the talents. It proves to be adverse here that they do not sufficiently take into account the conditions and the needs of the sport. The cadre system for tennis in Germany is too inflexible, and only within the last 3 years has it tended to abandon strict age criteria in order to design the system in a more flexible way. In France, cadre reconversion exists for athletes who have been in the highest cadre and have ended their career, and who now want incorporation into professional life. This kind of social protection has to be judged as very positive. Regular financial protection offers tennis talents security, so that financial support must be regarded as positive. Germany and the UK try to do justice to the specific needs of the talents by a complicated module system. The social situation is also of decisive importance for the support of talents, as well as performance level. Extensive financial support can be found in all countries, depending on the individual player. An acceptable system exists in the Czech Tennis Federation; yet here it is incumbent upon private supporters to promote talent financially. The athletes have hardly any planned security. The other acceptable system can be found in the French Tennis Federation. France must be mentioned very positively inasmuch as the talents can be exercised at all larger 'pôles'. The INSEP in Paris is exemplary: here a boarding school is directly in an area where various school-leaving qualifications can be taken. This is also made possible for some talents in the CR. In Germany there are only a restricted number of such facilities for tennis, whilst these institutions are mainly reserved for other sports.

The search for talent and support can be carried out in the most varied ways; in the countries examined they differ considerably in professionalism. The identification of the talents still causes considerable difficulties. The prognostic quality of the instruments for the determination of talents used is poor. The social barriers which must be overcome in systematic talent spotting are aggravating. More favourable conditions can be seen in centralist and authoritarian systems (France and, to a certain extent, the CR). But here also, the search for talent cannot at all be described as successfully organised. The promotion of talent appears to be still more problematic. In cooperation with the school system it could be considered satisfactory. The support, however, takes place only for a small group of children.

So what is to be done? Tennis in the countries examined is likely to become and remain an even more socially exclusive sport within the next few years. Talent Development will either be afforded by the public sport system, by private initiative or both, but TI and selection will be restricted to children from families with a good financial background.

In Germany there are relatively few people involved in Talent Identification, in relation to the size of the country and the number of registered members. Centrally controlled organisations responsible for TI like those in France are only possible if the federation can afford them. The Czech Republic cannot, so talented children are either discovered by chance or brought by their parents.

We know that talents need good teaching and learning conditions for their development and it is obvious that without good coaches, parental guidance and the right home environment, and adequate support from the national federations, a talent can never develop his/her skills over a long period of time. In this thesis, we have not come up with a new programme for TD, but for TI we can suggest that the federations identify clubs in their countries and support them directly, because the French model is too cost-intensive. If federations supported their clubs directly and gave them the responsibility for TI, more talents could be identified and developed nation-wide. In summary, there are many different pathways a player might follow to achieve top level in tennis; but all of them need a high investment of money. The question who is financing the talent is not so easy to answer. For that the selected countries in this research offer several possibilities. The national federations have national and regional training centres where players can develop; at these centres, players can train at low cost or free of charge. The family is often the most important source of financial support. All key agents mention this, but unfortunately only a low percentage of families can support their talented child. We think that the effect of this situation is that in the case of the majority of families the economic situation leads them to the decision not to invest in their children because the probability of achieving international success is not very high. The consequence is that if the "talent pool" is based on the low percentage of the population that can support the talented ones financially, a country will be missing out on most of the best talents. Cost plays a major role in top player development and this issue must not be ignored by the federations.

In all four countries examined, the content of their national TID programmes is valid in theory, but in practice neither applied by a majority of the coaches nor directly and entirely benefiting the individual players in their TD process. Therefore, I would suggest better communication between the key agents, the federations and their apparatus, the clubs, coaches, parents and players. It takes a child 10-15 years of commitment and effort to move from the beginning to the complex and difficult process later on, and as long as he/she remains in this development process, he/she should be embedded in the system and the national federation should support them. No matter how committed one is at the age of ten or eleven, if a player does not stick to the whole TD process over a number of years, he or she will be overcome by others who do continue.

In this study, I have concentrated on the TID programmes of different nations more or less from an outsider's point of view. However, given our position as a professional tennis coach in Germany I have been able to take into account the opinions of players, parents, coaches and administrators, regarding these programmes and it is obvious that financial resources are a key factor for the success of talent development in tennis. I hope that this research has provided information that might assist in the construction of more effective and more practicable talent identification and development programmes which give more consideration to the external factors.

A Professional and Practical Coda

Tennis federations in various countries may recommend their programme as the perfect programme, but the message of this chapter and the thesis overall has been that TID remains a dynamic process which appears to be determined by both innate and environmental factors, and that without family support, competent coaches and good physical resources an athlete will not achieve world class performance. I know from previous research that talent has a complex (multidimensional) nature and that the identification of talent is difficult, time-consuming, and ongoing. Research and observations have shown that there is no globally accepted model for Talent Identification in tennis (Bös & Wohlmann 1987; Elliot et al. 1990; Müller 1989; Gabler 1993; Reilly & Williams 2000; Schönborn 1993; Unierzyski 2003). In tennis, coaches and parents need time to recognise talent. It is not difficult to find scientific evidence suggesting that it is possible to identify an eventual Grand Slam champion at an early age. However, coaches provide much insight into what makes a successful player. It is the right combination of physical, mental and intangible skills. Elite players are 'freaks of nature' – the player who possesses all of the skills needed to play tennis at the highest level may come along only once in a coach's lifetime. With that said, it is always important to leave an opening for the player who does not fit into the 'traditional mould'. Every once in a while a player comes along who is completely different from everyone else at a high level (Roetert 2003).

There is a need to give tennis coaches and federations a simple and effective tool which will support their 'experienced eyes' and enhance TID programmes. Any process of talent identification should detect factors affecting performance in competitive tennis, but not just at a junior level. Additionally, every programme should predict the potential of future performance with a high degree of accuracy. Recognising environmental factors should form a part of every talent identification and development programme. Talent identification and development programmes must be looked upon as a process and not an event which requires constant updating. TID programmes should have an on-going longitudinal character with an interdisciplinary approach and the support of sport scientists, but with coaches playing the dominant role. Standardisation/profiling (a mixture of tests and judgements of coaches/experts) is the best tool to collect and analyse the data. Talented players in tennis should not have big deficits in their profile. On-court results before puberty cannot be used as 'predictors'; even good results at the junior level (e.g. gaining a ITF Ranking) do not guarantee achievements in professional tennis (on average only approximately 50% of the top 10 ITF ranked juniors achieve a top 100 ATP ranking, according to Reid and Crespo (2005). Therefore, talent identification and development cannot only be based on results; a player should reach a minimum level of motor abilities, features of body structure, and psychological properties at each stage of development/in each age group. It is crucial to consider individual differences in growth and maturation (e.g. biological and emotional age). Therefore, major (more scientific) screenings and decisions should be taken at the end of each stage of a player's development.

Again, due to the characteristics that a tennis player should have to reach the elite level, it is very difficult, probably impossible, to recognise or 'smell' talent based on a single observation by one person during a solitary testing/identification event (Christensen 2009). Therefore it is important for each national tennis federation to develop and use its own Talent Identification and Development programme and to link it with player development and coach training systems, which should act together as one integrated body.

This begs the question of what TID programmes should look like. Talent Identification and Development programmes in tennis are nowhere perfectly implemented and realized in practice, although they seem to be good and valid in theory in each country examined. In some countries, the approach to detecting, identifying and developing talent seems to be a little different and more effective in practice, as we have seen in the case of the Czech Republic and France. This is due to the fact that both the CR and France, with a rigid, success-oriented, centrally controlled tennis system, succeed better in implementing and realising their TID programmes, whereas in the UK and Germany, for various political, historical, cultural and social reasons, with too much autonomy 'outside' the tennis system and the control of the national federation, and many more individual TD possibilities, the TID programmes are losing efficacy. In the same way as it is important for a tennis federation to implement a TID programme, it is necessary to provide solutions for each individual and provide much better communication between parents, coaches, administrators, and even clubs.

Finally, I suggest the ideal tennis federation in which a programme's theory can be transferred into practice would be one in which the following conditions applied. The national centres would be open to children even at younger ages, like the French federation, which sends different age groups to regional training centres, with the subsidiary effect that the best players train together. In this federation, a talent development commission should be responsible for the talented players in the country, which includes the whole control of the training development of the talented ones in their different development stages. Communication between the key agents has to improve considerably. There must be clear and published guidelines about the development pathway to becoming a professional player with practical suggestions. A system is only as good as each individual actor in it. The tremendous spread of private tennis academies in the last 5 years reveals a certain general dissatisfaction with the national systems. Whether the TID of the private academies or that of the national tennis federations will succeed in the long run, the future alone will show.

Tennis, coaching, and talent identification and development 1995-2010: Personal reflections on a research journey

This research thesis was undertaken following several years working as a national and international professional tennis coach, including time spent as a 'sports expert' as part of the International Olympic Committee's Olympic Solidarity Programme. In what follows I will explain more about how my interest in Talent Identification and Development in tennis has developed and how my professional and research interests coincided through the production of this thesis. Talent Identification and Development in tennis (hereafter TID) is extremely difficult to do. It must be progressive and systematic. To ensure that the programme is meaningful, it must be done over a long period of time. It must take into account the most important and indispensable parameters of success.

The topic of TID in tennis first caught my attention in 1995 when I went to Bulawayo in Zimbabwe to participate in a privately organised project called "Tennis for underprivileged children in high density suburbs of Bulawayo". The environment was exactly as it might be expected to look like in a poor African suburb, although in between thousands of brick houses were two tennis courts.

The courts were those of the Emakhandeni Lawn Tennis Club, which had been founded by Aaron Mpofu (who later left the country and sought refuge in Newcastle in the UK in 2004). Together with Aaron I produced a TD programme to identify young players and coaches. Subsequent visits in 1995, 1996 and 1998, funded by private donations, the German Embassy in Harare and the German Ministry of Foreign Affairs, gave rise to several other notable outcomes from the project: the identification of a Davis Cup Player for Zimbabwe (Dumiso Khumalo), the production of seven tennis development coaches, tennis enthusiasts and talented children who achieved a good standard of play, for the African context. Unfortunately due to the political situation in Zimbabwe the tennis infrastructure has since nearly collapsed. Nonetheless at the time, the positive results from the programme in such a relatively poor infrastructure gave me the idea of comparing tennis coaching and TID programmes in Germany and Zimbabwe. In Germany I worked at a regional tennis club with eight courts (three indoor) and around 400 members, but the outcomes of this programme was I felt no way near as productive as the one at the Emakhandeni Lawn Tennis Club.

In 1999 I took the idea of producing a report on 'Training Practice and Talent Development in Tennis', a document that everybody could use no matter if they were in Zimbabwe or Germany, to the International Tennis Federation (ITF). The ITF did not appreciate the need for producing such a paper at the time, possibly because they had just published a set of coaching syllabuses. The ITF did however offer me the chance to produce a survey about school tennis programmes worldwide and I accepted. I developed a questionnaire, which was approved by the ITF and Miguel Crespo, the ITF Development Officer. The questionnaire was sent to all reachable member countries via email. I obtained feedback from more than 60% of ITF member associations; however the results have never been officially published. Doing this was a good experience for me; and I learned that the language of tennis was more or less the same all over. This motivated me further to produce a simple book about tennis 'talents' and how to develop them.

At my club in Germany I installed a talent group where I identified children at the age of 7 through their sense of playing. Later on the Swaziland Olympic and Commonwealth Games Association (SOCGA) through their General Secretary (Muriel Hofer) offered me a four-year contract (2001-2004) to work in Swaziland as General Manager of the OlympAfrica Centre, an Olympic partner organisation aiming to bring young people into sport and offer them education in one place. Additionally I was asked to implement a talent identification and development programme nationwide for tennis and to support the Swaziland National Tennis Federation with infrastructural advice. I also had to run a nine-module education course about sport coaching and science (including fundamental anatomy, planning of training, physical conditioning, etc). This was all funded by the IOC through their Olympic Solidarity Programme. I fulfilled the contract and spent eight months in Swaziland and 4 months in Germany (May-August) each year for four years. Whilst in Germany together with a colleague I implemented a talent development group, which was supported financially by the regional federation for about three years.

At this stage of my career I was confronted with a lot of responsibility and expectations from both the federation and myself. I wanted to know how I could implement a talent identification and development programme in a poor, developing, country where tennis was equally underdeveloped. I did the same as in Germany and I used a programme to identify children at schools through their basic motor skills and probed a little more deeply into their tennis specific skills. During my time I had contact with hundreds of pupils and I recorded the results. When I had identified a talented group and tried to bring them into clubs I discovered that the majority of them came from the poorest backgrounds, a similar situation to the one I came across in Germany. My TID programme in Swaziland was really not perfect but it was something.

I asked myself the question; am I really doing the right thing? Do parents, players, administrators or coaches understand that TID is more than running a programme? When I was back in Germany I began to feel that all these key actors did not have much of an idea about TID. In practice books and training manuals there are hundreds of scientifically written pages but only a few about

TID. Parents complain about their lack of knowledge, whilst screaming on their children through the fences as they are competing. Coaches mostly do not show interest in TID because it is a time consuming and financially risky part of their job. Administrators I feel really do just talk about programmes and decide about implementation in their policies. Whilst players, I suggest, do not really care most of time and will almost believe anything that people tell them. It is a real problem and unfortunately even a good development coach has little chance of counteracting informal conversations between parents where myths can become "half-truths" and knowledge about the best way of conducting TD for their children.

In sum, my national and international professional coaching experiences revealed that there was a big gap between the theory and practice in tennis regarding the Talent Identification and Development Process. There were many good coaches and administrators who still did not know exactly how to organise and run Talent Identification and Talent Development programmes in their federations and clubs. It occurred to me that practice seemed to be based more on 'trial and error' than anything else. However, it was also indisputable that almost every person involved in tennis – players, coaches, parents, officials, the media, and supporters – would like to see themselves, their children, and their players competing at the highest professional level. To achieve this high performance a long- term player development path is strongly recommended, as we know that the development of tennis specific skills is a complex process that continuously involves some degree of identification and selection (natural or formal) of talented players at all stages. Only an exclusive group of players that have a numerous set of specific characteristics required by the game have the ability to perform at the highest professional level. However, to identify and develop these 'talents' in tennis is as much an art as a science.

That was the point I had reached in 2003 when I made contact with Professor David Collins, then of the University of Edinburgh. He was well-known as an expert in the field of TID. In 2004 I officially registered at the University of Edinburgh as a part-time postgraduate student. The consequence for me was to see my supervisor several times a year while I spent my working and family life in

Germany. For almost the next two years I followed the ideas suggested by Professor Collins. The input I received from him was very helpful in initially focussing my research. His approach and expertise as a performance coach and psychologist meant that he was interested in seeing me produce a thesis that could be used practically by practitioners and other performance coaches. When Dave left Edinburgh in late 2005 to become UK Athletics' performance director principal supervision of my thesis was taken over by Dr John Horne (now Professor of Sport and Sociology at the University of Central Lancashire), a sociologist in the field of sport, and Dr Pat McLaughlin.

The change of supervisory team influenced my thesis, and the focus switched from a practically orientated piece of research to attempting a broader sociologically informed view about tennis TID in different European countries. My initial more empirical/practical approach shifted to an interest in seeing how TID worked in comparative perspective. As a part-time, non-native English-speaking student, normally resident in Germany, I encountered several challenges. For example it was not always easy to fly over for a few days to Edinburgh in order to work under the supervision of my supervisors at different stages of the research. Nonetheless I have been able to use my established contacts and language skills to undertake the research and hopefully through this thesis have produced an original and unrivalled contemporary overview of TID in tennis in selected European countries.

Bibliography

This Bibliography is in two sections. The first section contains reference to all published books, journal and magazine articles and other written documents consulted. The second section lists all website and information sources referred to in the thesis.

Section 1

Abbott, A. (2005). *Talent Identification and Development.* PhD Thesis. Edinburgh University.

Abbott, A. & Collins D. (2002). A theoretical and empirical analysis of a 'State of the Art' Talent Identification model. *High Ability Studies* 13 (2), 158.

Agassi, A. (2008). Wunderkinds. *Tennis.com 1,* 46.

Alfermann, D., Würth, S. & Saborowski, C. (2002). Soziale Einflüsse auf die Karriereentwicklung im Jugendleistungssport: Die Bedeutung von Eltern und Trainern. *Psychologie und Sport* 9 (2), 50-61.

Altmann, F. & Baratta, M. (2006a). *Der Fischer Weltalmanach. Tschechien.* Zahlen-Daten-Fakten. Fischer, Frankfurt, 796.

Altmann, F. & Baratta, M. (2006b). *Der Fischer Weltalmanach. Deutschland.* Zahlen-Daten-Fakten. Fischer, Frankfurt, 181-182.

Balyi, I. & Hamilton, A.(2003). Long-term athlete development, trainability and physical preparation of tennis players. *Strength and Conditioning for Tennis.* International Tennis Federation, London, 49-57.

Bar-Or, O. (1975). Predicting athletic performance. *Physician and Sports Medicine* 3, 81-85.

Bartmus, U., Neumann, E. & de Marees, H. (1987). The talent problem in sports. *International Journal of Sports Medicine* 8, 415-416.

Bernhard, B. (1987). Methodologische, pädagogische und psychologische Aspekte zu einem handlungsorientierten Ansatz der Talentforschung. *Spektrum der Sportwissenschaft,* 286-299.

Bette, K.-H. (1984). *Die Trainerrolle im Hochleistungssport. System- und rollentheoretische Überlegungen zur Sozialfigur des Trainers.* Richarz, Sankt Augustin.

Blahüs, P. (1975). For the prediction of performance capacity in the selection of sports talented youth. *Teorie a Praxe Telesne Vycsbovy 24,* 471-477.

Bloom, B. S. (1985). *Developing talent in young people.* Ballantine, New York.

Born, H. P., Fuchs H. & Tasch, T. (2002). *Talentförderung im Tennis. Sichtung, Auswahl, Grundlagenausbildung und Grundlagentraining von Talenten.* Deutscher Tennis Bund, Hamburg.

Bortz, J. & Döring, N. (1995). *Forschungsmethoden und Evaluation für Sozialwissenschaftler.* Springer-Verlag, Berlin.

Bös, K. & Schneider, W. (1997, 2003). *Vom Tennistalent zum Spitzenspieler. Eine Reanalyse von Längsschnittdaten zur Leistungsprognose im Tennis.* Schriften der Deutschen Vereinigung für Sportwissenschaft 131. Czwalina, Hamburg, 11-27.

Bös, K. & Wohlmann, R. (1987). *Allgemeiner Sportmotorischer Test.* Deutscher Tennis Bund, Hannover.

Bosch, G. (1986). *Boris.* Uhlstein, Frankfurt.

Böseler, T. (2005). Vom Talent zum Profi. *Tennismagazin* (6), 46-47.

Bourdieu, P. (1982). *Die feinen Unterschiede: Kritik der gesellschaftlichen Urteilskraft.* Suhrkamp, Frankfurt a. M.

Brabenec, J. (1996). Talent Identification. *Coaches Review 9.* International Tennis Federation, 10.

Breuer, C. (2006).*Sportentwicklungsbericht 2005/ 2006.* Analyse zur Situation der Sportvereine in Deutschland. Köln, 1-56.

Brown, J. (2001). *Sports Talent. How to identify and develop outstanding athletes.* Human Kinetics, Champaign, 300.

Brymann, A. & Bell, E. (2007). *Buisness Research Methods.* Oxford University Press.

Bungard, W. (1979). Methodische Probleme bei der Befragung älterer Menschen. *Zeitschrift für experimentelle und angewandte Psychologie 26,* 211-237.

Bussmann, G. & Pfaff, E. (2004). Karriereabbruch im Spitzensport. Drop-out-Risiken bei Tennisspielerinnen? *Tennissport* 11 (6), 4-7.

Butler, C.J. (1978). *Wachstumsfelder im Freizeitbereich*: Spezialstudie Tennis-Squash. Institut für Freizeitwirtschaft und Freizeitforschung, München, 101.

Cassidy, T., Jones, R. & Potrac, P. (2004).*Understanding Sports Coaching*. Routledge, Oxon.

Carlson, R. (1988). The socialization of elite tennis players in Sweden: An analysis of the players' backgrounds and development. *Sociology of Sport Journal*, 5 (3), 241-256.

Cachay, K. & Thiel, A. (1996). Sozialkompetenz für Trainerinnen und Trainer im Hochleistungssport. *Trainerakademie Köln und Verband Deutscher Diplom Trainer* 4, 8-15.

Christadler, M. & Uterwedde, H. (2005). *Länderbericht Frankreich. Geschichte, Politik, Wirtschaft, Gesellschaft* 2, Leske/ Budrich, Opladen.

Christensen, M. (2009). "An Eye for Talent": Talent identification and the "Practical Sense"of Top-Level Soccer Coaches. *Sociology of Sport Journal*, 26, 365-382.

Clerici, G. (1987). *500 Jahre Tennis*. Vom Spiel der Könige zum Milliardengeschäft. Frankfurt a.M.

Coakley, J. (2007). *Sports in Society: Issues & Controversies*. McGraw-Hill, New York.

Coakley, J. (2001). *Sport in Society: Issues & Controversies*. McGraw-Hill, Boston.

Conzelmann, A. (2003). *Karriereverläufe im Spitzentennis*. Universität Tübingen, Tübingen.

Conzelmann, A. (2004). Neuanfang im deutschen Tennis. *Deutsche Tennis Magazin* 10, 74-75.

Côté, J. (1999). The influence of the family in the development of talents in sports. *The Sports Psychologist* 13, 395-417.

Crespo, M. & Miley, D. (1998). Principles for talent search and detection. *Advanced Coaches Manual*. International Tennis Federation, London, 293.

Crespo, M. & McInerney, P. (2006). Historical background of TID in tennis. *Coaching & Sport Science Review* 39, 2-3.

Creswell, J. (2003). *Research Design: Qualitative, Quantitative, and Mixed Methods Approaches*. Sage Publications, California Thousand Oaks.

Csikszentmihalyi, M., Rathunde, K. & Whalen, S. (1993). *Talented teenagers: The roots of success and failure*. Cambridge University Press. New York.

Dahlgren, L. (1984). Talentbestimmung in Schweden. *Talentsuche und Talentförderung im Tennis*. Hamburg, 34-49.

Delforge, C. (2006). Analysis of parent-player relationships and the role of the coach. *Coaching & Sport ScienceReview* 14 (38), 5-6.

Deutscher Tennis Bund (1987). *Materialien für die Praxis*. Sportwissenschaftlicher Beirat, Hannover.

De Boer, J. (2007). Cardio-Tennis. *Coaching & Sport Science Review*. International Tennis Federation, 42, 13.

De Bosscher, V., De Knop, P. & Heyndels, B. (2003). Comparing Tennis Success Among Countries. *Journal of the International Society for Comparative Physical Education and Sport*, 25(1), 1-22.

DeVaus, D. (2002). *Surveys in Social Research*. Routledge, London.

Diener, U. (2006). *Grafstat*. Hamm.

Digel, H., Burk, V. & Fahrner, M. (2006). *Die Organisation des Hochleistungssports – ein internationaler Vergleich*. Schriftenreihe des BISP (115), Schorndorf.

Digel, H. (2006). *Trainer in der Krise*. Südwestpresse. Tübingen

Digel, H. & Fahrner, M. (2003a). *Hochleistungssport in Frankreich*. Bräuer, Weilheim/ Teck.

Digel, H. & Burk, V.(2003b). Sportinteresse- und Partizipation. *Hochleistungssport in Großbritannien und Nordirland*. Bräuer, Weilheim/ Teck.

Digel, H. (2001). Talentsuche und Talentförderung im internationalen Vergleich. *Leistungssport*, 4, 72-78.

Durand-Bush, N. & Salmela, J. H. (2000). The Development of Talent in Sport. *The Handbook of Sport Psychology*. New York, 269-287.

Elliot, B. & Ackland, T. (1990). A prospective study of physiological and kinanthropometric indicators of junior tennis performance. The *Australian Journal of Science and Medicine in Sport*, 22, 87-92.

Emrich, E., Güllich & W. Pitsch (2005). Zur Evaluation des Systems der Nachwuchsförderung im deutschen Leistungssport. *Beiträge zum Nachwuchsleistungssport 113*. Hofmann, Schorndorf, 75-138.

Ericsson, K.A.,Krampe, R.Th. & Tesch-Römer, C. (1993). The role of deliberate practice in the acquisition of expert performance. *Psychological Review* 100, 363-406.

Ericsson, K. A. (2003). The development of elite performance and deliberate practice: An update from the perspective of the expert-performance approach. J. Starkes and K. A. Ericsson (Eds.). *Expert performance in sport: Recent advances in research on sport expertise*. Human Kinetics, Champaign, 49-81.

European-Commission (2004). The citizens of the European Union and Sport. *Special EUROBAROMETER 213*, 5.

Fédération Française de Tennis (1998). Annual and monthly training process with 14&under players. *Developing young tennis players*. International Tennis Federation, Canada, 37.

Fédération Française de Tennis (2004). The French System. *Deutsche Tennis Magazin 3*, 22.

Franke, E. (1996). Zum Selbstbild des Trainerberufs im Spiegel seiner Verantwortung. *Leistungssport* 26, 21-24.

Gabler, H. & Zein, B. (1983). *Talentsuche und Talentförderung im Tennis*. Czwalina, Hamburg.

Gabler, H. (1993). Results of a Talent study in Tennis. *Talentsuche im Tennis*. Czwalina. Ahrensburg, 23-25.

Gabler, H. & Zein, B.(1993). Talent search and Talent development in tennis. *Beiträge zur Theorie und Praxis des Tennisunterrichts (8)*. Deutscher Tennis Bund. Hamburg, 9-13.

Geissler, R. (2002). *Die Sozialstruktur Deutschlands. Die Gesellschaftliche Entwicklung vor und nach der Wiedervereinigung*. Westdeutscher Verlag, Wiesbaden.

Geron, E. (1976). Psychological assessment of sport giftedness. In U. Simri (ed.), *Proceedings of the international symposium on psychological assessment in sport,* 216-231. Netanya, Israel.

Gillmeister, H. (2008). Tennis History. *Coaching and Sport Science Review 15 (46),* 16-18.

Gillmeister, H. (1997). *Tennis: A Cultural History.* Fink, München.

Gimbel, B. (1976). Possibilities and problems in sports talent detection research. *Leistungssport* 6, 159-167.

Gratton, C. & Taylor, P. (2000). *Economics of sport and recreation.* SponPress, London.

Guttmann, A. (2004). *Sports. The first five Millennia.* University of Massachusetts Press. Amherst and Boston.

Guttmann, A. (1994). *Games and Empires. Modern sports and cultural imperialism.* Columbia University Press. New York.

Guttmann,A. (1978). *From Ritual to Record.* Columbia University Press. NewYork.

Hamilton, B. (2000). East African running dominance: what is behind it? *British Journal of Sports Medicine,* 34, 391-396.

Hantrais, L. & Mangen, S. (1996). *Cross-National Research Methods in the Social Sciences.* Pinter, London/New York.

Harre, D. (1982). *Trainingslehre.* Sportverlag, Berlin.

Harris, H.A. (1972). Sport in Britain. *Geschichte der Leibesübungen (4).* Bartels & Wernitz, Berlin,134-181.

Hartmann-Tews, I. (1996). *Sport für alle?! Strukturwandel europäischer Sportsysteme im Vergleich. Bundesrepublik Deutschland, Frankreich, Großbritannien.* Hofmann, Schorndorf.

Hay, J. G. (1969). Rowing: An analysis of the New Zealand Olympic selection test. *Research Quarterly for Exercise and Sport* 40, 83-90.

Hellstedt, J.C. (1987). The Coach/ Parent/ Athlete Relationship. *The Sport Psychologist* 1, 151-160.

Hermann, H.-D. (1996). Persönlichkeit und Kommunikation. *Trainerakademie Köln und Verband Deutscher Diplom Trainer* 2, 4-6.

Hoare, D. (2001). *Talent Identification and Selection manual. Tennis*. Sports Information and Science Agency (SISA). Johannesburg (SA), 1-19.

Hofsäss, K. (2008). Was läuft im deutschen Tennis schief? *Deutsches Tennis Magazin* 8, 36.

Hohm, J. & Klavora, P. (1987). *Tennis: Play to win the Czech Way*. Sports Book Publisher, Toronto, 352.

Hohmann, A. & Seidel, I. (2003). Scientific aspects of talent development. *International Journal of Physical Education 40 (1)*, 9-20.

Hohmann, A. & Carl, K. (2002). Zum Stand der sportwissenschaftlichen Talentforschung. A. Hohmann, D. Wick & K. Carl (Ed.) *Talent im Sport*. Hofmann, Schorndorf, 3-30.

Hotz, A. (1990). Was zeichnet einen "guten" Trainer letztlich aus? *Leistungssport* 20 (5), 45-46.

Houlihan, B. (1997). *Sport, policy and politics: a comparative analysis*. Routledge, London.

Houlihan, B. & White, A. (2002). *The Politics of Sports Development*. Routledge, London, 196-203.

Howe, M.J., Davidson, J.W.& Sloboda, J.A. (1998). Innate talents: Reality or myth? *Behavioural & Brain Sciences*, 21, 399-442.

Hug, O. (1991). *Menschenführung und Gruppenprozesse. Situative Führung für Trainer*. Hofmann, Schorndorf.

International Tennis Federation (2002). *Developing young tennis players*. International Tennis Federation, London.

International Tennis Federation (2002). *Competitive Options for 14 & Under Players. Developing young tennis players*. International Tennis Federation, London, 32.

International Tennis Federation (1998). General framework for the long term development of a tennis player. *Advanced coaches manual*. International Tennis Federation, London, 202.

International Tennis Federation (1998a). *Leadership, Management and Administration Manual.* International Tennis Federation, London.

International Tennis Federation (1998b). *School Tennis Initiative (STI).* International Tennis Federation, London.

Joch, W. (1997). Rekrutierung, Wettkampfsysteme. *Das sportliche Talent: Talenterkennung – Talentförderung – Talentperspektiven* .Meyer und Meyer, Aachen, 167.

Jokl, E., Karvonen, M.J., Kihlberg, H., Koskela, A. & Noro, L. (1956). Sports in the cultural pattern of the world. *Institute of occupational health 1956.* Helsinki.

Judkin, J. (2005). Tennis Talent development in Russia. *Focus* 35, 98-101.

Kalinowski, A.G. (1985). The Development of Olympic Swimmers. Bloom, B. (Ed.), *Developing talent in young people.* Ballantine Books, New York, 139-192.

Kaminski, G., Mayer, R. & Ruoff, B.A. (1984). *Kinder und Jugendliche im Leistungssport.* Hofmann, Schorndorf

Kearney, J. T. (1999). *Talent identification and Development*: The foundation of Olympic success.

Killing, W. (2002). Der Trainerberuf in der Krise. *Leistungssport* 32 (3), 49-54.

Kuchařová, V. & Kroupa, A. (1999). Demographic and social structure. *Human Development Report of the Czech Republic 1999.* Prague: Research Institute for Labour and Social Affairs.

Lake, R. (2008). *Social Exclusion in British Tennis*: A History of Privilege and Prejudice. School of Sport and Education, Brunel University.

Lasserre, R. & Schild, J.(1997). *Frankreich – Politik, Wirtschaft, Gesellschaft, Reihe*: *(Grundwissen Politik 19).* Leske + Budrich, Opladen.

Lawn Tennis Association (2006). Coaches. *Blueprint for British Tennis.* West Kensington, Lawn Tennis Association, London, 8.

Lubbers, P. & Gould, D. (2003). Phases of world-class player development. *Coaching & Sport Science Review,* 30, 2.

Massias, J.C. (2006). Das Französische Tennis. *Das Deutsche Tennis Magazin* 8, 34.

MacCurdy, D. (2008). A Global Look at Top Player Development. *Coaching & Sport Science Review, 46*, 27-29.

Martin, D. & Renz, K. (1993). Development Practice/ Handbuch Training. *Handbuch Trainingslehre*. D. Martin. Schorndorf, Ausschuss Deutscher Leibeserzieher 100, 291-312.

Meinberg, E. (2001). *Trainerethos und Trainerethik*. Sport & Buch Strauß, Köln

Mignon, P. & Truchot, G. (2001). *Stat-Info. Bulletin de statistiques et d'études*. La France sportive. Premiers résultats de l'enquête – practice sportives 2000.

Miley, D. (2007). Tennis...Play and Stay. *Coaching & Sport Science Review*. International Tennis Federation, 42, 1-3.

Miranda, M. (2007). 'Getting More Children to Play Tennis in School'. *Coaching&Sports Science Review*. International Tennis Federation, 42, 5.

Monsaas, J.A. (1985). *Learning to Be a World-Class Tennis Player*. In: B.S. Bloom (Ed.) *Developing talent in young people*. Ballantine Books, New York, 211-269.

Müller, E. (1989). Sportmotorische Testverfahren zur Talentauswahl im Tennis. *Leistungssport* 2(19), 5-9.

Murray, A. (2008). *Andy Murray. Hitting Back*. Century, London, 85-115.

Ning, X. (2006). Wir handeln nach den drei Prinzipien. *Deutsches Tennis Magazin* 3, 24.

Pearson, J.L. (?) Marketing Research. *School of Business & Accountancy*, Ngee Ann Polytechnic.

Perrotta, T. (2008b). Wunderkinds. *Tennis.com* 1, 45-47.

Regnier, G. & Salmela J. (1982). Strategie für Bestimmung und Entdeckung von Talenten im Sport. *Leistungssport* 12, 431-440.

Regnier, G., Salmela J. & Russell, S.J. (1993). Talent Detection and development in sport. In R.N. Singer, M. Murphy & L.K. Tennant (Eds). *Handbook on research on sport psychology*. McMillan.New York, 371-425.

Reid, M. & Crespo, M. (2005). The ITF Junior Boys' Circuit and its role in professional Player Development. *Coaching & Sport Science Review* 13 (35), 2-3.

Reilly, T. & Williams, A. (2000). A multidisciplinary approach to talent identification in soccer. *Journal of Sports Sciences*, 18, 655-656.

Reitschuster, B. (2005). Die Russinnen kommen. *Focus* 35, 98-101.

Robinson (1998). *Crossing the Line: Violence and Sexual Assault in Canada's National Sport*. McCelland & Stewart Inc., Toronto.

Roetert, P. & Riewald, S. (2003). Talent Identification. *Applied Sport Science for High Performance Tennis*. International Tennis Federation, Vilamoura, 63-64.

Russell, K. (2000). *Ice time. A Canadian hockey journey*. Viking, Toronto.

Salmela, J.H. (1996). *Great job coach! Getting the edge from proven winners.* Potentium, Ottawa (CA).

Schneider, W. & Bös, K. (1993). *Leistungsprognose bei jugendlichen Spitzensportlern*. Göttingen, Hogrefe.

Schönborn, R. (1993). Leistungslimitierende und Leistungsbestimmende Faktoren. *Talentsuche und Talentförderung im Tennis*. Ahrensburg, 51-75.

Schwarzer, D. (2007). *Entwicklungsverläufe und Karrieremuster im internationalen Spitzentennis*. University of Heidelberg, Heidelberg.

Sharp, B. (2007). Tennis is a Sport for All – ITN. *Coaching&Sports Science Review*. International Tennis Federation, 42, 8.

Silvermann, D. (2000). *Doing qualitative research*. Sage Publications Ltd., London.

Sloane, K. (1985). Home Influence on Talent Development. In: Bloom, B. (Ed.). *Developing Talent in Young People*. Ballantine, New York, 439-477.

Statistisches Bundesamt Deutschland (2008). *Einkommen und Vermögen in Deutschland – Messung und Analyse Forum der Bundesstatistik* 32, Bonn.

Stemmler, T. (1988). Vom Jeu de Paume zum Tennis. Insel Verlag, Frankfurt.

Stojan, S. (1996). From Talent to Champion – The Role of the Coach. *Coaches Review*, 9, 14.

Sturm, G. (1997a). *Großbritannien*. Leske+Budrich. Opladen, 67-70.

Sturm, G. (1997b). *Großbritannien*. Leske+Budrich. Opladen, 132.

Teuber, S. (1990). *Talentförderung in Frankreich*. Czwalina, Ahrensburg.

Unierzyski, P. (2006). How to Recognise Tennis Talent? *14th ITF Worldwide Coaches Workshop, Turkey 2005 – "Quality Coaching for the Future"*. International Tennis Federation, Ali Bey Club.

Unierzyski, P. (2003). Motor Ability as a predictor of Future Tennis Performance – A study of Junior Grand Slam Winners. *Applied Sport Science for High Performance Tennis*. International Tennis Federation, Vilamoura, 132.

Unierzyski, P. (2003). Notational Analysis in Tennis as a Talent Identification Tool. *Applied Sports Science for a High Performance Tennis*. International Tennis Federation, Vilamoura.

Unierzyski, P. (1996). A Retrospective Analysis of Junior Grand Slam Winners. *ITF Coaches Review* 9, 2-3.

Van Bottenburg (1992). The Differential Popularization of sports in Continental Europe. *The Netherlands journal of Social Science 28*, 3-30.

Van Bottenburg (2001). *Global Games*. Urbana, Illinois.

Van Bottenburg (2005). *Sports Participation in the European Union*. DeltaHage, Den Haag.

Wiggins (1997). Great speed but little stamina. The historical debate over black athletic superiority. *The New American Sport History*. University of Illinois Press, Chicago, 312-338.

Würth, S. (2001). *Die Rolle der Eltern im sportlichen Entwicklungsprozess von Kindern und Jugendlichen*. Pabst Science Publishers, Lengerich.

Württembergischer Tennis Bund (2004). *Sichtungsbedingungen des WTB/ Bz.5*. Stuttgart, 2.

Wolstencroft, E. (2004). *Talent Identification and Development. An Academic Review*. SportsScotland, Edinburgh, 1-103.

Zháněl, J. (2004). TESTOVÁ BATERIE. *Fakulta tělesné kultury UP*, Olomouc, 1-18.

Section 2

Association of Tennis Professionals (2008a). *ATP Rankings Germany, 1-100*. Retrieved 20.10.2008, from http://www.atpworldtour.com/Rankings/Singles.aspx?d=20.10.2008&c=GER&r=1#.

Association of Tennis Professionals (2008b). *ATP Ranking Czech Republic; 1-100*. Retrieved 20.10.2008, from http://www.atpworldtour.com/Rankings/Singles.aspx?d=20.10.2008&c=CZE&r=1#.

Association of Tennis Professionals (2008c). *ATP Ranking France, 1-100*. Retrieved 19.10.2008, from http://www.atpworldtour.com/Rankings/Singles.aspx?d=20.10.2008&c=FRA&r=1#.

Association of Tennis Professionals (2008d). *ATP Ranking UK, 1-100*. Retrieved 20.10.2008, from http://www.atpworldtour.com/Rankings/Singles.aspx?d=20.10.2008&c=GBR&r=1#.

Association of Tennis Professionals (2005). *Professional Rankings*. Retrieved 19.01.2005, from http://www.atptennis.com/3/en/rankings.

British Olympic Association (2009). *Our Vision for the BOA*. Retrieved 1.7.2009, from http://www.olympics.org.uk/Documents/Our_Vision_toemail.pdf.

British Olympic Association (2005). *The British Olympic Association*. Retrieved 1.7.05. 2005, from http://www.olympics.org.uk/thisistheboa/thisistheboa.asp.

Bundesgesundheitsministerium (2008). *Prävention. Bewegung und Ernährung*. Retrieved 2.2.2008 from, http://www.bmg.bund.de/cln_117/nn_1168258/sid_9BCCA15C51476B38F9E76B54BCA28535/nsc_true/SharedDocs/Pressemitteilungen/DE/2008/Presse-3-2008/pm-09-07-08.html?__nnn=true.

Central Council of Physical Recreation (2008). *About Us*. Retrieved 20.10.2008, from http://www.ccpr.org.uk/aboutccpr/.

Central Council of Physical Recreation (2008a). *About CCPR*. Retrieved 20.10.2008, from http://www.ccpr.org.uk/.

Central Council of Physical Recreation (2008b). *Who are our members*. Retrieved 20.10.2008, from http://www.ccpr.org.uk/aboutccpr/.

Central Intelligence Agency (2008a). The *world fact book/ France*. Retrieved 22.9.2008, from https://www.cia.gov/cia/publications/factbook/geos/fr.html#Intro.

Central Intelligence Agency (2008b). *The world fact book/ UK*. Retrieved 22.9.2008, from https://www.cia.gov/cia/publications/factbook/geos/uk.html#Intro.

Central Intelligence Agency (2008c). *The world factbook/ Germany.* Retrieved 22.9.2008, from http://www.cia.gov/cia/publications/factbook/geos/gm.ht ml#Intro

Central Intelligence Agency (2008d). *The world factbook/ Czech Republic.* Retrieved 28.10.2008, from https://www.cia.gov/library/publications/the-world-factb ook/geos/ez.html#Intro.

Czech Republic (2008a) *All about Czech History.* Retrieved 24.11.2008, from http://www.czech.cz/en/czech-republic/history/all-about-czech-history

Czech Republic (2008b): *The Velvet Revolution and its consequences.* Retrieved 24.11.2008 from http://www.czech.cz/en/czech-republic/history/all-about-czech-history/the-velvet-revolution-and-its-consequences

Czech Republic (2008c). *Historical Development of sports and sports organisations in the Czech Republic.* Retrieved 1.12.2009, from http://czech.titio.cz/en/tourism-sport/sports/historical-development-of-sports-and-sports-organizations-in-the-czech-republic?i= .

Czech Sports Association (2009). *ČESKÝ SVAZ TĚLESNÉ VÝCHOVY CZECH SPORT ASSOCIATION.* Retrieved 1.12.2009, from http://www.cstv.cz/zpravodaj_otp.htm.

Czech Sports Association (2007). *Regionalni sdruzeni CSTV Jihlava.* Retrieved 10.7.2007, from www.cstv.cz/jihlava/english_version.htm.

Czech Statistical Office (2008a). Distribution by sex group in the Czech Republic Retrieved 23.11.2008 from, http://www.czso.cz/csu/2007edicniplan.nsf/engk apitola/1413-07--10.

Czech Tennis Association (2009). *Metodicka komise* CTS. Retrieved 5. Febuary 2005, from http://metodickakomise.cztenis.cz/?page_id=11.

Czech Tennis Association (2008). *Policy.* Retrieved 5. Febuary 2005, from http://www.cztenis.cz/index.php?id1=14&id2=2.

Czech Tennis Association (2008a). *CZtenis-oficialni stranky Ceskeho tenisoveho svazu.* Retrieved 1.12.2009, from http://www.cztenis.cz/starsi-zactvo/zebricky.

Czech Tennis Association (2008b). *The Czech Tennis Federation.* Retrieved 10.01.2005, from www.cztenis.cz.

Deutscher Olympischer Sport Bund (2009). *Richtig Fit*. Retrieved 1.12.2009, from http://www.richtigfit.de/.

Deutscher Olympischer Sport Bund (2009a). *Daten und Fakten*. Retrieved 1.12.2009, from http://www.dosb.de/de/organisation/organisation/

Deutscher Olympischer Sport Bund (2009b). *Bestandserhebungen*. Retrieved 5.07.2008, from http://www.dosb.de/fileadmin/fm-dosb/downloads/2007_DOSB_Bestandserhebung.pdf.

Deutscher Olympischer Sport Bund (2008). *Auf welchen Feldern in Sport und Gesellschaft ist der DSB aktiv*. Retrieved 8.10.2008, from http://www.dosb.de/index.php?id=349.

Deutscher Olympischer Sport Bund (2008a). *DOSB zur Verzehrstudie*. Retrieved 5.2.2008, from http://newsletter.dosb.de.

Deutscher Olympischer Sport Bund (2008b). *Sport für alle*. Retrieved 2.3.2005, from http://www.dsb.de/index.php?id=532.

Deutscher Olympischer Sport Bund (2008c). *Olympiastützpunkt*. Retrieved 28.10.2008, from http://www.dosb.de/de/leistungssport/olympiastuetzpunkte/

Deutscher Olympischer Sport Bund (2007). *Der Deutsche Sportbund und sein Aufgabenspektrum*. Retrieved 8.10.2007, from http://www.dosb.de/.

Deutscher Olympischer Sport Bund (2006). *Staatsziel Sport*. Retrieved 1.12.2009, from http://www.dosb.de/fileadmin/fm-dosb/downloads/dosb/Staatsziel_Sport_31.10.pdf.

Deutscher Sport Bund (2005). *Die soziale Offensive Sport steigert die Lebensqualität*. Retrieved 22.3.2005, from http://www.dsb.de/index.php?id=531.

Deutsche Sporthilfe (2008). *Stiftung Deutsche Sporthilfe*. Retrieved 28.10.2008, from http://www.sporthilfe.de/servlet/index?page=2

Deutsche Sporthilfe (2008a). Förderung. Aktuell geförderte Sportler. Retrieved 28.10.2008, from http://www.sporthilfe.de/sporthilfe.de/servlet/index?page=60.

Deutscher Tennis Bund (2009). *DTB Hauptamt*. Retrieved 21.1.2009, from http://www.dtb-tennis.de/7612.php?selected=1068&selectedsub=7961&selsubsub=7611.

Deutscher Tennis Bund (2009a). *Jugend.* Retrieved 29.11.2009, from http://www.dtb-tennis.de/16347.php?selected=16345.

Deutscher Tennis Bund (2009b). *Förderung.* Retrieved 29.11.2009, from http://www.dtb-tennis.de/8941.php?selected=1068&selectedsub=8940.

Deutscher Tennis Bund (2008). Leistungssportkonzeption. Retrieved 12.6.2008, from http://www.dtb-tennis.de/8947_9011.php?selected=1068&selectedsub=8940.

Deutscher Tennis Bund (2008a). *Mitgliederentwicklung.* Retrieved 30.12.2008, from http://www.dtb-tennis.de/downloads/Mitgliederentwicklung_seit_1948.pdf.

Deutscher Tennis Bund (2008b). *Tennisplätze.* Retrieved 30.12.2008, from http://www.dtb-tennis.de/2979_3022.php?selected=1101&selectedsub=2976.

.Deutscher Tennis Bund (2008c). *Landesverbände.* Retrieved 10.4.2008, from http://www.dtb-tennis.de/2979_6603.php?selected=1101&selectedsub=2976

Deutscher Tennis Bund (2008d). *Nachwuchs.* Retrieved 30.10.2008, from http://www.dtb-tennis.de/2979_3910.php?selected=1101&selectedsub=2976

Deutscher Tennis Bund (2008e). *Altersstruktur.* Retrieved 10.4.2008, from http://www.dtb-tennis.de/2979_3919.php?selected=1101&selectedsub=2976

Deutscher Tennis Bund (2008f). *Mannschaften.* Retrieved 30.10.2008, from http://www.dtb-tennis.de/2979_3910.php?selected=1101&selectedsub=2976.

Deutscher Tennis Bund (2008g). *Turniere.* Retrieved 30.10.2008, from http://www.dtb-tennis.de/14314.php?selected=3898&selectedsub=14312.

Deutscher Tennis Bund (2005). *DTB-Kaderliste 2005 der Damen/ Herren sowie der weiblichen und männlichen Jugend*, Retrieved 10.10.2005, from http://www.dtb-tennis.de/downloads/Kader.pdf.

English Golf Union (2008). *English Golf Union.* Retrieved 13.5.2008, from http://www.englishgolfunion.org.

European Tennis Association (2008). *Member Nations.* Retrieved 22.1.2008, from http://www.tenniseurope.org/TennisEurope/Te_Member_Nations.aspx.

European Union (2008). *2000-today*.Retrieved 20.1.2008, from http://europa.eu/abc/history/2000_today/index_en.htm.

Fédération Française de Tennis (2008). *Une histoire commencée au 19ème siècle.* Retrieved 20.03.2008, from http://www.fft.fr/cms-fft/?id=1296.

Fédération Française de Tennis (2008a). *Créer une élite pour la future.* Retrieved 8.2.2008, from http://www.fft.fr/cms-fft/?id=1397.

Fédération Française de Tennis (2008b). *Détection.* Retrieved 8.2.2008, from http://www.fft.fr/cms-fft/?id=1398.

Fédération Française de Tennis (2008c). *Les missions de la D.T.N.* Retrieved 9.2.2008, from http://www.fft.fr/cms-fft/?id=1399.

Football Association (2008). *The FA.com.* Retrieved 13.5.2008, from http://www.thefa.com/NewAwayKit.aspx.

Foreign and Commonwealth Office (2008). *The United Kingdom.* Retrieved 28.11.2008, from http://www.fco.gov.uk/.

Hahn, T. (1995). *The Turke and Sir Gawain.* Medieval Institute Publications. Michigan. Retrieved 24.2.2008 from http://www.lib.rochester.edu/camelot/teams/turkfrm.htm.

Hantrais, L. (1995). *Comparative Research Methods.* Retrieved 1.3.2009, from http://sru.soc.surrey.ac.uk/SRU13.html.

Hewitt P. (2004). *TUC Manufacturing Conference.* Retrieved 25.11.2008, from http://www.berr.gov.uk/dius/innovation/technologystrategyboard/tsb/competitions-for-funding/november2004/page12104.html.

Institut National de la Statistique et des études économiques (2008). *Bilan démographique 2007.* Retrieved 25.11.2008, from http://www.insee.fr/fr/themes/document.asp?ref_id=ip1170

International Tennis Federation (2009). *ITF Junior Rankings.* Retrieved 20.1.2009, from http://www.itftennis.com/juniors/rankings/index.asp

International Tennis Federation (2009a). *ITF Junior Rankings Germany.* Retrieved 3.12.2009, from http://www.itftennis.com/juniors/rankings/index.asp.

International Tennis Federation (2009b). *ITF Junior Rankings Czech Republic.* Retrieved 1.12.2009, from http://www.itftennis.com/juniors/rankings/index.asp.

International Tennis Federation (2009c). *ITF Junior Rankings France*. Retrieved 3.12.2009, from http://www.itftennis.com/juniors/rankings/index.asp.

International Tennis Federation (2009d). *ITF Junior Rankings Great Britain*. Retrieved 30.10.2008, from http://www.itftennis.com/juniors/rankings/index.asp.

International Tennis Federation (2008). National Federations. Retrieved 25.10.2008, from http://www.itftennis.com/abouttheitf/nationalassociations/

International Tennis Federation (2008a). *Grand Slams*. Retrieved, 19.10.2008, from http://www.itftennis.com/abouttheitf/worldwide/grandslams/index.asp

International Tennis Federation (2008b). *Play and Stay*. Retrieved 20.10.2008, from http://itftennis.com/playandstay/index.asp

International Tennis Federation (2007). Tour Ranking System. Retrieved 28.8.2007, from http://www.itftennis.com/shared/medialibrary/pdf/original/IO_39065_original.PDF.

International Tennis Federation (2006a). *History of ITF*. Retrieved 30.11.2009, from http://www.itftennis.com/abouttheitf/abouttheitf/history.asp.

International Tennis Federation (2006b). *Tennis Worldwide Overview*. Retrieved 30.11.2009, from http://www.itftennis.com/abouttheitf/worldwide/index.asp.

International Tennis Federation (2006c). *ATP*. Retrieved 30.11.2009, from http://www.itftennis.com/abouttheitf/worldwide/index.asp.

Kubista, A. (2007). *Martina Navratilova. We all had a name*. Retrieved 22.7.2007 from http://www.czech.cz/pdf.aspx?id=17835

Kuchařová, V. & Kroupa, A. (1999). Demographic and social structure. *Human Development Report of the Czech Republic 1999*. Prague: Research Institute for Labour and Social Affairs.

Leamington Tennis Club (2008). *Tennis History*. Retrieved 24.02.2008, from http://www.leamington-tennis-squash.co.uk/tennis.

Lawn Tennis Association (2008a). *The performance Programme*. Retrieved 12.2.2008 from http://www.lta.org.uk/Performance/?BSMGuid=6360a1d5-a071-4b33-95b6-a3ad467d3b04

Lawn Tennis Association (2008b). *Winning Player Pathway*. Retrieved 12.12.2008, from http://www.lta.org.uk/Global/Downloads/Player%20Resources/Winning%20Player%20Pathway.pdf.

Lawn Tennis Association (2008c). *National Tennis Centre*. Retrieved 20.10.2008, from http://www.lta.org.uk/about-us/National-Tennis-Centre/.

Lawn Tennis Association (2007). *Annual Reports 2007*. Retrieved 9.2.2008 from http://www.lta.org.uk/AboutUs/AnnualReports

Lawn Tennis Association (2007a). *Accounts 2007*. Retrieved 9.2.2008 from http://www.lta.org.uk/AboutUs/AnnualAccounts

Lawn Tennis Association (2006).Coaches. *Blueprint for British Tennis*. West Kensigton, London, Lawn Tennis Association, 1-20.

Lawn Tennis Association (2005). *Our vision...Our mission*. Retrieved 30.10.2005, from www.lta.org.uk.

Lawn Tennis Association (2004). *Performance Pathway*. Retrieved 29.11.2004, from http://www.lta.org.uk/ReachTheTop/PerformanceJourney/.

Leibniz Institut for Social Science (2003). New Europeans and Culture. *Eurobarometer 2003.1*. Retrieved 1.11.2008, from http://zacat.gesis.org/webview/index.jsp

Masters, J. (1997). *Traditional Games*. Retrieved 25.2.2008 from http://www.tradgames.org.uk/games/Tennis.htm.

MacCurdy, D. (2006). *Talent Identification around the world and Recommendations for the Chinese Tennis Association*. Retrieved 24.2.2008, from www.itftennis.com/shared/medialibrary/pdf/original/IO_18455_original.PDF.

Ministère des sports. (2008). *Les licences et les clubs des fédérations agréées en 2006*. Retrieved 12.12. 2008, from http://www.sports.gouv.fr/IMG/pdf/STAT-INFO_07-05.pdf

Office for National Statistics (2009). *Lifestyles and sport*. Retrieved 20.10.2009, from http://www.statistics.gov.uk/cci/nugget_print.asp?ID=2211.

Office for National Statistics (2008). *Population Estimates*. Retrieved 20.8.2008, from http://www.statistics.gov.uk/cci/nugget.asp?ID=6.

Perrotta, T. (2008). Wunderkinds: The future of the tennis prodigy. Retrieved 10.1.2008, from http://www.tennis.com/features/general/features.aspx?id=108988.

Professional Bowls Association (2008). *The Professional Bowls Association*. Retrieved 13.5.2008, from http://www.bowlspba.com.

Sport England (2008). *Active People Survey 2*. Retrieved 28.10.2009, from http://www.sportengland.org/research/active_people_survey/active_people_survey_2.aspx.

Sport England (2004). *Participation in Sport-results from the GHS 2002*. Retrieved 5.10.2007, from http://www.sportengland.org/research/archive.aspx

Statistisches Bundesamt (2009). Bevölkerung und Geschlecht. Retrieved 31.11.2009, from http://www.destatis.de/jetspeed/portal/cms/Site/destatis/Internet/DE/Navigation/Statistiken/Bevoelkerung/Bevoelkerungsstand/Bevoelkerungsstand.psml.

Tennis Europe (2009). *The Czech Tennis Association*. Retrieved 1.12.2009, from http://www.tenniseurope.org/TennisEurope/Te_Member_Nations_detail.aspx?id=17.

Tennis Europe (2008a). *The Lawn Tennis Association*. Retrieved 22.05.2008, from http://www.tenniseurope.org/TennisEurope/Te_Member_Nations_detail.aspx?id=22.

Tennis Europe (2008b). *Fédération Française de Tennis*. Retrieved 21.12.2008, from http://www.tenniseurope.org/TennisEurope/Te_Member_Nations_detail.aspx?id=20

Tyzack A. (2005). The True Home of Tennis. *Country Life, 22 June 2005*. Retrieved 25.2.2008 from http://www.countrylife.co.uk/news/culture/article/79487/The_True_Home_of_Tennis.html).

United Kingdom Sports (2008). *Sport in the UK*. Retrieved 20.10.2008, from http://www.uksport.gov.uk/pages/sport_in_the_uk/.

United Kingdom Sports (2008a). *Introducing UK Sports*. Retrieved 28.10.2008, from http://www.uksport.gov.uk/assets/File/Generic_Template_Documents/About_UK_Sport/UK%20Sport%202%20pager%20updated%20new%20-%20Sepo7.pdf

Women's Tennis Association (2009). *Sony Ericsson WTA Tour*. Retrieved 29.11.2009, from http://www.sonyericssonwtatour.com/page/Home/0,,12781,00.html.

Women's Tennis Association (2009a). *Rankings Germany, 1-100*. Retrieved 29.11.2009, from http://www.sonyericssonwtatour.com/page/RankingsNSingles/0,,12781~0~68,00.html.

Womens's Tennis Association (2009b). *Rankings Czech Republic, 1-100*. Retrieved 29.11.2009, from http://www.sonyericssonwtatour.com/page/RankingsNSingles/0,,12781~0~49,00.html

Women's Tennis Association (2009c). *Rankings France, 1-100*. Retrieved 29.11.2009, from http://www.sonyericssonwtatour.com/page/RankingsNSingles/0,,12781~0~64,00.html.

Women's Tennis Association (2009d). *Rankings UK, 1-100*. Retrieved 29.11.2009, from http://www.sonyericssonwtatour.com/page/RankingsNSingles/0,,12781~0~70,00.html.

Youth Sport Net (2008). *Relations between the Ministry of Education and sport and civic associations*. Retrieved 25.11.2008, from www.youth-sport.net/fileadmin/fm-youthsport/Czech/Go-ngo.doc.

Appendices

Appendix A: Four Examples of Questionnaires   228

Appendix B: Names of Interviewees and Date of Interviews   275

Questionnaire parents

Comparative Analysis of Talent Identification and Talent Development in Tennis (CATIT)

Introduction to the survey

This survey is part of my research being conducted for a doctoral thesis (PhD) registered at the University of Edinburgh (UK).

- Seeking way to find ways of optimising talent identification in tennis

- Comparing practice in four European countries

- Seeking views of coaches, parents, players and administrators

- Personal experience as a tennis coach

All findings and sources of information supplied will be treated in strict confidence.

Thank you very much for participating in this research survey.

Michael Seibold
Contact address:
Scheefstr. 37/1
72074 Tübingen
Phone +49707124402
Mobil +4901727433927

April 2006

1) **Date of Interview**
_____

2) **Personal Data**

country
_____

3) **When did your child start playing tennis?**

one response

[ ]a 3years

[ ]b 4years

[ ]c 5years

[ ]d 6years

[ ]e 7years

[ ]f over 8 years

4) **How was your child identified?**

multiple response

[ ]A coach

[ ]B father

[ ]C mother

[ ]D relatives

[ ]E other

5) Has been your child identified as talented for tennis?

multiple response

[ ]A yes

[ ]B no

[ ]C explain

6) What or who was the main influence on your child starting playing tennis?

multiple response

[ ]A parents

[ ]B relatives

[ ]C own initiative

[ ]D friends

[ ]E enviroment

[ ]F good coaches

[ ]G good practice available

[ ]H financially attractive

[ ]I school

[ ]J other

7) Do you have any goals for your child in tennis?

multiple response

[ ]a professional level

[ ]b national level

[ ]c regional level

[ ]d club level

[ ]e having fun

[ ]f no

[ ]g other

8) How far you have been usually travelled for the daily training sessions?

one response

[ ]a less than 2km

[ ]b 2-10km

[ ]c 11-20km

[ ]d 21-30km

[ ]e 31-40km

[ ]f 41-50km

[ ]g more than 50 km

[ ]h other

9) Do you think your child is practicing enough?

multiple response

[ ]A less 5 h/week

[ ]B 6 hours/ week

[ ]C 7hours/ week

[ ]D 8hours/ week

[ ]E 9hours/ week

[ ]F 10hours/ week

[ ]G more than 10hours/ week

[ ]H please describe

10) Has your child placed in a talent development group before the selection into a regional squad?

multiple response

[ ]A yes

[ ]B no

[ ]C not selected

[ ]D explain

11) Please judge the first coach for your child who has trained more than 1 year your child?

multiple response

[ ]A cooperative
[ ]B authoritive
[ ]C command
[ ]D very interested
[ ]E good training
[ ]F hard
[ ]G very success orientated
[ ]H like a friend
[ ]I other

13) Did your child change the coach in the past years? If yes, please describe the age and the reasons?

multiple response

[ ]A no
[ ]B yes
[ ]C explain

14) Do you recall any positive influences on the tennis development of your child?

multiple response

[ ]A no
[ ]B yes
[ ]C explain

15) Do you recall any negative influences on the tennis development of your child?

multiple response

[ ]A no

[ ]B yes

[ ]C explain

16) Who are mainly the sparring partners for your child?

one response

[ ] -2 much lower

[ ] -1 lower level

[ ] 0 same

[ ] 1 better

[ ] 2 much better

17) What support in your opinion is most important in the development process from your child?

multiple response

[ ]A Finance

[ ]B Coach

[ ]C Parents

[ ]D National federation

[ ]E regional federation

[ ]F club

[ ]G private

[ ]H other

18) Did/ do your child achieved any support regarding -money/ equipment, sponsors-in the recent years?

multiple response

[ ]A yes

[ ]B no

[ ]C explain

19) How do you estimate the biological age of your child?

multiple response

[ ]A accelerated

[ ]B retarded

[ ]C normal

20) Did your child even in young age practice any sport (not tennis)?

multiple response

[ ]A 2 years:_____

[ ]B 3 years:_____

[ ]C no

[ ]D explain:_____

21) Do you have any opinion about the talent development system in your federation?

please describe

_____
_____
_____
_____

22) **What has been the highest ranking your child achieved as a junior U12?**

one response

[ ]a no ranking

[ ]b Top 100 national

[ ]c Top 30 regional

[ ]d other

23) **What has been the highest ranking your child achieved as a junior U14?**

one response

[ ]a no ranking

[ ]b Top 100 national

[ ]c Top 20 regional

[ ]d other

24) **What has been the highest ranking your child achieved as a junior U16?**

one response

[ ]a no ranking

[ ]b Top 100 national

[ ]c Top 20 regional

[ ]d other

25) **What is the current ranking from your child?**

one response

[ ]a no ranking

[ ]b Top 100 national

[ ]c Top 20 regional

[ ]d other

26) How you judge the support from your federation?

one response

[ ]-2 no support

[ ]-1 less support

[ ]0 average

[ ]1 good support

[ ]2 very good

27) What factors do you think characterise your child in tennis?

multiple response

[ ]A Motivation

[ ]B Interest

[ ]C psychological behavior

[ ]D performance

[ ]E physique/ physique maturity

[ ]F physiology

[ ]G other

28) In your opinion is there an existing talent development programme in your federation for children?

multiple response

[ ]A yes

[ ]B no

[ ]C explain

29) Do you have any advice for other parents?

please describe

_____

_____

30) Do you think your child has enough sessions?

multiple response

[ ]A do not know

[ ]B yes

[ ]C no

[ ]D explain

31) Do you think the annual planning up to day for your child is or has been perfect?

multiple response

[ ]A do not know

[ ]B no

[ ]C yes

[ ]D explain

32) How important is a annual planning?

multiple response

[ ]A very important

[ ]B important

[ ]C not important

[ ]D other

33) Does the coach or regional/ national federation hold regular performance and evaluation interviews with you regarding the development of your child?

multiple response

[ ]A yes

[ ]B no

[ ]C explain

34) Are you influenced by anecdotes and stories from the development from other world class players?

multiple response

[ ]A no
[ ]B yes
[ ]C explain

35) Do you think the NTF support is necessary for the career development of your child?

multiple response

[ ]A do not know
[ ]B no
[ ]C yes
[ ]D explain

36) Do you recognise some strengths in the development of your child?

please describe

_____
_____

37) Do you recognise some weakness in the development of your child?

please describe

_____
_____

38) **How important is tennis in your family?**

one response

[ ]A very important

[ ]B important

[ ]C average

[ ]D less important

[ ]E not important

39) **What is your aspiration for your child's future in tennis?**

please describe

_____
_____
_____
_____
_____

40) **We are interested in your personal opinion. If you like to make same notes, you can do it know. Thank you.**

please describe

_____
_____
_____
_____
_____

41) Please rate this questionnaire

one response

[ ] A not important

[ ] B less important

[ ] C good

[ ] D very good

[ ] E excellent

Thank you

Questionnaire Players

Comparative Analysis of Talent Identification and Talent Development in Tennis (CATIT)

Introduction to the Survey

This survey is part of my research being conducted for a doctoral thesis (PhD) registered at the University of Edinburgh, Scotland.

- Seeking to find ways of optimising talent identification in tennis

- Comparing practice in four European countries

- Seeking views of coaches, parents, players and administrators

- Personal experience as a tennis coach

All findings and sources of information supplied will be treated in strict confidence.

Thank you very much for participating in this research survey.

Michael Seibold
Contact address:
Scheefstasse 37/1
72074 Tübingen
Germany
Phone +49707124402
Mobile +491727433927

April 2006

1) **Personal Data**

Country

_____

2) **At what age did you start to play tennis?**

one answer

[ ]a 3

[ ]b 4

[ ]c 5

[ ]d 6

[ ]e 7

[ ]f 8

[ ]g 9

[ ]h 10

[ ]i later then 10

3) **What has been the reason to start playing tennis?**

Select all that apply

[ ]A relatives

[ ]B parents

[ ]C own interest

[ ]D friends

[ ]E club

[ ]F infrastructure

[ ]G school

[ ]H media

[ ]I other

4) What do you think about the amount of your training?

[ ]A I could train more

[ ]B I could train little more

[ ]C It is ok like that

[ ]D I would train less

[ ]E I would train much less

5) How do you judge the intensity of your training?

one response

[ ]A I would like to train more intensively

[ ]B It is ok like that

[ ]C I would like to train less intensively

6) What is your personal goal in tennis?

select all that apply

[ ]A international ranking

[ ]B national ranking

[ ]C regional ranking

[ ]D to play as good as possible

[ ]E tennis as a life time sport

[ ]F please explain

7) Which international ranking do you think to achieve in the future?

one response

[ ]a Top 1000

[ ]b Top 500

[ ]c Top 200

[ ]d Top 100

[ ]e Top 50

[ ]f Top 20

[ ]g other

8) Did you think of stopping playing tennis?

one response

[ ]a no

[ ]b yes, sometimes

[ ]c yes, often

[ ]d explain

9) Do you have already stopped playing tennis and than started again?

one response

[ ]a yes, once

[ ]b yes, often

[ ]c no

10) If you thought stopping playing tennis, what have been the reasons?

one response

[ ]a no succees in tennis
[ ]b family problems
[ ]c problems with friends
[ ]d problems in school
[ ]e injury
[ ]f bad training conditions
[ ]g problems with the training group
[ ]h it has been too much
[ ]i no more motivation
[ ]j other reasons

11) Do you like to travel to tournaments?

one response

[ ]1 very much
[ ]2 much
[ ]3 little
[ ]4 do not like it

12) Are you involved in decisions about your training and competition planning?

please select all that apply

[ ]A I can always decide / in training
[ ]B I can decide many things / in training
[ ]C I can decide sometimes during the training
[ ]D I can not decide anything in training
[ ]E I can always decide about the competition
[ ]F I can decide in many competitions
[ ]G I can decide sometimes in competition
[ ]H I can not decide anything in competition

13) Is there a confidential person to talk about your problems (not only tennis)?

   one response
   [ ]a no
   [ ]b yes
   [ ]c explain if you like

14) How many days per month you are injured or ill in average?

   one response
   [ ]a 0-1 day
   [ ]b 2-4 days/ month
   [ ]c 5-10 days/ month
   [ ]d 11-15 days/ month
   [ ]e more than 15 days/ month

15) Please judge your coach as a tennis expert?

   one response
   [ ]1 very good
   [ ]2 good
   [ ]3 medium
   [ ]4 rather bad
   [ ]5 very bad

16) Please judge your coach as a human?

   one response
   [ ]1 very good
   [ ]2 good
   [ ]3 medium
   [ ]4 rather bad
   [ ]5 very bad

17) Why do you train with this coach?

please select all that apply

[ ] A he is available

[ ] B he is a professional

[ ] C there is no other

[ ] D I do not know

[ ] E other

18) How many hours did you practice each week in your first year of playing tennis? Do you remember?

please select all that apply

[ ] A 1 hour

[ ] B 2 hours

[ ] C 3 hours

[ ] D 4 hours

[ ] E more then 5 hours

[ ] F other

19) Have you been identified as talented?

one response

[ ] a yes

[ ] b no

[ ] c I do not know

20) How important is/ was your coach?

one response

[ ] 1 very important

[ ] 2 important

[ ] 3 not important

21) Why do you have chosen your coach?

please select all that apply

[ ]A No choice

[ ]B he is a professional

[ ]C he is like a friend

[ ]D I can learn many things

[ ]E he has good experience

[ ]F no idea

[ ]G other

22) How many coaches you have had in your career until today?

one response

[ ]a 1

[ ]b 2

[ ]c 3

[ ]d 4

[ ]e 5

[ ]f more than 5

23) Did you recognise that you are a part of a Talent Development programme in your country?

one response

[ ]a yes

[ ]b no

[ ]c I do not know

24) Have you been in a squad?

one response

[ ]A club level

[ ]B district level

[ ]C regional level

[ ]D national level

[ ]E no squad

[ ]F other

25) Did you receive any financial support during your development?

please select all that apply

[ ]A club

[ ]B regional federation

[ ]C National Federation

[ ]D private

[ ]E parents

[ ]F other

26) Do you receive explicit guidelines and information on what is expected from you with regard to an elite players programme?

please select all that apply

[ ]A annual plan

[ ]B selection criteria's

[ ]C medical support

[ ]D players evaluation

[ ]E travel support

[ ]F other

27) Do the Club/ NTF hold regular performance and evaluation interviews with you?

please select all that apply

[ ]A once a year

[ ]B twice a year

[ ]C every 3 months

[ ]D no

[ ]E other

28) If any support, do you think the NTF support is necessary for your career development?

one response

[ ]a yes

[ ]b no

[ ]c I do not know

29) If you do not train enough, why it is so?

one response

[ ]a no money

[ ]b no coach

[ ]c no facility

[ ]d no club

[ ]e no partner

[ ]f no family support

[ ]g other

30) How many hours do you currently practice each week?

please select all that apply

[ ]A less than 10 hours

[ ]B 12 hours

[ ]C 14 hours

[ ]D 16 hours

[ ]E 20 hours

[ ]F more than 20 hours

[ ]G other

31) In your career did you follow a specific training programme?

one response

[ ]a yes

[ ]b no

[ ]c I do not know

32) If you look back in your development process, did you train enough?

please select all that apply

[ ]A yes

[ ]B no

[ ]C could be more

[ ]D too much

[ ]E sometimes

[ ]F I do not know

[ ]G explain

33) (Ex-players only) What has been the reasons stopping playing tennis?

please select all that apply

[ ]A money

[ ]B facilities

[ ]C school

[ ]D friends

[ ]E parents

[ ]F motivation

[ ]G injury

[ ]H no coach

[ ]I no partners

[ ]J others

34) Do you start playing tennis to achieve professional standard?

one response

[ ]a yes

[ ]b no

[ ]c I do not know

35) Please describe the strengths of your Talent identification and development process in the recent years

please describe

_____
_____
_____
_____

36) Please describe the weakness of your Talent identification and development process in the recent years

please describe

_____
_____
_____
_____

37) We are at the end of this questionnaire. We are very thankful for your support. If you like to ad your personal statement or give same advice, please feel free to do so!

please describe

_____
_____
_____
_____

Questionnaire Administrators

Comparative Analysis of Talent Identification and Talent Development in Tennis (CATIT)

Introduction to the Survey

This survey is part of my research being conducted for a doctoral thesis (PhD) registered at the University of Edinburgh, Scotland.

- Seeking to find ways of optimising talent identification in tennis

- Comparing practice in four European countries

- Seeking views of coaches, parents, players and administrators

- Personal experience as a tennis coach

All findings and sources of information supplied will be treated in strict confidence.

Thank you very much for participating in this research survey.

Michael Seibold
Contact address:
Scheefstrasse 37/1
72074 Tübingen
Germany
Phone +49707124402
Mobil +491727433027
Email: mb.seibold@t-online.de

April 2006

1) Personal Data

name

_____

2) Function

please describe

_____

3) Date of Interview

_____

4) Could you give me an overview of what you do as a administrator?

please describe

_____

_____

_____

_____

5) What are your priorities and why?

please describe

_____

_____

_____

_____

6) How are talented players recruited?

multiple response

[ ] A at kindergarden
[ ] B primary schools
[ ] C clubs
[ ] D academies
[ ] E public events
[ ] F tournaments
[ ] G through rankings
[ ] H somebody say so
[ ] I I do not know
[ ] J other

7) Where do they train and why is it done this way?

please describe

_____
_____
_____
_____

8) Are you using a concept for the Talent Identification and development process in your federation?

multiple response

[ ] A yes
[ ] B no
[ ] C please describe

9) Which agencies are mainly responsible for talent identification and talent development?

multiple response

[ ]A club

[ ]B regional federation

[ ]C national federation

[ ]D private people

[ ]E others

10) Which agency is coordinating the talent searching process?

multiple response

[ ]A national

[ ]B regional

[ ]C clubs

[ ]D Individuals

[ ]E schools

[ ]F private

[ ]G other

11) At which age does the national/ regional federation starts with active talent searching?

one response

[ ]1 under 6 years

[ ]2 under 8 years

[ ]3 under 10 years

[ ]4 under 12 years

12) Is there a regular evaluation about identified talents regarding there performance?

one response

[ ] a yes

[ ] b no

[ ] c I do not know

13) How far the parents are involved into this process?

one response

[ ] a regular feedback once a year

[ ] b regular feedback twice a year

[ ] c regular feedback every month

[ ] d no feedback

[ ] e other

14) What factors do you think characterise someone who has the potential to become elite?

multiple response

[ ] A skill

[ ] B strategy

[ ] C emotion

[ ] D enviroment

[ ] E physiology

[ ] F psychology

[ ] G character

[ ] H money

[ ] I friends

[ ] J parents

[ ] K coach

[ ] L other

15) Why are these factors important?

please describe

_____
_____
_____
_____

16) What characterise the development of an athlete from novice to elite status in tennis?

multiple response

[ ]A enviroment

[ ]B facilities

[ ]C parents

[ ]D financial background

[ ]E coaches

[ ]F tournaments

[ ]G results

[ ]H ranking

[ ]I other

17) Which environment do you think could be very helpful to create elite players?

please describe

_____
_____

18) Is there only one way of making it?

one response

[ ]a yes

[ ]b no

[ ]c please, describe

19) What other pathways are possible?

multiple response

[ ]A look for private sponsors

[ ]B go to academies

[ ]C stay in the club

[ ]D other

20) Does your NTF/ RTF offer clear guidelines as to the levels/ skills etc. expected?

multiple response

[ ]A yes

[ ]B no

[ ]C I do not know

[ ]D if yes, please describe

21) Do scouts go out directly to tennis clubs to identify young talents?

multiple response

[ ]a yes

[ ]b no

[ ]c please explain

22) How effective do you think current Talent Development processes are in tennis from your point of view as an administrator?

one response

[ ]1 very effective

[ ]2 effective

[ ]3 sometimes effective

[ ]4 seldom effective

[ ]5 not effective

23) Do young talents get explicit guidelines on what is expected from them?

one response

[ ]a yes

[ ]b no

[ ]c explain

24) Does the National or regional tennis federation identify tennis clubs which are doing talent development plans?

one response

[ ]a yes

[ ]b no

[ ]c I do not know

[ ]d other

25) Does the NTF give financial and other forms of assistance to tennis clubs with regard to talent development? If yes do you know a number in percent of the annual budget?

multiple response

[ ]A no

[ ]B yes

[ ]C budget in %_____

26) How important do you think is a ranking system?

one response

[ ] 1 not important

[ ] 2 less important

[ ] 3 sometimes important

[ ] 4 important

[ ] 5 very important

27) Do you think most of the players in clubs have the knowledge how to get a ranking?

one response

[ ] a yes

[ ] b no

[ ] c I do not know

28) What kind of selection criteria's into squads are most important?

multiple response

[ ] A results

[ ] B technique

[ ] C tactical

[ ] D behaviour

[ ] E physiology

[ ] F contacts

[ ] G other

29) **If there were more resources available to you, would you organise the Talent Development process differently?**

one response

[ ]a yes
[ ]b no
[ ]c please explain

30) **How many of 1,000 identified talented children can achieve a world ranking?**

one response

[ ]a less than 1%
[ ]b less than 10%
[ ]c less than 30%
[ ]d less than 50%
[ ]e less than 75%
[ ]f less than 90%
[ ]g 100%
[ ]h please explain

31) **Why it is like that?**

please describe

_____
_____

32) Could you describe the general characteristics of tennis culture in your country?

please describe

_____
_____
_____
_____

33) Can everybody play tennis? Or is it a socially exclusive sport?

please describe

_____
_____
_____
_____

34) How does tennis compare in terms of popularity among the other sports in the country?

multiple response

[ ] A Top 1-3
[ ] B Top 4-5
[ ] C Top 6-10

35) What are the strengths of the current TiD process in your federation?

please describe

_____
_____
_____

36) What is the main weakness of the current TiD process in your country?

please describe

_____

_____

37) Do you have any suggestions to improve Talent identification IN YOUR COUNTRY with regard to better tennis performance at international level?

please describe

please describe

_____

_____

_____

38) How many players are parts of the national development programme?

multiple response

[ ] A 20-50

[ ] B 50-100

[ ] C 100-120

[ ] D 120-150

[ ] E more than 150

39) How important is a questionnaire like that?

one response

[ ] -2 not important

[ ] -1 less important

[ ] 0 average

[ ] 1 important

[ ] 2 very important

40) That's the end of this questionnaire. We appreciate your support. If you have any advice or like to make some statements about this research, please feel free to do so! Thank you

please describe

_____

_____

Questionnaire coaches

Comparative Analysis of Talent Identification and Talent Development in Tennis (CATIT)

Introduction to the Survey

This survey is part of my research being conducted for a doctoral thesis (PhD) registered at the University of Edinburgh, Scotland.

- Seeking to find ways of optimising talent identification in tennis

- Comparing practice in four European countries

- Seeking views of coaches, parents, players and administrators

- Personal experience as a tennis coach

All findings and sources of information supplied will be treated in strict confidence.

Thank you very much for participating in this research survey.

Michael Seibold
Contact address:
Scheefstr. 37/1
72074 Tübingen
Phone +49707124402
Mobil +4901727433927

April 2006

1) 1 Personal Data

country

_____

_____
_____

2) Could you describe what you do as a coach?

mutiple response

[ ]A club coach

[ ]B district coach

[ ]C regional coach

[ ]D national coach

[ ]E private coach

[ ]F professional coach

[ ]G other

3) What are your priorities and why?

multiple response

[ ]A Talent Identification

[ ]B Talent Development

[ ]C to have winning players

[ ]D to help young people have fun

[ ]E to help young people develop (physically, psychologically, socially)

[ ]F please, describe

4) **How do you know that's correct practice of what you are doing?**

multiple response

[ ]A experience

[ ]B success of own players

[ ]C the other say so

[ ]D I do not know

[ ]E other

5) **What are your personal reasons for coaching?**

multiple response

[ ]A to be involved in a sport I like

[ ]B to earn a living

[ ]C to have power

[ ]D to be in charge

[ ]E to be with people I like

[ ]F to give something back to sport

[ ]G to gain public recognition

[ ]H to enjoy myself

[ ]I   to demonstrate my knowledge and skill in the sport

[ ]J to help people to develop physically

[ ]K to help athletes develop psychologically

[ ]L to help people develop socially

[ ]M other

6) **What kind of coach you are?**

one response

[ ]A submissive

[ ]B command

[ ]C cooperative

7) Do you run a regular specific talent identification program for children?

one response

[ ]a yes

[ ]b no

8) Why do you run this kind of programme?

multiple response

[ ]A I learnt it so

[ ]B experience

[ ]C I learnt it from an other coach

[ ]D its the guideline of the National Federation

[ ]E manual

[ ]F other

9) What is the main targeted group in your club/ country/ academy?

multiple response

[ ]A under 10 years

[ ]B under 12 years

[ ]C under 14 years

[ ]D under 16 years

[ ]E senior players

[ ]F leisure players

[ ]G other

10) Why do you target this group of athletes?

please describe

_____

_____

_____

11) **Please describe how talent identification and talent development is organised in your country**

please describe

_____

_____

_____

12) **If you run a specific program, is there any financial support for the programme?**

multiple response

[ ]A club

[ ]B district

[ ]C regional federation

[ ]D national federation

[ ]E private

[ ]F others

13) **Does the national or regional federation regulate the program (reports, interviews, feedbacks)?**

multiple response

[ ]A yes

[ ]B no

[ ]C other

14) **What stages are important for each talent development process in tennis?**

multiple response

[ ]A 6 to 10 years

[ ]B 11 to 13 years

[ ]C 14 to 18 years

15) What characterises a talented child at beginner level?

multiple response

[ ] A motivation

[ ] B interest

[ ] C psychological behaviour

[ ] D performance

[ ] E physique

[ ] F physiology

16) Which factors are important to produce optimal performance?

multiple response

[ ] A skill

[ ] B strategy

[ ] C emotion

[ ] D enviroment

[ ] E physiology

[ ] F psychology

[ ] G character

[ ] H money

[ ] I friends

[ ] J parents

[ ] K coach

[ ] L other

17) Is your Talent Development programme influenced by any models drawn from the sport science literature?

multiple response

[ ] A yes

[ ] B no

[ ] C please describe

18) Are you familiar with the talent developing models of Bloom and Ericsson?

one response

[ ]a yes

[ ]b no

19) Is your Talent development practice influenced by anecdotes and stories about top-level stars?

multiple response

[ ]A yes

[ ]B no

[ ]C explain

20) Do you try to model your athletes on the careers of world-class players?

multiple response

[ ]A yes

[ ]B no

[ ]C please describe

21) What kind of methods are you using to identify talented people?

multiple response

[ ]A testing on motor skills

[ ]B watching them play

[ ]C I just train them

[ ]D other

22) **What kind of methods are you using to develop talented people in tennis?**

multiple response

[ ]A principles of training

[ ]B Model of Bloom

[ ]C manuals

[ ]D try and error

[ ]E technique training

[ ]F only hard drills

[ ]G other

23) **In your opinion are there better pathways than yours to develop young athletes?**

multiple response

[ ]A yes

[ ]B no

[ ]C explain

24) **Does it matter what pathways are taken?**

multiple response

[ ]A yes

[ ]B no

[ ]C explain

25) **How important is the influence of a coach for the athletes' development?**

one response

[ ]-1 not important

[ ]0 less important

[ ]1 important

[ ]2 very important

26) How important do you think is a ranking system?

one response

[ ]1 not important

[ ]2 less important

[ ]3 important

[ ]4 very important

27) Do you know how to bring your talented people into international rankings?

one response

[ ]a yes

[ ]b no

28) What kind of selection criteria into squads is most important?

multiple response

[ ]A results

[ ]B technique

[ ]C tactics

[ ]D behaviour

[ ]E physiologhy

[ ]F contacts

[ ]G other

29) How effective do you think the current Talent Identification and Development processes are in tennis?

one response

[ ]1 not effective

[ ]2 less effective

[ ]3 effective

[ ]4 very effective

30) If there were more resources available to you would you organise Talent identification and Development differently?

multiple response

[ ]A yes

[ ]B no

[ ]C explain

31) If you have identified 1000 children, how many of them can make it into professional level?

one response

[ ]a less than 1%

[ ]b less than 10%

[ ]c less than 30%

[ ]d less than 50%

[ ]e less than 75%

[ ]f less than 90 %

[ ]g 100%

[ ]h other

32) Please describe the strengths of the national talent development programme

please describe

_____
_____
_____
_____

33) **Please describe the weakness of the national development programme**

please describe

_____

_____

_____

_____

34) **That's the end of this questionnaire. We appreciate your support. If you have any advice or like to make some statements about this research, please feel free to do so! Thank you**

please describe

_____

_____

Appendix B

Interviews with key actors in Germany and the Czech Republic

Anonymised list

Players from Germany

anonymised	Date of Interview
Pascale	18.4.2006/Questionnaire
Markus	20.11.2006
Stefan	15.6.2006
Eduard	22.7.2006
Fabienne	25.5.2006
Karin	27.5.2006

Players from the Czech Republic

anonymised	Date of Interview
Milena	1.6.2007
Radana	1.6.2007
Andreas	1.6.2007
Richard	20.4.2006
Daria	25.6.2006

Parents from Germany

anonymised	Date of Interview
Erich	2.8.2006
Markus	22.6.2006
Thomas	30.7.2006/Questionnaire
Susanne	30.7.2006/Questionnaire
Ira	20.12.2006
Martina	29.7.2006
Beate	12.12.2006

Parents from the Czech Republic

anonymised	Date of Interview
Aijka	25.6.2006
Marina	20.4.2006
Martin	19.6.2006
Ondrej	20.4.2006

Administrators from Germany

anonymised	Date of Interview
Uli	22.5.2006
Carsten	30.5.2006/ Questionnaire
Maria	01.05.2006
Wolf	28.10.2007

Administrator from the Czech Republic

anonymised	Date of Interview
Miroslav	18.12.2007/Questionnaire

Coaches from Germany

anonymised	Date of Interview
Andre	20.11.2006
Boris	20.5.2006
Chris	29.4.2006/ Questionnaire
Darren	29.10.2006
Eric	20.7.2006
Frank	20.7.2006
Gustav	20.12.2006

Coaches from Czech Republic

anonymised	Date of Interview
Andreas	30.5.2006
Bohdan	25.6.2006
Cyril	25.6.2006
David	7.5.2006
Emil	23.7.2006

***ibidem*-**Verlag

Melchiorstr. 15

D-70439 Stuttgart

info@ibidem-verlag.de

www.ibidem-verlag.de
www.ibidem.eu
www.edition-noema.de
www.autorenbetreuung.de

www.ingramcontent.com/pod-product-compliance
Lightning Source LLC
Chambersburg PA
CBHW072126290426
44111CB00012B/1790